David Brainerd:

A Flame for God

VANCE CHRISTIE

CHRISTIAN
FOCUS

Vance Christie is a pastor and author specializing in missionary biographies. He lives in Aurora, Nebraska, and has previously written for the 'Heroes of the Faith' series. He has also written *John & Betty Stam* (ISBN 978-1-84550-376-5) in the Historymakers series.

All Scripture quotations are taken from the *King James Version*.

ISBN 1-84550-478-X
ISBN 978-1-84550-478-6

© Vance Christie 2009

10 9 8 7 6 5 4 3 2 1

Published in 2009
by
Christian Focus Publications, Ltd,
Geanies House, Fearn, Ross-shire,
IV20 1TW, Great Britain.

www.christianfocus.com

Cover design by Daniel Van Straaten

Printed and bound by
Norhaven A/S, Denmark

CONTENTS

DEDICATION

To my brother, Randy,
my boyhood idol,
cherished friend in adulthood,
esteemed fellow minister of the Gospel

FOREWORD

David Brainerd was a living illustration of how, in order to confound the mighty and the wise, our God delights to use those whom this world might deem weak and foolish (1 Cor. 1:26-29). Brainerd was a feeble, sickly man, prone to difficult bouts with severe depression. He was orphaned at age fourteen and dismissed from Yale before graduating (because he remarked that one of his tutors had no more grace than a piece of furniture). Brainerd nevertheless continued privately studying for the ministry and in time obtained a license to preach.

His whole ministry was spent laboring in obscurity as a missionary to Native Americans. He died of tuberculosis before his thirtieth birthday. He had completed only about four years of ministry among the people he loved and wanted to reach.

For a man with such a short career in a pioneer work, Brainerd's influence as a missionary was remarkable. At the close of the Great Awakening, many American Indians under Brainerd's ministry were powerfully and dramatically converted to Christianity.

Yet Brainerd's greatness, and the main reason we remember him today, lay in the character of his private life. The publication of his diary after his death is what revealed the heart of this great man to the world. And for generations, Christians have rightly honored him for the strength and quiet passion of his devotion to the pursuit of God's glory.

Jonathan Edwards was David Brainerd's first biographer. Brainerd had succumbed to complications from tuberculosis and, after being bedridden and steadily growing weaker for some time, died in Edwards' home. *An Account of the Life of the Late Rev. David*

Brainerd, Edwards' famous work, is one of the classic biographies of both American and evangelical history.

A wave of remarkable influence began with the original publication of that book. Since that time, Brainerd's life has made a profound impact on generation after generation of Christians, especially many young people who have seen Brainerd's resolute single-mindedness and been moved to emulate his holy zeal. The ranks of the evangelical missionary force are continually being replenished with young people, and large numbers of them have been profoundly and directly influenced by the testimony of David Brainerd. Thus Brainerd's life and labor have continued to reap fruit in great abundance for two and a half centuries since his death.

In this marvelous new biography, Vance Christie has given us a thorough, engaging, meticulously documented but wonderfully readable chronicle of the life of David Brainerd. Christie makes Brainerd live and breathe for the twenty-first century reader in a vivid, colorful account of the young man's heart, mind, and work. This is a splendid volume, full of insight into what drove Brainerd to give his life in the Lord's service – despite several obstacles that would seem insurmountable to the typical person today.

This retelling of Brainerd's story is a much-needed and strategic answer to many of the current generation's spiritual needs. Brainerd's devotion to serving others for God's glory makes a sharp contrast with the shallowness and self-centeredness of our postmodern culture, and points to a better, more Christlike way. Brainerd's own words, quoted frequently but always strategically by Christie, reveal Brainerd as a real and honest man, with struggles, discouragements, and bouts of depression that, if anything, make our postmodern woes seem paltry by comparison. The Appendix deals in detail with Brainerd's battle against frequent and crippling waves of depression, and is one of the most valuable chapters of the book.

I know you will enjoy this book, as I did. My prayer is that you will also be moved by it to a more earnest walk with Christ and a deeper devotion to Him, and above all that you will catch something of David Brainerd's passion to see Christ glorified.

John MacArthur

INTRODUCTION

At the end of a somewhat discouraging Sunday of ministry, David Brainerd, one of the earliest missionaries to Colonial American Indians, wrote in his diary: 'In the evening I was grieved that I had done so little for God. Oh, that I could be "a flame of fire" in the service of my God!' His allusion was to Hebrews 1:7: 'And of the angels He saith, "Who maketh His angels spirits, and His ministers a flame of fire."'

Of his inner thoughts and longings four evenings later, immediately following an intense, protracted season of private prayer, he wrote similarly: 'But oh, with what reluctancy did I find myself obliged to consume time in sleep! I longed to be as "a flame of fire," continually glowing in the divine service, preaching and building up Christ's kingdom to my latest, my dying moment.' The next day he recorded that he 'longed to burn out in one continued flame for God.'

Such was the white-hot intensity and devotion of a man who came to be regarded as one of the most eminent missionaries and among the most consecrated disciples of Christ in the history of the Church. He wished that, like the angels, he could burn brightly and continually in untiring service to the Lord. He wanted his heart, like theirs, ever to be aflame with undiminished zeal and love for God. In his Gospel preaching ministry he desired to be a bright, unfailing source of spiritual light to others.

God used this servant of such remarkable devotion in truly outstanding ways. Though he served as a missionary but four short years before his untimely death at age twenty-nine, in that brief span of time his ministry was blessed with an astounding period of converting revival among Indians who previously had known only abject paganism. That revival marked a belated dramatic epilogue to America's Great Awakening.

Following his death, the esteemed Puritan pastor, Jonathan Edwards, published extensive segments of Brainerd's private spiritual journal. Edwards knew it accurately reflected the intense and consistent spirituality and consecration he and many others had witnessed in their beloved friend. He realized the tremendous spiritual benefit that could come to others through a consideration of Brainerd's life and personal spiritual reflections.

What Edwards had no way of knowing was the vast and long-lasting extent of the good that would be accomplished through the publication of the missionary's personal journal. Since the earliest accounts of Brainerd's life and journal were published over two hundred and fifty years ago, they have never failed to remain in print in one form or another. For more than a quarter of a millennium Christian people throughout the world have been greatly encouraged, instructed and challenged through the contemplation of his exceptional example and perspectives.

Others, especially those who do not seem to share Brainerd's evangelical convictions, tend to depict him as an extremist who is of historical interest but not an appropriate model for spiritual emulation. Such a portrayal requires careful evaluation and correction.

It cannot be denied that in some senses Brainerd was an extremist. This appears to have been in keeping with both his upbringing and natural temperament. His rigorous Puritan upbringing, which of course played a formative role in the development of his outlook on and approach to life, seems extreme to more casual modern sensibilities. His feelings were very intense. With regard to his beliefs, he had strong convictions and definite views. But while he actively sought to win others to his point of view, he habitually did so in a gentle, patient and respectful fashion.

He was extreme in what he expected and demanded of himself, most often to a fault. As a result, he severely chastised himself for his shortcomings and mercilessly drove himself to fulfill his duty, even in the face of tremendous hardship and self-sacrifice. Too late in his brief ministry career he came to realize that he had carried out devotion to duty at the expense of his own health, and thereafter sought to moderate his habits somewhat.

But his radicalism was always firmly tethered and completely subjected to his considerable intellect and his Christlike spirit. Other than one brief period during his college career, he never strayed into thinking or behavior that was considered fanatical and perhaps less than spiritual. His thinking consistently manifested exceptional depth, clarity, wisdom and spirituality. His conduct was above reproach, being characterized by evident godliness and all variety of the fruit of Christ's Spirit.

On the whole, his radicalism was of a type worthy of emulation. His extremism exemplified the characteristics that Christ in His Word calls His disciples to pursue and promote: deep devotion to God; fervent worship of Him; sacrificial service of Christ and man; thoroughgoing holiness; active evangelism and missionary enterprise.

Though Brainerd himself never drew such parallels, his radical commitment mirrored that of another extremist Christian, the Apostle Paul. Like Paul, Brainerd's all-out devotion led him to endure numerous hardships in serving Christ. So consuming was his commitment to serving his Lord that, like the Apostle, he willingly chose to forego marriage and other legitimate earthly pleasures. He shared the Apostle's heart for zealously preaching the Gospel and actively expanding Christ's kingdom among previously unreached peoples. Paul's statement of himself in Philippians 1:21 was just as true of Brainerd: 'For to me to live is Christ, and to die is gain.'

For fullest exposure to and benefit from Brainerd's personal spiritual reflections, one of the editions of Jonathan Edwards' work, *The Life of David Brainerd*, may be read. (See the brief bibliography at the end of this volume for a description of three different editions of that work.) The edition most frequently cited in this volume is the Yale University Press edition of 1985, edited by Norman Pettit.

That edition has rendered a tremendous service to readers by including in brackets the references for the numerous Scripture passages that Brainerd freely cited (but normally did not identify) in his diary. Those bracketed Bible references have been retained in the present work. While the vast majority of the bracketed references in the Yale edition are accurate, occasionally an alternate reference has been substituted when further consideration of a particular biblical citation deemed it appropriate to do so.

Most of the quotations from Brainerd's journal are not referenced in the chapter endnotes of this volume. The specific chronological designations in the main text usually make it clear where the citations are to be found in Edwards' *The Life of David Brainerd*. When the location of a quotation is not altogether clear (as when it is displaced from an earlier or later portion of *The Life*), it has been referenced in a chapter endnote.

1

BOYHOOD AND CONVERSION

In 1649 an eight-year-old orphan named Daniel Brainerd was brought from Essex, England, to Hartford, Connecticut. It is not known what had happened to his family in the homeland or which vessel carried him to the New World.[1] Perhaps those unknown individuals who looked after the vulnerable young boy hoped his fortunes would improve and he would be able to make something of himself in America. If that was the case, their hopes for the lad were amply realized in the end.

Daniel lived in Hartford with a family named Wadsworth until he was twenty-one. He then joined twenty-seven other land seekers in traveling a score of miles down the scenic Connecticut River to establish the community of Haddam. The tract those early pioneers settled was twelve miles square and was divided nearly equally on the east and west sides of the river. Daniel prospered there, eventually becoming not only Haddam's chief landholder, but also its constable, surveyor, assessor and collector, as well as a Commissioner for the General Court and a justice of the peace.

Two years after the settling of Haddam, which soon grew to be a community of some sixty families, Daniel married Hannah Spencer. She bore him seven sons and a daughter. The youngest of their sons, Hezekiah, was born in 1681. He inherited the largest portion

1. Many of the details presented here concerning David Brainerd's ancestors and early childhood are gleaned from: Norman Pettit, *The Life of David Brainerd* (New Haven and London: Yale University Press, 1985), pp. 33-5, 99-100; David Wynbeek, *David Brainerd, Beloved Yankee* (Grand Rapids: Eerdmans, 1961), pp. 13-15.

of his father's estate, including the family homestead with its house in the country located two miles upriver from Haddam. The house stood just one hundred feet above the Connecticut's west bank.

Hezekiah went on to become quite prominent. In addition to being a country squire, a regiment commander and, like his father, a justice of the peace at Haddam, he served in the Connecticut government. He was a Representative to the General Assembly, Speaker of the House for two years, and a member of the Senate from 1723 till his untimely death four years later.

Thomas Brainerd, a descendant of Hezekiah's brother, James, described Hezekiah as a man 'of great personal dignity and self-restraint, of rigid notions of parental prerogative and authority, of the strictest puritanical views as to religious ordinances, of unbending integrity as a man and a public officer, and of extreme scrupulousness in his Christian life.'[2]

On October 1, 1707, Hezekiah married Dorothy Hobart Mason, the young widow of Daniel Mason. Dorothy came from a family that had produced a number of ministers. Her paternal grandfather, Peter Hobart, after suffering persecution as a Puritan preacher in England, moved his family to Hingham, Massachusetts, where he continued his ministry. Four of his five sons followed in their father's ministerial footsteps, serving churches in New England.

Hobart's second son, Jeremiah, was Dorothy's father. After serving at Hempstead on Long Island, a pastorate made difficult, in the words of Edwards, 'by reason of numbers turning Quakers, and many others being so irreligious that they would do nothing towards the support of the gospel,' Jeremiah became Haddam's first minister. He pastored there till his death at age eighty-five in 1715.

Dorothy's maternal grandfather was the cultured Puritan minister Samuel Whiting who served congregations in Boston of Lincolnshire, England, and Lynn, Massachusetts. In addition to his daughter, Dorothy's mother, Whiting had three sons, all of whom devoted their lives to the ministry. An uncle of Dorothy's

2. Pettit, *Life of David Brainerd*, p. 99; Thomas Brainerd, *The Life of John Brainerd* (Philadelphia: Presbyterian Publication Company, 1865), p. 30.

14

mother, Oliver St John, served as Chief Justice of England under the eminent Puritan political leader, Oliver Cromwell.

When Dorothy married Hezekiah Brainerd she already had a two-year-old son, Jeremiah Mason, by her first husband. Hezekiah and Dorothy's union was blessed with nine children of their own: Hezekiah (born 1708), Dorothy (1710), Nehemiah (1712), Jerusha (1714), Martha (1716), David (1718), John (1720), Elizabeth (1722) and Israel (1725). David, the sixth child and third son of his parents, was born one week after Easter, on Sunday, April 20, 1718.

Details are sketchy about David Brainerd's upbringing. He and his siblings were doubtless expected to share fully in the numerous chores to be carried out around the farm and home. They also needed to attend carefully to their schooling and religious duties. But life was not all work for them. They likely hiked and hunted in the forested hills that made up their portion of the Connecticut River valley. Nearby streams and the river would have afforded opportunities for summertime fishing and swimming as well as wintertime skating.

The Brainerd children likely received much of their education at home. Subjects commonly emphasized during that era included reading, writing, arithmetic and the catechism. The town records of Haddam reveal that money was provided for a community schoolhouse in 1728, so it is possible, though far from certain, that David Brainerd was one of its early pupils. Whether educated at home or in a local schoolhouse, the fact that he was later admitted to Yale College and there rose to the top of his class makes clear that he received a sound basic education as a boy.

Certainly daily religious instruction and weekly church attendance figured prominently in the life and routine of the Brainerd family. Puritan families commonly had both morning and evening family devotions. Brainerd's paternal grandfather, Daniel, served as one of the original deacons when the Congregational Church was formed in Haddam in 1700. As has already been mentioned, his other grandfather, Jeremiah Hobart, was the first pastor of that congregation. David Brainerd's strict, dutiful father doubtless saw to it that all his family members were punctilious in their church attendance.

The building where the Brainerds attended church was erected in 1721. Congregants enjoyed singing psalms, but did so without the aid of an organ, as organs had not yet come into use by Congregational churches of that period. The meetinghouse had neither lights nor a fire for heat. Worship services were held Sunday morning and afternoon, and it was not at all uncommon for the pastor's sermons to run up to two hours in length.

Neighboring Indians had the right to hunt and fish in the countryside, so the sight of natives would have been one to which the Brainerd children were accustomed. For years a large tribe of superstitious, devil-worshiping Indians had resided a short distance downriver, near East Haddam. The natives called that location Machemoodus, meaning 'the place of noises,' so named for the rumblings and strange sounds that emanated from deep within the base of nearby Mount Tom. The aborigines believed the mountain to be the residence of Hobbamock, the spirit of evil and the author of all human plagues and calamities.

Looking back near the end of his life, David Brainerd would write that he did not remember having any significant conviction of sin before he was seven or eight years old. Then he became deeply convicted of his sin, concerned about the condition of his soul and terrified at the thought of dying. By that sudden spiritual agitation he was 'driven to the performance of duties,' presumably including more conscientious endeavors at personal prayer and Bible reading. Those legalistic efforts, however, proved to be 'a melancholy business that destroyed my eagerness for play.' As it turned out, that early period of spiritual concern was short-lived.

He further revealed that from his youth he was 'somewhat sober, and inclined rather to melancholy than the contrary extreme.' His propensity toward dejection was doubtless deepened by a stunning loss he suffered when he was but nine years of age. At that time his half-brother, Jeremiah Mason, was twenty-two and engaged to be married to Mary Clark. Their wedding day was set for May 24, 1727, and Phineas Fiske, Haddam's second pastor, performed the ceremony. The happiness of the occasion was shattered, however, when news arrived that Hezekiah Brainerd, while attending to senatorial duties in Hartford, had suddenly passed away earlier in the day. That same day was Hezekiah's birthday; he was only forty-six.

Throughout the next few years David Brainerd was relatively unconcerned about and satisfied with his spiritual condition. That abruptly ended during the opening months of 1732, however, when he became greatly excited over 'a mortal sickness' which visited Haddam. Once again he became frequent and fervent in his perceived spiritual duties. He also found delight in reading Christian books, especially James Janeway's *Token for Children*. Janeway was a Nonconformist minister who served in London, before dying of consumption in 1674 at age thirty-seven.[3] His *Token for Children*, subtitled *Being an Exact Account of the Conversion, Holy and Exemplary Lives, and Joyful Deaths of Several Young Children*, urged young people to live in a serious, devout fashion so that they might be prepared to enter heaven should they die.

That March, a month before his fourteenth birthday, another dark season came into his young life. His mother's death at age fifty-two left him 'exceedingly distressed and melancholy.' After her passing his religious concern began to decline and gradually he slipped back into a state of relative complacency.

The year that followed brought many changes for the Brainerd family. Brainerd's oldest brother, Hezekiah, had married Phineas Fiske's daughter, Mary, in January of 1731. Their first child was born in July of 1732 in the homestead which Hezekiah, Jr., had inherited. Nehemiah graduated from Yale that fall, and in December David Brainerd's favorite sister, Jerusha, married Samuel Spencer of East Haddam. Just days before his fifteenth birthday the following April, he moved into Samuel and Jerusha's home in the village of East Haddam.

During the four years that he lived there he cultivated a degree of religious devotion by maintaining his private spiritual duties. He also tried to avoid spending too much time with other young people because of the detrimental effect he perceived it had on his spiritual life:

3.   Pettit, *Life of David Brainerd*, pp. 101-2.

> I was not exceedingly addicted to young company, or frol-
> icking, as it is called. But this I know, that when I did go
> into such company, I never returned from a frolick in my life
> with so good a conscience as when I went. It always added
> new guilt to me, and made me afraid to come to the throne of
> grace, and spoiled those good frames I was wont sometimes
> to please myself with.

In April of 1737 he turned nineteen and received his portion of
the family inheritance, a farm near Durham, about ten miles west
of Haddam. He tried his hand at farming for a few months, but
found it did not appeal to him. Instead, more in keeping with
his 'natural inclination' toward studies, he frequently longed to
attend college and pursue a liberal arts education.

Hezekiah, Jr., who would shortly become Haddam's Clerk
and a justice of the peace, had three years earlier taken his father's
place as Representative to the General Assembly, a post he would
occupy almost continually for forty years. Nehemiah had entered
the ministry, following in the footsteps of several of his relatives.
As Brainerd approached his twentieth birthday, he decided that
he, too, would pursue a ministerial career.

He returned to Haddam in April, 1738, in order to live and study
with Phineas Fiske, who was then in his twenty-third year of
ministry there. About that same time one of Fiske's six daughters,
Elizabeth, was married to Brainerd's brother, Nehemiah. The
somber older pastor gave the aspiring ministerial student an
interesting bit of advice that it would appear he hardly needed,
but was careful to heed: 'he advised me wholly to abandon young
company and associate myself with grave elderly people, which
counsel I followed.'

In less than a year Brainerd read twice completely through
the Bible. In addition, he devoted considerable time each day to
prayer and other secret duties, and gave careful attention to the
Bible messages he heard at church, endeavoring to retain as much
of them as possible. He also met with a group of young people
(presumably with Fiske's approval) on Sunday evenings for
a time of religious devotions. After those meetings and sometimes
again on Monday mornings, he would rehearse to himself the

sermons he had heard that Sabbath. 'In short,' he later said of himself, 'I was a very good Pharisee, i.e., had a very good outside, but rested entirely on my duties, though I was not sensible of it.'

Fiske passed away in the fall of that year, after which Brainerd continued his studies under the tutelage of his brother, Nehemiah. He remained constant in his religious duties and was often amazed at and troubled over the carelessness of others with regard to spiritual matters. 'Thus I proceeded a considerable length on a self-righteous foundation, and should have been entirely lost and undone, had not the mere mercy of God prevented.'

God graciously began to dismantle his self-righteousness one Sunday morning late that year as he went out walking to spend some time in private prayer. Suddenly, unexpectedly he was overwhelmed with a view of his own sin and vileness, as well as with a sense of his being in imminent danger of the wrath of God. This left him greatly distressed and dejected for days and caused him to spend much time alone.

In February of 1739 he set apart a day for secret fasting and prayer. He spent the entire day crying to God for mercy and asking Him to open his eyes to see the evil of sin and the way of life by Jesus Christ. God used the day to help him see the sinful condition of his own heart and, to some degree, his spiritual helplessness. 'But still I trusted in all the duties I performed.'

Sometimes he became spiritually apathetic, not having any significant convictions of sin for days at a time. Afterwards, however, conviction would return to seize him even more strongly. He later described one such occasion that was especially distressing:

> One night I remember in particular, when I was walking solitarily abroad, I had opened to me such a view of my sin that I feared the ground would cleave asunder under my feet and become my grave, and send my soul quick (alive) into hell, before I could get home. And though I was forced to go to bed, lest my distress should be discovered by others, which I much feared; yet I scarce durst sleep at all, for I thought it would be a great wonder if I should be out of hell in the morning.

His considerable spiritual perplexity and distress led him to start virulently finding fault with God's ways of dealing with mankind. He thought it unfair that Adam's sin had been imputed to all human beings and wished for some other way of salvation than by Christ. He pondered various schemes ('strange projections, full of atheism') by which he might escape God's notice, thwart God's decrees concerning him and escape the divine wrath his sins deserved. Often he wished there was no God. He even wished there were some other Divine Being with whom he might 'join and fight against the living God!'

He considered four aspects of Christian doctrine related to salvation especially irksome. First, he took issue with God's law as being unreasonably rigid. If it regulated only his outward conduct he thought he could bear with it and possibly fulfill it. But he realized it condemned also the evil thoughts and other sins of his heart that he could not possibly prevent. Secondly, he resisted Scripture's teaching that faith alone was the condition of salvation. Having been 'very conscientious in duty' and 'exceeding religious' for such a long time, he could not abide the thought that all he had done should count for nothing toward his own salvation.

In the third place, he was frustrated by his inability to ascertain precisely what was involved in believing and coming to Christ. Having pondered Christ's call to the weary and heavy laden to come to Him, Brainerd could discover no way that the Savior directed them to do that. He read Solomon Stoddard's *Guide to Christ* but ended up frustrated with it. Though the volume did an excellent job of describing the exact condition of his own heart while under conviction, it failed to tell him anything he could '*do*' that would bring him to Christ. As he would later state of himself, he had not yet learned 'that there could be no way prescribed whereby a natural man could, of his own strength, obtain that which is supernatural.'

Solomon Stoddard (1643–1729) was Jonathan Edwards' father-in-law and his predecessor as the pastor at Northampton, Massachusetts. *A Guide to Christ, Or the way of directing souls that are under the work of conversion* was originally published in Boston in

1714.[4] In the end, that work played a central role in Brainerd's being brought to salvation. He testified that the book was the instrument 'which, I trust, in the hand of God was the happy means of my conversion.'

Fourthly, he had great inward opposition toward the doctrine of God's sovereignty over salvation. He refused to accept that teaching because he feared that God intended to condemn him.

God's Spirit, however, continued to work powerfully in his heart, pressing him to relinquish his hopes of commending himself to God through his own good deeds. Finally one morning while walking and meditating near a secluded hazel grove, he suddenly and conclusively realized that all his plans and efforts to bring about salvation for himself were utterly hopeless. He was brought to a complete standstill by the stunning comprehension that he was totally lost spiritually speaking. 'I had thought many times before that the difficulties in my way were very great: But now I saw in another and very different light, that it was forever impossible for me to do anything towards helping or delivering myself.' Surprisingly, perhaps, once that realization was made, the spiritual tumult he had been experiencing eased somewhat.

He remained in that frame of mind from a Friday morning till the following Sunday evening, July 12, 1739, when he again walked in the same secluded grove. Being in a very melancholy mood that evening, he struggled unsuccessfully for about half an hour to pray. Though not distressed, he was disconsolate, feeling as if nothing in heaven or earth could make him happy. Presently, God broke through in saving grace to his soul.

Brainerd's conversion experience was an unusual one. It involved, as his own attempt at describing the occurrence reveals, something of an inner vision of God's surpassing glory:

> And having been thus endeavoring to pray (though being, as I thought, very stupid and senseless) for near half an hour ..., then, as I was walking in a dark thick grove, unspeakable glory seemed to open to the view and apprehension of my soul. I do not mean any external brightness, for I saw no

4. Pettit, *Life of David Brainerd*, p. 123.

21

such thing. Nor do I intend any imagination of a body of light somewhere away in the third heavens, or anything of that nature; but it was a new inward apprehension or view that I had of God, such as I never had before, nor anything which had the least resemblance of it.

I stood still, wondered, and admired! I knew that I never had seen before anything comparable to it for excellency and beauty: It was widely different from all the conceptions that ever I had had of God, or things divine. I had no particular apprehension of any one Person in the Trinity, either the Father, Son, or Holy Ghost; but it appeared to be divine glory that I then beheld. And my soul 'rejoiced with joy unspeakable' (1 Pet. 1:8) to see such a God, such a glorious Divine Being; and I was inwardly pleased and satisfied that He should be God over all for ever and ever. My soul was so captivated and delighted with the excellency, loveliness, greatness, and other perfections of God, that I was even swallowed up in Him; at least to that degree that I had no thought (as I remember) at first about my own salvation, and scarce reflected there was such a creature as myself.

His conversion left him not only with a willing acceptance of God's sovereign rule over all, but also filled with desire to properly glorify Him, and completely satisfied with the way of salvation through faith in Jesus Christ alone:

Thus God, I trust, brought me to a hearty disposition to exalt Him and set Him on the throne, and principally and ultimately to aim at His honor and glory, as King of the universe. ...

At this time, the way of salvation opened to me with such infinite wisdom, suitableness, and excellency, that I wondered I should ever think of any other way of salvation; was amazed that I had not dropped my own contrivances, and complied with this lovely, blessed, and excellent way before. If I could have been saved by my own duties, or any other way that I had formerly contrived, my whole soul would now have refused. I wondered that all the world did

not see and comply with this way of salvation, entirely by
the 'righteousness of Christ' (Rom. 3:22; 1 Cor. 1:30).

For the next several days he continued to relish almost constantly
the thoughts and feelings he had had about God and the way of
salvation through Christ at the moment of his conversion. From
the time he arose in the morning till he retired each night he 'could
not but sweetly rejoice in God.'

Not long after his conversion, he faced two dark periods of the
soul. These, he was careful to clarify, differed from the distress
he had experienced while under conviction as a lost sinner. At
first he came under 'thick darkness' and 'great distress' due to
a pressing sense of his ongoing sinfulness and guilt before God.
Before long, following a season of heartfelt repentance, his joy in
God was restored.

Toward the end of August he became troubled not so much
over his own spiritual condition, but instead at a seeming absence
of God's close presence in his life. To Brainerd, with his passionate
spirit that was given to extremes of perception, 'it seemed as if the
presence of God was clean gone forever.' Thankfully, that sense
soon passed: 'But it pleased the Lord to return graciously to me,
not long after that.'

2

Spiritual Awakening at Yale

Early in September of 1739, less than two months after his conversion, Brainerd entered Yale College in New Haven, Connecticut. He did so somewhat reluctantly, fearing that he would not be able to lead 'a life of strict religion in the midst of so many temptations.' His fears were not totally unfounded.

At that time some forty-five resident students lived in the College Hall, a three-story frame building which was 165 feet long and 22 feet wide. In addition to dorm rooms, the structure had a hall, a library and a kitchen. Freshmen enjoyed little privacy and were subjected to continual hazing by upperclassmen who compelled them to perform menial services upon the slightest demand. To make matters worse for Brainerd, since two-thirds of the freshmen were between the ages of thirteen and seventeen, he, at age twenty-one, was older than most of the seniors. This made his subjection to younger upperclassmen all the more humbling and trying.

Nor was the general spiritual tenor among the student body at all encouraging. Jonathan Edwards, while attending Yale two decades earlier, reported that students participated in night-time forays when they visited taverns, stole hens, geese, turkeys and pigs, broke out windows, played with cards, and used 'cursing, swearing and damning.' Just one year before David Brainerd entered the school, a sophomore named Ezra Clapp described one such nocturnal romp: 'Last night some of the freshmen got six quarts of rum and about two pails full of cider and about eight pounds of sugar and made it in to Samson ... and we made such prodigious rout ... and yelled and screamed so that a body would have thought that they were killing dogs there.'[1]

That January, 1740, a measles epidemic broke out at the college. Brainerd was laid low by the disease and had to go home to Haddam, though he soon recovered and was able to return to New Haven. Because of the demands placed on him by his diligent studies and harassing upperclassmen, he was not able to devote as much time to spiritual duties as he desired. He revealed: 'by reason of hard and close studies and being much exposed on account of my freshmanship, I had but little time for spiritual duties. My soul often mourned for want of more time and opportunity to be alone with God.'

Happily, the spring and summer that followed brought him increased opportunities for such periods of devotional retirement. He also had to wrestle, however, with his own ambition to excel in his studies, a desire that he confessed 'greatly wronged the activity and vigor of my spiritual life.' Yet still, as a rule, he was able to say, like the psalmist, 'in the multitude of my thoughts within me, thy comforts delight my soul' (Ps. 94:19). He added of those divine inner comforts, 'these were my greatest consolations day by day.'

Of one especially sweet season of personal communion with God at that time he wrote:

> One day I remember in particular (I think it was in June, 1740), I walked to a considerable distance from the college, in the fields alone at noon, and in prayer found such unspeakable sweetness and delight in God that I thought, if I must continue still in this evil world, I wanted always to be there, to behold God's glory: My soul dearly loved all mankind, and longed exceedingly that they should enjoy what I enjoyed. It seemed to be a little resemblance of heaven.

This word of personal testimony reveals that his intense private devotional relationship with the Lord did not cause him to be

---

1.   Wynbeek, *Beloved Yankee*, p. 20. Clapp's antiquated spelling has been modernized.

uninterested in or withdrawn from his fellow men. Throughout his life he would hunger after and actively pursue regular times of private fellowship with God. This would always be a pronounced aspect of his Christian life. But such an emphasis did not lead him to become a spiritual recluse. Instead, as here, he regularly expressed in his personal diary his great love and concern for other people, even all mankind. He strongly desired all people to enjoy the blessed personal communion that he himself experienced with God.

While participating in a communion service on July 6 he experienced 'some divine life and spiritual refreshment.' He also revealed of that occasion: 'When I came from the Lord's Table, I wondered how my fellow students could live as I was sensible most did.' Far from betraying an inappropriately censorious spirit, his observation reveals a spiritual sensitivity the majority of his fellow students lacked at that time. His incredulity over this state of affairs was completely understandable. Thankfully, though he had no way of knowing it at the time, before long he would witness a widespread spiritual transformation in the college's student body.

His intense personality, seriousness of purpose and desire to excel academically led him to continue to prosecute his studies with utmost, even excessive, diligence. As a result, by August he was completely exhausted and became seriously ill. That month he began to spit blood, the first indication of the tuberculosis that would end his life just seven years later. He followed the advice of his tutor who urged him to go to his home in Haddam and disengage his mind from his studies as much as possible.

Three months later he had recovered his health well enough to return to college. Doing so was not a welcome prospect for him, as he explained: 'I now so longed after God and to be freed from sin that when I felt myself recovering and thought I must return to college again, which had proved so hurtful to my spiritual interest the year past, I could not but be grieved, and I thought I had much rather have died. For it distressed me, to think of getting away from God.'

A very pleasant surprise, however, awaited him upon his arrival back at school. He found all but a few of his fellow students under a deep concern for the salvation of their souls following the recent visit, on October 27, of George Whitefield to the New Haven campus.

Whitefield, a young Anglican priest and evangelist from England, was the human instrument most widely used by God to spread the Great Awakening throughout the American colonies. That year, 1740, at age twenty-six, he had preached his way from Georgia and South Carolina, through Philadelphia and the Middle Colonies, then up to Boston and more than thirty other New England towns. In Boston, as a result of Whitefield's ministry, taverns were closed for lack of patrons and ministers were besieged by anxious inquirers of all ages and stations in life.

Leaving Boston, Whitefield traveled to Northampton, where he spent four days, October 17-20, in Jonathan Edwards' home and preached five times from his pulpit. From there the itiner-ant followed the Connecticut River down into Connecticut, ministering in towns along the way. On Monday, October 27, he preached to the Yale students in New Haven. There, too, the Spirit fell with mighty convicting power, so much so that when Brainerd returned to school in early November, spiritual condi-tions were largely altered on campus. Earnest concern about spir-itual matters had replaced the indifference and even irreverence toward them that had previously prevailed.

Brainerd himself had not had the opportunity to hear Whitefield preach. But based on the reports he had heard of the evangelist's message and lifestyle, he was encouraged by and supportive of him.

When Brainerd returned to school he received permission to board off campus at the home of Isaac Dickerman. Dickerman served as deputy to the General Assembly from 1718 to 1757 and was made captain of the militia in 1722. His third son, Isaac Jr., a 1736 graduate of Yale, died in 1740 at the age of twenty-five, and Brainerd may have occupied his room.[2]

His personal spiritual life remained strong his first several weeks back at Yale: 'I returned to college about November 6 and,

2. Pettit, *Life of David Brainerd*, p. 149.

through the goodness of God, felt the power of religion almost daily for the space of six weeks.' After an 'unspeakably' refreshing time of evening devotions on November 28 in which he reflected on Hebrews 12:22-24, he wrote, 'My soul longed to wing away for the paradise of God; I longed to be conformed to God in all things.' Following another meaningful season of personal devotions on December 9, he declared, 'Oh! one hour with God infinitely exceeds all the pleasures and delights of this lower world.'

Toward the end of January, 1741, however, he 'grew more cold and dull in religion' as his old ambition to excel academically reasserted itself. But personal satisfaction and fulfillment from those pursuits alluded him:

> But after this, some time in February following, the Lord was pleased to throw me into a strong, unusual frame so that I enjoyed neither comfort in things divine and spiritual nor pleasure in things temporal. My studies yielded me no satisfaction. Indeed there seemed to be no satisfying good for me to enjoy either in heaven or earth. It was some degree of despair I was under at times. I was held in this disconsolate condition near three weeks, especially at turns ...

That period of spiritual decline was brought to an end through a continued stirring of God's Spirit at Yale: 'But through divine goodness, a great and general awakening spread itself over the college about the latter end of February, in which I was much quickened and more abundantly engaged in religion.'

The following month, March of 1741, the flames of revival on campus were further fanned through the ministry of Gilbert Tennent, a thirty-eight-year-old Presbyterian pastor from New Brunswick, New Jersey, and that colony's leading English revivalist. Encouraged to do so by Whitefield, Tennent undertook an evangelistic tour of the New England Colonies. A group of Boston ministers reported that in three months' time Tennent had been visited by more than one thousand individuals who were concerned for their souls. Besides ministering in Boston, Tennent preached in twenty other Massachusetts and Connecticut towns, reportedly with even greater effect than Whitefield had experienced.

A tall, fiery Irishman with long flowing hair, Tennent preached with the force of an Old Testament prophet. His messages majored on the demands of God's law and on stern warnings about His justice. After hearing Tennent preach in New York on November 14, 1739, Whitefield recorded in his personal journal: 'He went to the bottom indeed, and did not daub with untempered Mortar. ... Hypocrites must either soon be converted or enraged at his preaching. He is a son of thunder, and I find doth not fear the faces of men.'[3]

Tennent spent a week in New Haven, preaching seventeen times from Joseph Noyes' pulpit in the First Church and delivering several more sermons in the College Hall. When the revivalist moved on to Milford, some ten miles away, a group of thirty Yale students followed him on foot to listen to him preach there also.

But not everyone was supportive of Whitefield and Tennent's itinerant ministries and the stir they were creating. One such individual was Yale's arch-conservative rector, Thomas Clap. A 1722 Harvard graduate, Clap had served for fourteen years as the faithful but overbearing pastor in Windham, Connecticut, before assuming his rectoral responsibilities at Yale. Though learned and capable, he was unduly strict and despotic.

Like many staid ministers in New England, Clap stoutly opposed any type of perceived 'enthusiasm,' the eighteenth-century term for religious emotionalism or fanaticism. He and others of his ilk disapproved of the fervent preaching styles of these evangelists and viewed with suspicion the strong emotional responses their messages often elicited. Desiring to protect the students from what he perceived to be unhealthy extremism, Clap forbad them to attend Tennent's meetings in Milford. When some of the students failed to comply with his order, he fined them for doing so.

About that same time David Brainerd and two other undergraduates, Samuel Buell and David Youngs, began paying personal visits to their fellow students to inquire about their spiritual life. Samuel Hopkins, who would go on to become New England's

3. Pettit, *Life of David Brainerd*, p. 38.

greatest theologian, second only to Jonathan Edwards, was then a senior at the college. Years later he recorded in his *Memoirs* that Brainerd distinguished himself in his zeal in visiting the students 'for conversation and prayer.' He also indicated that his own conversion immediately followed the occasion of Brainerd's visit with him.

Hopkins confessed that at first he resented the visit, but afterwards he returned to his room in tears. There he took up Isaac Watts' modified version of the psalter, turned to Psalm 51 and read, as he described it, 'with strong affections, and made it all my own language, and thought it was the language of my heart to God.' Among other sentiments he personalized through the reading of Watts' versification of that psalm were these lines:

> Great God, create my heart anew,
> And form my spirit pure and true.

> Jesus, my God, thy blood alone--
> Thy blood can make me white as snow.

> A broken heart, my God, my King,
> Is all the sacrifice I bring.[4]

Ebenezer Pemberton, a 1721 Harvard graduate and pastor of the First Presbyterian Church in New York City, was invited to speak at Yale on April 19. An eyewitness report of his trip by one of his parishioners reveals something of the spiritual revival that was stirring in New England at that time:

> Whole colleges are under conviction, and many savingly converted. Our minister (Mr Pemberton of New York), being sent for to Yale College on account of the many distressed persons there, in his going and coming preached twice a day on the road, and even children followed him to his lodgings, weeping and anxiously concerned about the salvation of their souls.[5]

4. Wynbeek, *Beloved Yankee*, p. 23.
5. Ibid.

Pemberton was well received by the students at Yale. His sermon delivered in the College Hall on 1 Corinthians 2:2 – 'For I determined not to know any thing among you, save Jesus Christ, and him crucified' – made a profound impression on the students and was immediately published under the title *The Knowledge of Christ Recommended*. A list of 100 subscribers appended to the publication reveals that all but three Yale students ordered copies of the address. Brainerd, Buell and Youngs subscribed for six copies apiece while Hopkins ordered eight copies.

The day after Pemberton's address in the College Hall, April 20, 1741, was Brainerd's twenty-third birthday. Perhaps with the inspiring challenge of Pemberton's sermon still fresh in his mind and heart, he pledged himself 'to be wholly the Lord's, to be forever devoted to His service.'[6]

---

6. This pledge was preserved through an entry he made in his diary exactly one year later, on his twenty-fourth birthday. In that entry he recorded the commitment he had made on his previous birthday.

3

COLLEGE CONFLICT

Three parties soon formed in the early stages of the Great Awakening. Preachers who supported the religious renewal were dubbed 'New Lights' or 'New Side' by their opponents. This was a somewhat derisive term intended to imply that the so-called spiritual light of the itinerating evangelists was a recent innovation rather than part of the historic Christian faith. Those who regarded the religious commotion as not being of God came to be called 'Old Lights.'

Members of the New Light camp became either Separatists or moderates. Separatists were quick to judge their ministers as unbelievers if they were not fully supportive of the revival and believed that they needed to leave their established churches to start separate congregations. Some 400 churches existed in New England before the Awakening. Approximately 100 new congregations were formed as a result of the revival, most of those by Separatists.

Since there were not enough trained ministers to lead all the new churches, many 'Separate' meetings were led by self-appointed lay preachers and, in some cases, even by women exhorters. Many lay exhorters denigrated the importance of book learning and having trained clergy. They only thought it necessary that an individual could preach 'in the Spirit.'

Moderates, such as Jonathan Edwards, supported the Awakening in the main as being a work of God's Spirit but sought to curb its human flaws and excesses. They warned against hyper judgmentalism and divisiveness. Moderates discouraged ministry by untrained lay exhorters while insisting on the need for pastors to be formally educated. They also cautioned against uncontrolled emotionalism and dependence upon visions or strong impressions on the mind as legitimate sources of spiritual guidance.

In July, 1741, David Brainerd's brother, Nehemiah, wrote a letter to Eleazer Wheelock, another of the prominent preachers in the Awakening, asking him to come and help lead a series of revival meetings that Nehemiah was planning for his own church in Eastbury. Eastbury was located ten miles southeast of Hartford and eighteen miles northwest of Lebanon, where Wheelock pastored the Second or North Parish. It was said of the thirty-year-old Wheelock that during that time he preached a hundred more sermons than there are days in the year.[1]

Interestingly, Nehemiah's letter to Wheelock revealed, 'If you can't come till the week after next, probably our Friend Buel and my Brother will be here.'[2] This statement shows that David Brainerd was an acquaintance of Wheelock and that his fellow student, Samuel Buell, was a personal friend of both Wheelock and Nehemiah Brainerd. It may also suggest that Nehemiah anticipated that the two collegiates would play some supportive role in the upcoming special meetings.

A crisis occurred in New Haven in September of 1741 when Wheelock's brother-in-law, James Davenport, came to preach in that town. The twenty-five-year-old Davenport was a 1732 graduate of Yale and pastor of the Presbyterian congregation of Southold, Long Island. His great-grandfather, John Davenport, had been the founder-minister of the New Haven colony a century earlier, and his father had served as the pastor at nearby Stamford.[3] James Davenport likely was invited to speak in New Haven due to these respectable family ties.

Davenport had taken leave of his Southold congregation earlier that summer to itinerate in Connecticut. He quickly proved to

1. Iain H. Murray, *Jonathan Edwards, A New Biography* (Edinburgh: Banner of Truth, 1996), p. 168.
2. Wynbeek, *Beloved Yankee*, p. 28.
3. Pettit, *Life of David Brainerd*, p. 40; Wynbeek, *Beloved Yankee*, p. 30.

be an inflammatory, radical Separatist. When he preached from Joseph Noyes' own pulpit in September he left the First Church and all of New Haven in an uproar by denouncing the pastor as a wolf in sheep's clothing, an unconverted hypocrite and a devil incarnate. A split in the church soon became imminent after Davenport advised the congregation to leave Noyes for good.

A number of Yale students, David Brainerd apparently being one of them, were adversely affected by Davenport's influence. The students became increasingly dissatisfied with having to listen to Noyes' sermons. Disparaging statements were also made about the spiritual condition of the school's rector as well as its trustees and tutors. As a result, when the trustees met during commencement week that same month, they passed this resolution: 'Voted, that if any student of this college shall directly or indirectly say, that the Rector, either of the trustees or tutors are hypocrites, carnal or unconverted men, he shall for the first offence make a public confession in the Hall, and for the second offence be expelled.'

Jonathan Edwards was invited to give the baccalaureate sermon at the college's Commencement on September 10. Probably the school's governors hoped his influence would have a moderating effect on the perceived extremism that had developed among some of the students. Doubtless Yale officials were only partially pleased with the perspectives he shared on that occasion.

He took as his primary text 1 John 4:1 – 'Beloved, believe not every spirit, but try the spirits whether they are of God: because many false prophets are gone out into the world.' From that chapter of Scripture he delineated some of the characteristics of a genuine work of God's Spirit. He then stated his conclusion that 'the extraordinary influence that has lately appeared causing an uncommon concern and engagedness of mind about the things of religion is undoubtedly, in the general, from the Spirit of God.' He further suggested that the irregular and even the objectionable features of the present revival did not reveal that the movement on the whole was not a work of God's Spirit.

He urged all Christians to do their utmost to promote the reformation rather than doing anything that would oppose or hinder it. But he also admonished the zealous supporters and promoters of the revival 'to give diligent heed to themselves to avoid all errors and misconduct ... and to give no occasion to those who stand ready to reproach [the work].' Before the end of that year Edwards' address was published under the title, *The Distinguishing Marks of a Work of the Spirit of God*.

Sometime that same winter Brainerd privately violated the resolution the trustees had passed during commencement week. He did so in the following manner: One day he and a couple of his close friends lingered in the College Hall following a student prayer meeting. That particular meeting had been led by one of the school's tutors, Chauncey Whittelsey, who, that day, had been unusually fervent in his prayers.

Whittelsey, just six months Brainerd's senior, had started teaching at Yale at the same time as David arrived there as a student. In addition to being an instructor in Hebrew, Greek and Latin, Whittelsey possessed a wide range of learning in both liberal arts and sciences, and was considered Yale's most capable tutor at that time. But he belonged to a family that condemned the Awakening in Connecticut, which probably accounted for his normal moderation in public prayer. In addition to six years of teaching at Yale, Whittelsey's ministerial career eventually included nearly three decades of service as Joseph Noyes' successor as pastor of New Haven's First Church.[4]

Since the three friends were alone in the room following the prayer meeting, one of Brainerd's companions ventured to ask his opinion of Whittelsey. Indicating the chair he was leaning on at that moment, Brainerd responded candidly but critically, 'He has no more [saving] grace than this chair.'

A freshman standing just outside the hall overheard the remark. He informed a woman in town of the statement and shared his suspicion that it had been made of one of the college's governors. The lady hastened with the news to Rector Clap who, in turn, summoned the freshman and questioned him about the matter. Having learned who was with Brainerd in the room when he made the remark, Clap sent for those friends. They were extremely unwilling to relate the contents of what they considered to be a private conversation, but the rector demanded they divulge exactly what Brainerd said and about whom he had spoken.

Clap then insisted that Brainerd make a public confession before the entire student body in the College Hall, but he refused to do so. Edwards later reported: 'Brainerd looked on himself greatly abused in the management of this affair; and thought that what he said in private was injuriously extorted from his friends, and that then it was injuriously required of him (as it was wont to be of such as had been guilty of some open notorious crime) to make a public confession, and to humble himself before the whole college in the Hall, for what he had said only in private conversation.'

The rector had two other grievances against him. Not long before, he had attended one of the 'Separate' meetings in New Haven that Clap had specifically forbidden. Furthermore, someone else had reported to the rector that Brainerd had said he wondered Clap 'did not expect to drop down dead for fining the scholars who followed Mr Tennent to Milford.' While Brainerd had to admit he had attended the Separate meeting, he had no recollection of ever having made any such statement about Clap.

From the rector's rigid perspective there was nothing to be done with Brainerd, whom he doubtless viewed as a troublesome, unrepentant and insubordinate enthusiast, but have him expelled from school. That is precisely what Yale officials did the winter of his third year at college.

In writing of these events years later, Edwards certainly did not approve of or try to cover over Brainerd's faults and excesses during his student days at Yale. With considerable frankness he states:

> But yet he was afterwards abundantly sensible that his religious experiences and affections at that time were not free from a corrupt mixture, nor his conduct to be acquitted from many things that were imprudent and blameable; which he greatly lamented himself, and was willing [desirous] that others should forget, that none might make an ill improvement of such an example.

However, Edwards did offer the following explanation on Brainerd's behalf:

> It could not be otherwise than that one whose heart had been so prepared and drawn to God, as Mr Brainerd's had been, should be mightily enlarged, animated and engaged, at the sight of such an alteration made in the college, the town and land, and so great an appearance of men's reforming their lives, and turning from their profaneness and immorality, to seriousness and concern for their salvation, and of religion's reviving and flourishing almost everywhere. But as an intemperate imprudent zeal, and a degree of enthusiasm soon crept in, and mingled itself with that revival of religion; and so great and general an awakening being quite a new thing in the land, at least as to all the living inhabitants of it; neither people nor ministers had learned thoroughly to distinguish between solid religion and its delusive counterfeits; even many ministers of the Gospel, of long standing and the best reputation, were for a time overpowered with the glaring appearances of the latter: And therefore surely it was not to be wondered at, that young Brainerd, but a sophomore at college, should be so; who was not only young in years, but very young in religion and experience, and still less for observation of the circumstances and events of such an extraordinary state of things: A man must divest himself of all reason to make strange of it. In these disadvantageous circumstances, Brainerd had the unhappiness to have a tincture of that intemperate, indiscreet zeal, which was at that time too prevalent; and was led, from his high opinion of others that he looked upon better than himself, into such errors as were really contrary to the habitual temper of his mind.

Brainerd's own perspectives on these affairs were mixed. Concerning how Yale officials handled his situation, Edwards reports, 'he ever, as long as he lived, supposed himself much abused in the management of it, and in what he suffered in it.' At the same time, for the rest of his life Brainerd deeply regretted and readily acknowledged his own unwise and inappropriate attitudes and actions during that period at college. As Edwards observed:

> ... how greatly his mind was soon changed, and how exceedingly he afterwards lamented his error, and abhorred himself for his imprudent zeal and misconduct at that time, even to the breaking of his heart, and almost to the overbearing and breaking the strength of his nature; and how much of a Christian spirit he shewed, in his condemning himself for that misconduct.[5]

Furthermore, with the help of God's Spirit, he was able to work through this traumatic incident with genuine humility and with a remarkable absence of malice.

Brainerd kept a careful diary in two small books from the end of January, 1741, through February of 1742. So pained was he over some of their contents, however, that shortly before his death he insisted those two volumes be destroyed. Edwards reveals:

> ... when he lay on his deathbed, he gave order (unknown to me till after his death) that these two volumes should be destroyed, and in the beginning of the third book of his diary, he wrote thus (by the hand of another, he not being able to write himself): 'The two preceding volumes, immediately following the account of the author's conversion, are lost. If any are desirous to know how the author lived, in general, during that space of time, let them read the first thirty pages of this volume; where they will find something of a specimen of his ordinary manner of living, through that whole space of time, which was about thirteen months; excepting that here he was more refined from some imprudencies and indecent heats, than there; but the spirit of devotion running through the whole was the same.'[6]

The hand of Providence must also be acknowledged in the unfolding of these events in Brainerd's life. Through them God

5. The above quotations of Edwards concerning Brainerd's questionable conduct at and expulsion from Yale are taken from Pettit, *Life of David Brainerd*, pp. 94, 153-6.
6. Ibid., pp. 153-4.

redirected His servant into an altogether different and more far-reaching avenue of ministry. John Piper's analysis to that effect is insightful: 'Instead of a quiet six years in the pastorate or lecture hall followed by death and little historical impact for Christ's kingdom, God meant to drive him into the wilderness that he might suffer for His sake and have an incalculable influence on the history of missions.'[7]

A fascinating historical footnote to Brainerd's experience at Yale concerns a subsequent change of conviction undergone by none other than Thomas Clap. By 1750 the rector had reversed his stand and joined New Siders in supporting the revivals!

---

7.   John Piper, *The Hidden Smile of God: The Fruit of Affliction in the Lives of John Bunyan, William Cowper, and David Brainerd* (Wheaton: Crossway, 2001), p. 129.

4

Awaiting God's Direction

In the spring following his expulsion from Yale, Brainerd went to live with Jedediah Mills, the pastor at Ripton (now Shelton), ten miles west of New Haven. Mills, a 1722 graduate of Yale, for eighteen years had earned a meager living and a widespread reputation as a capable teacher by helping to prepare young men for college. By 1742, however, he had fallen into disfavor with Yale officials because of his strong evangelistic preaching and committed friendship with various New Side leaders.[1]

Under Mills' supervision, Brainerd continued his studies for the ministry. The majority of his time during the four months that followed was spent at Ripton with Mills, though he frequently ventured on horseback to visit other neighboring ministers, especially Samuel Cook of Stratfield, John Graham in Southbury and Joseph Bellamy at Bethlehem.

On April 1 he began recording the third small book of his diary. The predominant focus of his private journal was on the condition of his personal spiritual life. This portion of the diary contained scant references to the events of his life, and generally only as those related to his spiritual status. It appears his exclusive purpose in keeping the diary at this time was to carefully analyze, with a view to improving, his personal spiritual state and his relationship with the Lord.

That he never intended for his diary to be read by others became clear at the end of his life when, only with considerable difficulty,

1. Pettit, *Life of David Brainerd*, p. 51.

his close associates dissuaded him from having it destroyed following his death. Precisely because he was composing a private journal, he wrote with utter frankness. He made no attempt to conceal or justify his own spiritual shortcomings and struggles, but spoke of them in the plainest and severest terms. Nor did he rein in the expression of his most intense spiritual devotion for fear that others would think him self-aggrandizing.

The unbridled passion and the unvarnished truth of his private journal are two of the primary factors that give it its attractiveness and power. Those same two factors make the reading of his diary an alternately delightful and painful experience.

Not surprisingly, some of the opening entries of book three of the diary reveal that his recent trials had had a dampening effect on his spiritual life. He longed for the sense of sweet, intimate fellowship with God that he had enjoyed before that turn of events:

> Friday, April 9. Most of my time in morning devotion was spent without sensible sweetness; yet I had one delightful prospect of arriving at the heavenly world. I am more amazed than ever at such thought; for I see myself infinitely vile and unworthy. I feel very heartless and dull; and though I long for the presence of God, and seem constantly to reach towards God in desires, yet I can't feel that divine and heavenly sweetness that I used to enjoy. No poor creature stands in need of divine grace more than I, and none abuse it more than I have, and still do.

Another matter much on his mind was the course of Christian service into which God would lead him. Apparently for some time he had been contemplating the possibility of being used of God to bring the Gospel to the Indians. But likely in light of his recent troubles at college, that possibility now seemed less likely. However, as he continued to pray about the matter, he seemed to grow in assurance that the Lord might yet use him in that capacity.

> Friday, April 2. ... Some time past I had much pleasure in the prospect of the heathens [Indians] being brought home to

Christ, and desired that the Lord would improve me in that work: But now my soul more frequently desires to die, 'to be with Christ' (Phil. 1:23).

Tuesday, April 6. ... I could think of undergoing the greatest sufferings in the cause of Christ, with pleasure; and found myself willing (if God should so order it) to suffer banishment from my native land, among the heathen, that I might do something for their souls' salvation, in distress and deaths of any kind. ... I felt weaned from the world and from my own reputation amongst men, willing to be despised, and to be a gazing stock for the world to behold.

Monday, April 12. This morning the Lord was pleased to 'lift up the light of his countenance upon me' (Ps. 4:6) in secret prayer, and made the season very precious to my soul. And though I have been so depressed of late, respecting my hopes of future serviceableness in the cause of God; yet now I had much encouragement respecting that matter. I was specially assisted to intercede and plead for poor souls, and for the enlargement of Christ's kingdom in the world, and for special grace for myself, to fit me for special services. I felt exceeding calm, and quite resigned to God, respecting my future improvement, when and where He pleased.

One week later he devoted an entire day to fervent fasting and prayer about these matters:

Monday, April 19. I set apart this day for fasting and prayer to God for his grace, especially to prepare me for the work of the ministry, to give me divine aid and direction in my preparations for that great work, and in His own time to 'send me into His harvest' (Matt. 9:38; Luke 10:2). Accordingly, in the morning, endeavored to plead for the divine presence for the day, and not without some life. In the forenoon, I felt a power of intercession for precious immortal souls, for the advancement of the kingdom of my dear Lord and Savior in the world; and withal, a most sweet resignation, and even consolation and joy in the thoughts of suffering hardships, distresses, and even death itself, in the promotion of it; and had special enlargement in pleading for the enlightening and conversion of the poor heathen. In the afternoon, God 'was with me of a truth' (1 Cor. 14:25). Oh 'twas blessed company indeed! God enabled me so to agonize in prayer that I was quite wet with sweat, though in the shade, and the wind cool. My soul was drawn out very much for the world; I grasped for multitudes of souls. I think I had more enlargement for sinners than for the children of God; though I felt as if I could spend my life in cries for both. I enjoyed great sweetness in communion with my dear Savior.

The next day was his birthday. Looking back, he felt that he had fallen far short in giving the Lord the consecrated service he had pledged a year earlier. He earnestly rededicated himself to serving God with singular devotion in the future:

Tuesday, April 20. This day I am twenty-four years of age. Oh, how much mercy have I received the year past! How often has 'God caused His goodness to pass before me' (Exod. 33:19)! And how poorly have I answered the vows I made this time twelve-month [a year ago], to be wholly the Lord's, to be forever devoted to his service! The Lord help me to live more to His glory for time to come. This has been a sweet, a happy day to me: Blessed be God. I think my soul was never so drawn out in intercession for others as it has been this night. ... I hardly ever so longed to 'live to God' (Rom. 14:8), and to be altogether devoted to Him; I wanted to wear out my life in His service and for His glory.

Another sentence from that same diary notation reveals a further issue he was prayerfully working through at that time: 'Had a most fervent wrestle with the Lord tonight for my enemies.' Quite likely this is a reference to those who had recently expelled him from school. He was endeavoring to respond to their perceived mistreatment of him as Christ had instructed in Matthew 5:44 and Luke 6:28.

The following Sunday, while praying for greater Christlikeness, he again interceded for those who had wounded him:

> Felt much pressed now, as frequently of late, to plead for the meekness and calmness of 'the Lamb of God' (John 1:29) in my soul: Through divine goodness felt much of it this morning. Oh, 'tis a sweet disposition, heartily to forgive all injuries done us; to wish our greatest enemies as well as we do our own souls! Blessed Jesus, may I daily be more and more conformed to Thee.

That evening, as he meditated on a number of texts from the book of Revelation, his soul became enraptured at the prospect of going to heaven, being made perfect like his beloved Savior, and joining the angels in pouring out zealous praise to Him. His diary entry that night included poetry of his own composition that helped to express his devotional sentiments:

> I wished and longed for the coming of my dear Lord: I longed to join the angelic hosts in praises, wholly free from imperfection. Oh, the blessed moment hastens! All I want is to be more holy, more like my dear Lord. Oh, for sanctification! My very soul pants for the complete restoration of the blessed image of my sweet Savior; that I may be fit for the blessed enjoyments and employments of the heavenly world.

> Farewell, vain world; my soul can bid adieu:
> My Savior's taught me to abandon you.
> Your charms may gratify a sensual mind;
> Not please a soul wholly for God designed.
> Forbear to entice, cease then my soul to call:
> 'Tis fixed, through grace; my God shall be my all.
> While He thus lets me heavenly glories view,
> Your beauties fade, my heart's no room for you.

> Lord, I'm a stranger here alone;
> Earth no true comforts can afford:
> Yet, absent from my dearest One,
> My soul delights to cry, my Lord!
> Jesus, my Lord, my one love,

Possess my soul, nor thence depart:
Grant me kind visits, heavenly dove;
My God shall then have all my heart.

At that time he regularly devoted two or three extended periods per day to his 'secret duties' of Scripture meditation and prayer. In some of these times of personal devotion he experienced intense, intimate fellowship with the Lord. But at other times he was distressed over a decline in his devotional intensity or at his own sinfulness. Sometimes he would experience both extremes on the same day:

> Tuesday, April 27. Retired pretty early [in the morning] for secret devotions; and in prayer God was pleased to pour such ineffable comforts into my soul that I could do nothing for some time but say over and over, 'Oh, my sweet Savior! Oh, my sweet Savior!' 'Whom have I in heaven but Thee? And there is none upon earth that I desire beside Thee' (Ps. 73:25). If I had had a thousand lives, my soul would gladly have laid 'em all down at once to have been with Christ. My soul never enjoyed so much of heaven before; 'twas the most refined and most spiritual season of communion with God I ever yet felt: I never felt so great a degree of resignation in my life: I felt very sweetly all the forenoon. In the afternoon I withdrew to meet with my God, but found myself much declined, and God made it a humbling season to my soul: I mourned over 'the body of death' (sin, Rom. 7:24) that is in me: It grieved me exceedingly that I could not pray to and praise God with my heart full of divine heavenly love. Oh, that my soul might never offer any dead cold services to my God! In the evening had not so much sweet divine love as in the morning; but had a sweet season of fervent intercession.

Events during the week of May 9-15 set off a spiritual firestorm in his heart. That week, for the first time since his expulsion from Yale, he returned to visit friends in New Haven. He also met with several ministers in Hartford who desired to have him reinstated as a student at the college. His diary the day before he set out on that journey reveals the spiritual turmoil that the approaching week had stirred up within him:

Lord's Day, May 9. I think I never felt so much of the cursed pride of my heart, as well as the stubbornness of my will before. Oh, dreadful! What a vile wretch I am! I could not submit to be nothing and to lie down in the dust! Oh, that God would humble me in the dust! I felt myself such a sinner, all day, that I had scarce any comfort. Oh, when shall I be 'delivered from the body of this death' (Rom. 7:24)? I greatly feared lest through stupidity and carelessness I should lose the benefit of these trials. Oh, that they might be sanctified to my soul! Nothing seemed to touch me but only this, that I was a sinner.

He did not spell out the particular issues of proud heart and stubborn will that he experienced at that time. Doubtless he had the very human desires of having his reputation cleared in the Yale affair and of being thought well of by others once again. He likely also desired to be readmitted to the college and to complete his formal training for the ministry. Perhaps he had not been able to mortify lingering, secret ambitions to gain recognition through academic achievement and the attainment of ministerial status. He did not divulge such ambitions, but even the most consecrated Christian ministers sometimes wrestle with them.

The next day he rode to New Haven where he was comforted to pray with some of his friends and to hear of God's goodness to them since he had last seen them. But throughout the course of that week he was distressed by the 'pride and enmity and vileness' of his heart as well as 'greatly exercised' by the lack of opportunity to spend time alone with God. Thursday evening he wrote: '... had some refreshment and comfort in religious exercises with Christian friends; but longed for more retirement. Oh, the closest walk with God is the sweetest heaven that can be enjoyed on earth!'

Similar sentiments would appear repeatedly in his diary in the years to follow. Of them Edwards commented after his death:

Though he was of a very sociable temper, and loved the company of saints, and delighted very much in religious conversation and in social worship; yet his warmest affections and their greatest effects on animal nature [emotional senses], and his sweetest joys, were in his closet devotions and solitary transactions between God and his own soul; as is very observable through his whole course, from his conversion to his death. He delighted greatly in sacred retirements; and loved to get quite away from all the world to converse with God alone in secret duties.[2]

Friday he met in Hartford with a group of ministers who were concerned about the treatment he had received at the hands of Yale officials. After hearing his side of the affair, the ministerial council determined to intercede in an effort to have him restored to his former position as a student at the college. But when the council appealed to the school's governors at an undisclosed later date it had no success.

As he journeyed southeast to Hebron on Saturday he was again downcast over the sense of his own heart's wickedness that had lain so heavily on him throughout the week. After visiting Christian acquaintances in other towns in eastern Connecticut – Lebanon, Norwich and Millington – he eventually returned to New Haven, perhaps stopping to visit his relatives around Haddam along the way. Over the course of several days his heart came to be at peace again, and he felt joyously resigned to whatever God's will for his life should prove to be.

He arrived back at Jedediah Mills' home in Ripton on Tuesday, June 1. Though Brainerd was feeling very weak physically, when a group of young people came to visit him that evening, he had prayer with them.

Ripton had been the site of considerable excitement during his recent absence. Mills had invited the controversial itinerant James Davenport to conduct a series of evangelistic meetings at his church. Davenport was accompanied by Benjamin Pomeroy of Hebron. The evangelist, who had a weakness in his legs, called Pomeroy his 'armour-bearer' because he frequently leaned on him for support.

Soon after their arrival in Ripton, serious complaints surfaced that their preaching was inflammatory. As a result they were both

2. Pettit, *Life of David Brainerd*, p. 509.

arrested and called before the Connecticut General Assembly at Hartford. The excitement over their arrest was so great that only with difficulty was the sheriff at Hartford able to conduct them to their lodgings. A militia of forty armed men was called out to protect the Assembly in case any of the evangelists' supporters became hostile.

After a three-day trial that began the same day Brainerd returned to Ripton, Pomeroy was acquitted. Davenport, however, was declared by the Assembly to be 'under the influence of enthusiastical impressions and impulses, and thereby disturbed in the rational faculties of his mind, and therefore to be pitied and compassionated, and not to be treated as otherwise he might be.' The Assembly ordered him to be sent back home, so one week later the sheriff and two columns of militiamen armed with muskets escorted him to the bank of the Connecticut River where he was put on a boat bound for Long Island.[3]

Throughout the month of June, Brainerd returned to his routine of ministerial studies and protracted daily time spent alone with God. He continued to devote entire days to prayer and fasting in an intense effort to gain God's direction and blessing for his future ministerial endeavors:

Monday, June 14. ... I set apart this day for secret fasting and prayer, to entreat God to direct and bless me with regard to the great work I have in view, of 'preaching the Gospel' (Luke 9:6); and that the Lord would return to me and 'show me the light of his countenance' (Ps. 4:6). Had little life and power in the forenoon; Near the middle of the afternoon, God enabled me to wrestle ardently in intercession for absent friends; But just at night, the Lord visited me marvelously in prayer; I think my soul never was in such an agony before: I felt no restraint; for the treasures of divine grace were opened to me: I wrestled for absent friends, for the ingathering of souls, for multitudes of poor souls, and for many that I thought were the children of God, personally, in many distant places. I was in such an agony, from sun half an hour high [before setting] till near dark, that I was all over wet with sweat; but yet it seemed to me that I had wasted away the day and had done nothing. Oh, my dear Jesus did 'sweat blood' (Luke 22:44) for poor souls! I long for more compassion towards them. Felt still in a sweet frame, under a sense of divine love and grace; and went to bed in such a frame, with my heart set on God.

After another soul-refreshing season of private fellowship with God the following Tuesday evening, he recorded this memorable perspective: 'It appeared such a happiness to have God for my portion that I had rather be any other creature in this lower creation than not come to the enjoyment of God: I had rather be a beast than a man without God, if I were to live here to eternity.'

During part of July he again visited ministerial acquaintances in the area, including Joseph Bellamy at Bethlehem and John Graham in Southbury. His diary entry the day he returned to Ripton reveals his characteristic response to the kind hospitality shown him by fellow Christians along the way:

Thursday, July 22. Journeying from Southbury to Ripton, called at a house by the way, where being very kindly entertained and refreshed, I was filled with amazement and shame that God should stir up the hearts of any to show so much kindness to 'such a dead dog as I' (2 Sam. 9:8); was made sensible, in some measure, how exceeding vile it is not to be wholly devoted to God. I wondered that God would suffer any of His creatures to feed and sustain me, from time to time.

Since his expulsion from Yale he had spent four months at Ripton, studying and awaiting God's direction for his future. He was about to receive heartening confirmation that, despite his perceived shortcomings and past mistakes, the Lord still intended to use him as a minister of the Gospel.

5

LICENSED TO PREACH

A group of New Side pastors, dissatisfied with the revival-resisting New Haven Consocation of ministers, had banded together to form their own ministerial body, the Association of the Eastern District of Fairfield County. This association met on Thursday, July 29, 1742, in Danbury, not quite twenty miles northwest of Ripton, to examine David Brainerd and a Yale graduate named Rueben Judd. Both men were granted a ministerial license, which allowed them to preach in the churches of that association but not to administer baptism or the Lord's Supper.

The very next day Brainerd preached his first sermon at John Graham's church in Southbury, expounding on 1 Peter 4:8, 'And above all things have fervent charity among yourselves: for charity shall cover the multitude of sins.' Afterward he divulged to his diary: 'Had much of the comfortable presence of God in the exercise: I seemed to have power with God in prayer, and power to get hold of the hearts of the people in preaching.' His next opportunity to preach came nine days later, on Sunday, August 8, when he spoke at both the services of Joseph Bellamy's congregation in Bethlehem on Job 14:14, 'If a man die, shall he live again?'

Bellamy was a year younger than Brainerd, but had already served as Bethlehem's pastor for three years. A gifted young man, Bellamy had graduated from Yale at age sixteen, then studied under Jonathan Edwards for two years before being licensed to preach and accepting the call as Bethlehem's first pastor when eighteen. He was a large, well-built man with a commanding appearance. His smooth, strong voice could, with little apparent effort, fill the largest meetinghouse, including the barn where the Bethlehem congregation worshiped at the time of Brainerd's visit. Highly intelligent, confident and outspoken, Bellamy quickly became an outstanding moderate New Light leader. He went on to faithfully serve his parish at Bethlehem for fifty years.[1]

Brainerd had his first opportunity to minister to Native Americans the following Thursday, August 12. He and Bellamy rode fifteen miles northwest of Bethlehem to an Indian village named Scaticock, not far from Kent on the Housatonic River. As would often prove to be the case throughout his ministerial career, Brainerd suffered marked inner conflicts immediately before effectively proclaiming the Word that day. He wrote of that occasion:

> This morning and last night was exercised with sore inward trials: I had no power to pray; but seemed shut out from God. I had in a great measure lost my hopes of God's sending me among the heathen afar off, and of seeing them flock home to Christ. I saw so much of my hellish vileness that I appeared worse to myself than any devil: I wondered that God would let me live, and wondered that people did not stone me, much more, that they would ever hear me preach! It seemed as though I never could nor should preach any more, yet about nine or ten o'clock the people came over, and I was forced to preach: And blessed be God, He gave me His presence and Spirit in prayer and preaching: so that I was much assisted, and spake with power from Job 14:14. Some Indians cried out in great distress, and all appeared greatly concerned.

After concluding his address, he and Bellamy prayed with the natives and 'exhorted them to seek the Lord with constancy.' They also hired an Englishwoman, probably from nearby Kent, to start a school for the Indians. Early that afternoon they left to return to Bethlehem.

This was not the first time the Scaticock natives had encountered Christians and the Gospel. A number of the Indians per-

---

1. Wynbeek, *Beloved Yankee*, pp. 41-2.

formed menial chores for the white people of the Kent church. Another young licensee of the eastern Fairfield ministerial association, Benaiah Case, had ministered to them the previous spring and had expressed his desire to settle among them.

Even before that, Moravian Christian missionary Henry Rauch evangelized the Indians of Scaticock and saw at least three of them profess faith in Christ. In February Rauch had taken his first native converts, whom he christened Abraham, Isaac and Jacob, to Olney, Pennsylvania, for an ecumenical conference of German colonists that was being held under the direction of Moravian leader Count Nicolaus Ludwig von Zinzendorf. The baptism of the three Indians had been the high point of the conference.[2]

Back in Bethlehem the following week, Brainerd's spirit again sank at the memory of his past faults and excesses at college:

> Tuesday, August 17. Exceedingly depressed in spirit. It cuts and wounds my heart to think how much self-exaltation, spiritual pride, and warmth of temper I have formerly had intermingled with my endeavors to promote God's work: And sometimes I long to lie down at the feet of opposers and confess what a poor imperfect creature I have been and still am. Oh, the Lord forgive me, and make me for the future 'wise as a serpent' and 'harmless as a dove' (Matt. 10:16)! Afterwards enjoyed considerable comfort and delight of soul.

Those painful memories may have been triggered by his anticipation of a return visit to New Haven later that same week. Thursday he left Bethlehem and, after a stop at Ripton en route, arrived at New Haven on Saturday. There he spent the remainder of the month, enjoying the company of like-minded friends and preaching at least once. The next to the last day of that visit he shared in a number of seasons of earnest prayer and fellowship with friends in various private homes.

On Wednesday, September 1, he traveled to Judea (now Washington), five miles west of Bethlehem, for the installation of his fellow-licensee, Rueben Judd, as the pastor of the new church

2. Wynbeek, *Beloved Yankee*, p. 43.

there. Bellamy invited Brainerd to preach to the Bethlehem congregation the following afternoon and evening as well as at all services the following Sunday.

Saturday evening of that same weekend he spent some time in fervent prayer for his younger brother, John, who was about to begin his first year of studies at Yale in preparation for the ministry: 'pleaded earnestly for my own dear brother John, that God would make him more of a pilgrim and stranger on the earth, and fit him for singular serviceableness in the world; and my heart sweetly exulted in the Lord, in the thoughts of any distresses that might alight on him or me, in the advancement of Christ's kingdom.' That prayer proved to be somewhat prophetic in light of the sacrificial ministry to Indians that the two brothers would later share.

Brainerd received an unsettling report as the new week got under way:

> Monday, September 6. Was informed that they only waited for an opportunity to apprehend me for preaching at New Haven lately, that so they might imprison me: This made me more solemn and serious, and to quit all hopes of the world's friendship: It brought me to a further sense of my vileness and just desert of this, and much more, from the hand of God, though not from the hand of man: Retired into a convenient place in the woods and spread the matter before God.

The Connecticut General Assembly had passed legislation the previous May aimed at curbing the number of 'strolling exhorters' (i.e., itinerant evangelists), who were seen as being the chief cause of the unrest in that colony's parishes during the past year. A law had been passed forbidding even licensed clergymen to preach in any parish other than their own unless they first received permission from the resident minister. Brainerd's detractors apparently felt he had violated that law by preaching while in New Haven recently, and desired to have him arrested and imprisoned as a result.

He had planned for quite some time to return to visit with friends during Yale's commencement that week. Accordingly, on

Tuesday he journeyed back to New Haven, but stayed at a friend's house a distance from town so that his presence might remain undetected. Wednesday he revealed: 'Though some time ago I reckoned upon seeing my dear friends at commencement, yet being now denied the opportunity, for fear of imprisonment, I felt totally resigned, and as contented to spend this day alone in the woods, as I could have done if I had been allowed to go to town.' Of the next day's events he wrote:

> Thursday, September 9. Spent much of the day alone: Enjoyed the presence of God in some comfortable degree: Was visited by some dear friends, and prayed with them: Wrote sundry letters to friends; felt religion in my soul while writing: Enjoyed some sweet meditations on some Scriptures. In the evening, went very privately into town, from the place of my residence at the farms, and conversed with some dear friends; felt sweetly in singing hymns with them; and made my escape to the farms again without being discovered by any enemies, as I knew of. Thus the Lord preserves me continually.

It is not clear from his diary how many days he remained in the country outside of New Haven, nor where he went in the weeks that immediately followed. The final day of that month found him feeling burdened over 'some disorders' he had been observing among Christians. While he did not specify what the disorders were, they likely included some of those discussed in chapter 3 that commonly accompanied the Awakening. At an unidentified location he sought to address those concerns in a sermon:

> Thursday, September 30. Still very low in spirits, and did not know how to engage in any work or business, especially to correct some disorders among Christians; felt as though I had no power to be faithful in that regard. However, towards noon, preached from Deuteronomy 8:2, and was enabled with freedom to reprove some things in Christians' conduct that I thought very unsuitable and irregular; insisted nearly two hours on this subject.

An entry in his private journal after the delivery of another sermon two and a half weeks later again revealed the spiritual conflict that accompanied the opportunity:

> Lord's Day, October 17. Had a considerable sense of my helplessness and inability; saw that I must be dependent on God for all I want; and especially when I went to the place of public worship: I found I could not speak a word for God without His special help and assistance: I went into the assembly trembling, as I frequently do, under a sense of my insufficiency to do anything in the cause of God, as I ought to do. But it pleased God to afford me much assistance, and there seemed to be a considerable effect on the hearers. ... I scarce ever preach without being first visited with inward conflicts and sure trials. Blessed be the Lord for these trials and distresses, as they are blessed for my humbling.

Despite such feelings of personal inadequacy that he regularly recorded in conjunction with his preaching ministry, it must not be assumed that he lacked ability in that area. Very much to the contrary, Jonathan Edwards later testified that Brainerd possessed 'extraordinary gifts for the pulpit.' He described the missionary's manner of preaching as being 'clear and instructive, natural, nervous [marked by strength of thought, feeling or style], forceable and moving, and very searching and convincing.' In addition, stated Edwards, Brainerd 'nauseated [detested] an affected noisiness and violent boisterousness in the pulpit, and yet much disrelished a flat and cold delivery, when the subject of discourse and matter delivered required affection and earnestness.'[3]

The next Saturday, October 23, he set out on a 175-mile preaching itineration. His first stops were at Simsbury and Turkey Hills to the northeast of Bethlehem. Inner conflicts raged worse than ever as he prepared to speak at West Suffield:

> Tuesday, October 26. Underwent the most dreadful distresses, under a sense of my own unworthiness: It seemed to me I deserved rather to be driven out of the place than to

3. Pettit, *Life of David Brainerd*, pp. 544-5.

have anybody treat me with any kindness, or come to hear me preach.... Oh, what 'dust and ashes' (Job 30:19) I am, to think of preaching the Gospel to others! Indeed, I never can be faithful for one moment, but shall certainly 'daub with untempered mortar' (Ezek. 13:10, 11) if God don't grant me special help. In the evening I went to the meetinghouse, and it looked to me near as easy for one to rise out of the grave and preach, as for me. However, God afforded me some life and power, both in prayer and sermon: God was pleased to lift me up and show me that He could enable me to preach. Oh, the wonderful goodness of God to so vile a sinner!

While preaching the following afternoon he faced a different challenge: 'But there was some noise and tumult in the assembly that I did not well like, and endeavored to bear public testimony against, with moderation and mildness, through the current of my discourse.' He was likely attempting to rein in excessive emotionalism in the service.

After visiting at Suffield, he traveled south and east to Eastbury, Hebron and Lebanon. His brother, Nehemiah, had served as the pastor at Eastbury for two years, but was quickly approaching death from tuberculosis. Brainerd next ventured to Millington, located nine miles east of his hometown of Haddam. There his heart was full of passionate desires for complete personal holiness and heaven:

Lord's Day, November 7. It seemed as if such an unholy wretch as I never could arrive at that blessedness, to be 'holy, as God is holy' (Lev. 11:44-45; 19:2; 1 Pet. 1:16). At noon, I longed for sanctification and conformity to God. Oh, that is the ALL, the ALL! The Lord help me to press after God forever.

Monday, November 8. Towards night, enjoyed much sweetness in secret prayer, so that my soul longed for an arrival in the 'heavenly country' (Heb. 11:16), the blessed paradise of God. Through divine goodness I have scarce seen the day, for two months, but death has looked so pleasant to me, at one time or other of the day, that I could have rejoiced the present should be my last, notwithstanding my pressing inward trials and conflicts ...

Jonathan Edwards, in editing Brainerd's diary, summarized the entries for the next ten days by stating that 'every day he appears to have been greatly engaged in the great business of religion and living to God, without interruption.' No indication is given of where he spent those days. He may have returned to Eastbury for a final visit with Nehemiah, who passed away on Tuesday, November 9, at age thirty. Perhaps he also stopped to see friends and relatives in and around Haddam.

It was while visiting friends in New Haven several days later that he received a correspondence that would lead to the determining of his future course of ministry.

6

Appointed as a Missionary

Protestant Christians who settled the American colonies had as one of their primary goals in doing so the evangelization of native Indians. The Massachusetts Bay charter of 1630, for instance, pledged to 'wynn and incite the natives of the Country to the Knowledge and obedience of the only true God and Savior of Mankinde, and the Christian fayth.' That colony's seal, reflecting the Apostle Paul's Macedonian vision of Acts 16:9, bore the figure of an Indian crying out, 'Come over and help us.'

New England ministers John Eliot and Thomas Mayhew Sr. and Jr., followed by grandson Experience Mayhew, were fruitful evangelists to native Americans along the Massachusetts seaboard throughout the latter half of the 1600s. Eliot and the Mayhews, in their respective ministries, each saw hundreds of Indians profess faith in Christ. But King Philip's War (named after the Wampanoag chief who initiated the fighting against the New England settlers) of 1675–6 decimated whole tribes of Indians. The spiritual work that had been carried out among those natives never really recovered. During the first quarter of the eighteenth century most Indians migrated far inland, and colonial Christians failed to maintain a missionary enterprise to them.

In 1701 the Society in Scotland for Propagating Christian Knowledge, commonly called the Scottish Society, was organized.[1] For decades it carried out active evangelistic ministry in the

---

1. The following description of the early endeavors of the Scottish Society is taken from Pettit, *Life of David Brainerd*, pp. 28-9.

Highlands of Scotland, where Roman Catholicism and sheer ignorance were the primary opponents. In 1730 the Scottish Society offered a generous bequest to Massachusetts authorities for the purpose of sending three missionaries to the 'infidels' (Indians). Governor Jonathan Belcher and 'other gentlemen of character and influence' were commissioned to form a Boston Board of managers to oversee the affair.

Three missionaries – Joseph Seccombe, Ebenezer Hinsdale and Stephan Parker – were sent to separate frontier military posts. Their ministries in that setting proved ineffective because the Indians were constantly coming and going. In addition, the Jesuit influence on the Indians in those locations proved dominant. After three years the project was abandoned.

In the fall of 1734 the Commissioners of Indian Affairs at Boston, the colonial agents for the London Society for Propagating the Gospel in Foreign Parts, appointed John Sergeant to establish an Indian town among the Mahican Indians (also called Mohegans) in the Housatonic River valley at Stockbridge, Massachusetts. As will be seen, Sergeant went on to have considerable success in that undertaking.

In 1740 the Scottish Society set up the New York Board to oversee missionary activities to the Indians in the Middle Colonies. This board was composed of Presbyterian ministers, but its first missionaries were New England Congregationalists. In 1741 the board commissioned Azariah Horton to serve among several scattered tribes on Long Island. More than a year later, toward the end of 1742, that board contacted David Brainerd.

He received the correspondence from the president of the board commissioners, Ebenezer Pemberton, while at New Haven: 'Friday, November 19. Received a letter from the Rev. Mr Pemberton of New York, desiring me speedily to go down thither and consult about the Indian affairs in those parts, and to meet certain gentlemen there that were entrusted with those affairs.'

His mind 'was instantly seized with concern' over that prospect. By immediately going to prayer about the matter with two or three Christian friends there in New Haven, he was able to recommit his future and all his concerns to God. In the days that followed he sometimes felt oppressed by the weight of the affair that had been placed before him, but he sought to continually cast that burden on the Lord.

Leaving from Ripton on Monday, he journeyed the eighty-five miles to New York City in three days. Of his feelings as he arrived at the bustling city of 11,000, he wrote: 'Wednesday, November 24. Came to New York; felt still much concerned about the importance of my business; put up many earnest requests to God for his help and direction; was confused with the noise and tumult of the city; enjoyed but little time alone with God; but my soul longed after Him.'

The next day he met with the commissioners of the New York Board – Ebenezer Pemberton of New York City, Jonathan Dickinson of Elizabethtown, New Jersey, and Aaron Burr of Newark, New Jersey. They examined him with regard to his spiritual life and Christian service experience as well as his acquaintance with theology and other branches of learning. That same day he preached a sermon, probably at Pemberton's church in Wall Street, 'to a considerable assembly, before some grave and learned ministers.'

The commissioners found him to be a highly suitable candidate for missionary service. They appointed him as a missionary of the Scottish Society and indicated their desire that he go as soon as would be convenient to minister to Indians living near the Forks of the Delaware River and along the Susquehanna River in Pennsylvania.

During the two weeks that followed he spent several days back in Haddam, likely in part to attend to personal business in anticipation of commencing missionary service. Saturday, December 11, found him in Southbury, where he had preached in John Graham's church immediately after being licensed. There he visited with a young man from Stratford, Nehemiah Greenman, who had shown interest and promise in pursuing a theological education.

Brainerd had been contemplating what to do with the remainder of the estate his father had earlier left him. Thinking he would have no use for it now that he was about to embark on missionary work, he was considering how he might best invest the funds for the advancement of Christ's kingdom. Consequently, he now proposed to Greenman his willingness to underwrite the cost of his training at Yale. Greenman accepted his generous offer and, in time, went on to graduate from the college in 1748. He eventually served as pastor of the Presbyterian Church at Piles Grove (later Pittsgrove), New Jersey, from 1753 to 1779.[2]

The day after making his proposal to Greenman, Brainerd preached twice to Joseph Bellamy's congregation in Bethlehem. In the morning he expounded on a text that had doubtless been much on his mind as of late, Matthew 6:33: 'But seek ye first the kingdom of God, and his righteousness; and all these things shall be added unto you.' His message on Romans 15:30 that afternoon likely was preached as an earnest personal request of the Bethlehem believers as he contemplated his upcoming missionary service: 'Now I beseech you, brethren, for the Lord Jesus Christ's sake, and for the love of the Spirit, that ye strive together with me in your prayers to God for me.' Apparently the Bethlehem Christians were noticeably moved by that message, for the preacher reported afterward, 'There was much affection in the assembly.'

When he said farewell to his Southbury friends three days later they 'supposed it might be likely we should not meet again till we came to the eternal world.' They were not just being melodramatic. Pennsylvania, where he intended to minister, was a distant frontier to the colonists of that day. Diseases and other dangers made it not unlikely that he might very well lay down his life while serving in such a remote location.

He spent Christmas, which was not celebrated by New Englanders, in New Haven. From there he returned to Haddam, where, over the course of the next two weeks, he suffered through a period of marked depression. While spending three days at Hebron and Lebanon he had some relief from his melancholy and enjoyed considerable spiritual comfort. Then, however, came an extremely dark and challenging day:

> Friday, January 14, 1742-3 (1743). My spiritual conflicts to-day were unspeakably dreadful, heavier than the mountains

2.   Pettit, *Life of David Brainerd*, p. 190.

and overflowing floods: I seemed enclosed, as it were, in hell itself. I was deprived of all sense of God, even of the being of a God; and that was my misery! I had no awful apprehensions of God as angry. This was distress, the nearest akin to the damned's torments that I ever endured: Their torment, I am sure, will consist much in a privation of God, and consequently of all good. ... My soul was in such anguish I could not eat, but felt as I supposed a poor wretch would that is just going to the place of execution. I was almost swallowed up with anguish when I saw people gathering together to hear me preach. However, I went in that distress to the house of God, and found not much relief in the first prayer; it seemed as if God would let loose the people upon me to destroy me, nor were the thoughts of death distressing to me, like my own vileness. But afterwards, in my discourse from Deut. 8:2, God was pleased to give me some freedom and enlargement, some power and spirituality; and I spent the evening something comforted.

Early the next week he traveled north to Coventry, then east to Canterbury. In that region of Connecticut religious extremism and judgmentalism had run wild. So while preaching at Canterbury on Wednesday afternoon he 'exhorted the people to love one another, and not to set up their own frames as a standard to try all their brethren by.' The next day he rode southwest to 'my brother's house between Norwich and Lebanon,' where he preached to a number of people in the evening. This was probably the home of his half-brother Jeremiah Mason.

Friday he stopped to visit in Lebanon, this time with Solomon Williams, pastor of the First Church, rather than with Eleazer Wheelock of the Second or North Parish. Williams was a Harvard graduate, a respected New Light and a first cousin of Jonathan Edwards. Brainerd spent several hours with him and was 'greatly delighted with his serious, deliberate and impartial way of discourse about religion.'

The missionary appointee again wrestled with overwhelming feelings of unworthiness the following Sunday:

> Lord's Day, January 23. Scarce ever felt myself so unfit to exist, as now: I saw I was not worthy of a place among the Indians, where I am going, if God permit: I thought I should be ashamed to look them in the face, and much more to have any respect shown me there. Indeed, I felt myself banished from the earth, as if all places were too good for such a wretch as I: I thought I should be ashamed to go among the very savages of Africa; I appeared to myself a creature fit for nothing, neither heaven nor earth.

Despite such severe self-deprecations, God used him the very next week to carry out a ministry of crucial importance. On Monday he rode to Stonington in the southeastern corner of Connecticut. That was the parish of Joseph Fish, a 1728 graduate of Harvard. Fish, a scholarly preacher whose sermons were said to have 'smelt of the lamp,' had enjoyed ten good years of pastoral ministry at Stonington until controversial James Davenport came to town in 1741. Under Davenport's evangelistic ministry 104 people were converted and added to the church, but fanaticism was rampant. When Fish, who had been active in the revivals, objected to the extremism, many turned against him and left his congregation. All this left the resident minister in personal turmoil. By December of 1742 he had become extremely distressed about his own salvation and, for a period of six weeks, stopped preaching to his congregation.[3]

Brainerd arrived in Stonington toward the end of Fish's absence from his pulpit. The middle of that week he addressed the troubled congregation:

> Wednesday, January 26. Preached to a pretty large assembly at Mr Fish's meetinghouse: Insisted on humility and steadfastness in keeping God's commands, and that through humility we should prefer one another in love, and not make our own frames the rule by which we judge others. I felt sweetly calm and full of brotherly love; and never more free from party spirit. I hope some good will follow, that Christians will be freed from false joy, and party zeal, and censuring one another.

3. Wynbeek, *Beloved Yankee*, pp. 50-1.

Fish later testified that just before he found relief from his spiritual distress, he was favored with Christian conversation from which he derived benefit. On February 7, less than two weeks after Brainerd's visit, he returned to his pulpit, choosing as his text for the occasion Jeremiah 1:6, 'Then said I, Ah, Lord God! Behold I cannot speak; for I am a child.' That humbling experience was said to have made him 'an excellent guide thereafter.' Seven years later another church invited him to become its pastor, but the loyal members of his own congregation utterly refused to give him up. He went on to serve as Stonington's minister for a total of fifty years. It is commonly and not unreasonably suggested that Brainerd's visit with Fish and his sermon at Stonington likely played a timely and significant role in restoring that pastor to his congregation.

Brainerd discovered similar dissatisfactory conditions in the church at New London, ten miles to the west, when he ventured there later that same week:

> Friday, January 28. Here I found some fallen into some extravagances, too much carried away with a false zeal and bitterness. Oh, the want of a Gospel temper is greatly to be lamented! Spent the evening in conversing with some about some points of conduct in both ministers and private Christians; but did not agree with them; God had not taught them with 'briers and thorns' (Judg. 8:16) to be of a kind disposition toward mankind.

He next traveled to East Haddam, where he spent a few days visiting with friends and relatives. The evening of Tuesday, February 1, he preached his farewell sermon at the house of an elderly man who had been unable to attend public worship services for quite some time.

The following day he set out for East Hampton on the southeast side of Long Island. The commissioners of the Scottish Society's New York Board had determined that winter was not the appropriate time for their new appointee to venture into the frontier wilderness with all its attendant hardships. Instead, he was to spend the remainder of the winter ministering to the congregation at East Hampton. In addition, his time on Long

Island would provide him opportunity to observe the ministry efforts of fellow missionary, Azariah Horton.

A messenger from East Hampton accompanied Brainerd as he traveled to Lyme at the mouth of the Connecticut River. Not altogether surprisingly, he was oppressed by thoughts of what he was giving up and the hardships he would have to bear in undertaking his new ministry:

> On the road I felt an uncommon pressure of mind: I seemed to struggle hard for some pleasure in something here below, and seemed loath to give up all for gone; but then saw myself evidently throwing myself into all hardships and distresses in my present undertaking; I thought it would be less difficult to lie down in the grave: But yet I chose to go rather than stay.

After waiting two days at Lyme, he and his companion were able to find a passage over the Long Island Sound to Oyster Ponds (now Orient), and from there they crossed the island to East Hampton. Originally named Maidstone when it was first settled in 1648, East Hampton was a prosperous whaling town.

For forty-three years the East Hampton congregation had been served by Nathaniel Huntting. Now sixty-seven years old and in failing health, Huntting wished to retire. He, too, had had his ministry disrupted through the influence of James Davenport, who lived just across the island at Southold. Though Huntting was not opposed to the Awakening, he spoke out against its excesses, so some of his parishioners judged him as being resistant to the work of God's Spirit. The East Hampton people were quite divided among themselves over those matters.

Though he immediately entered actively into ministerial duties, Brainerd felt extremely dejected during his first ten days on the island. But on Tuesday, February 15, he was able to write in his diary: 'In the evening, had divine sweetness in secret duty: God was then my portion, and my soul rose above those "deep waters" (Ps. 69:2, 14) into which I have sunk so low of late ...' Somewhat unexpectedly, just two days later he wrote, 'I find my soul is more refined and weaned from a dependence on my frames and spiritual feelings.'

Saturday he was 'exceeding infirm,' suffering from a severe headache and dizziness that left him scarcely able to sit up. He still felt very poorly the next day, but was able to testify: '... the Lord strengthened me, both in the outward and inward man, so that I preached with some life and spirituality, especially in the afternoon, wherein I was enabled to speak closely against selfish religion that loves Christ for His benefits, but not for Himself.'

The two weeks that followed proved to be peaceful, pleasant ones for him. Then on Wednesday, March 9, he rode sixteen miles to Montauk Point, on the eastern tip of Long Island. Azariah Horton ministered to 162 Indians who resided in two towns there.

Along the road that day Brainerd experienced 'some inward sweetness,' but once he arrived at the point and saw the Indians he felt 'something of flatness and deadness.' He may have been depressed by the conditions he found the natives living in or by the vivid reminder the situation gave him of the significant personal sacrifices he would have to make in order to carry out missionary work among such people. Or perhaps, as often was the case just before he was to preach, he was suddenly smitten with a sense of his own unfitness to minister. The latter interpretation of his feelings on that occasion seems to be borne out by what he recorded next in his diary:

> I withdrew and endeavored to pray, but found myself awfully deserted and left, and had an afflicting sense of my vileness and meanness. However, I went and preached from Isaiah 53:10. Had some assistance; and, I trust, something of the divine presence was among us. In the evening, again I prayed and exhorted among them, after having had a season alone, wherein I was so pressed with the blackness of my nature that I thought it was not fit for me to speak so much as to Indians.

He returned to East Hampton the following day. That brief one-day visit to Montauk Point was his only occasion to have in-person contact with Azariah Horton and his Long Island Indians.

Horton, a 1735 graduate of Yale, ministered to some 400 Indians scattered along one hundred miles of Long Island's southern coast. These natives represented four different tribes – Nantics, Mahicans, Pequots and Naragansetts. Horton eventually baptized thirty-five adults and forty-four children, but in the end only twenty of those showed lasting evidence of genuine conversion. Many of the natives fell away because of their weakness for liquor. In 1750 Horton left the island to assume the pastorate at South Hanover (now Madison), New Jersey.[4]

Brainerd was in poor health the remainder of the week following his visit to Montauk Point. On Sunday, March 13, he was so weak he doubted he would be able to preach. As he offered the opening prayer he felt scarcely able to stand. But as the service progressed, God strengthened him, so that he ended up preaching for nearly an hour and a half on Genesis 5:24, 'And Enoch walked with God.' He afterward noted: 'I was sweetly assisted to insist on a close walk with God, and to leave this as my parting advice to God's people here ... May the God of all grace succeed my poor labors in this place!'

At ten o'clock the next morning he bid a fond farewell to the 'dear people' of East Hampton. He experienced a mixture of conflicting emotions at that parting: 'My heart grieved and mourned and rejoiced at the same time.'

He rode nearly fifty miles to the township of Brook Haven in the middle of Long Island, where he spent the night and enjoyed a 'refreshing conversation with a Christian friend.' This unidentified friend may have been David Youngs, pastor of the Presbyterian Church in the village of Setauket at Conscience Bay. It will be remembered that Youngs, along with Samuel Buell, joined Brainerd in visiting their fellow students for spiritual conversation and prayer during the time of revival at Yale.

After reaching and spending a day in New York City, Brainerd continued on to Jonathan Dickinson's home at Elizabethtown, New Jersey, arriving there on Friday. The fifty-five-year-old Dickinson was not only a commissioner for the Scottish Society but also the leading Presbyterian minister in New Jersey at that time. A 1707 Yale graduate, he had been ordained as pastor of Elizabethtown in

4.   Wynbeek, *Beloved Yankee*, pp. 54-5.

1709. He led the church in leaving its Congregational roots in 1717 to join the Presbytery of Philadelphia. After a schism occurred in the Presbyterian Church in 1741 between Old Lights and New Siders, Dickinson took the lead in organizing the independent, pro-Awakening Synod of New York. A moderate New Sider, he keynoted love as the greatest of Christian virtues. In addition to being a pastor and Christian statesman, he was a popular author, practiced medicine and worked his glebe with profit.[5]

On Saturday afternoon Brainerd rode to Newark, where he was encouraged by a time of conversation and prayer with Aaron Burr, another Scottish Society correspondent. Short of stature and very handsome, Burr was also devout, brilliant, winsome and contagiously cheerful. He later married Jonathan Edwards' daughter, Esther, and their son, Aaron Burr, Jr., became the third Vice-President of the United States.

Only two years older than Brainerd, Burr had been a classmate of Joseph Bellamy at Yale, graduating in 1735 at age nineteen. He was installed as pastor of the Presbyterian Church of Newark in 1738. His keen mind and moderate spirit left both Old and New Lights favorably disposed toward him. In fact, just nine months before Brainerd's present visit to Newark, Rector Clap, acting in an official capacity, had asked Burr to serve as the associate pastor of New Haven's First Church.[6] While Burr declined that invitation, he was likely flattered by it. Brainerd may have felt flattered when Burr had him preach to his congregation on the Sunday morning and evening of his Newark visit.

The next day, Monday, March 21, he met with the Scottish Society commissioners at Woodbridge, several miles south of Elizabethtown. There he was informed of another change in plans for his immediate future. The commissioners had recently learned of an ongoing land dispute between settlers and Indians at the Forks of the Delaware. The conflict made it seem unlikely that a missionary would be accepted among the natives at that time.

5. Wynbeek, *Beloved Yankee*, pp. 91-2.
6. Ibid., pp. 56-7.

Furthermore, the commissioners had recently received word from John Sergeant, missionary to the Stockbridge Indians, that a fruitful work might be carried out among the natives at Kaunaumeek, New York, twenty miles northwest of his ministry base in Massachusetts. For those reasons it was determined that, for the time being, Brainerd should go to Kaunaumeek to minister to the Indians there while studying the Algonquian language under the tutelage of Sergeant at Stockbridge.

Over the course of the next ten days he made his way from Woodbridge in New Jersey, up through southeastern New York and western Connecticut, to Stockbridge. Along the way, on Sunday, March 27, he preached to the same group of natives at Scaticock, near Kent, in Connecticut, that he and Joseph Bellamy had ministered to the previous August. He was detained there on Monday by heavy rains.

Throughout most of the journey he felt 'dejected and very disconsolate.' Probably he was disappointed not to be headed immediately to the unreached Indians on the frontier for whom he had been praying for such a long time. Perhaps also he was wrestling again with doubts about his own fitness for this type of ministry. The possibility that intense spiritual warfare was being waged against him just as he embarked on his missionary career cannot be discounted. Whatever the reason, as he rode toward Stockbridge on the final day of his journey – Thursday, March 31 – his mind was 'overwhelmed with an exceeding gloominess and melancholy.' (See the Appendix at the close of this volume for further perspectives on Brainerd's persistent despondency.)

Exactly one year had passed since he had started penning the third small book of his diary at Jedediah Mills' home in Ripton. Since being licensed to preach, then commissioned as a missionary, he had visited, sometimes repeatedly, about three dozen towns and had preached some sixty sermons. In his ministerial travels throughout Connecticut as well as to New York, Long Island, New Jersey and Massachusetts, he had ridden over 1,200 miles on horseback.

7

A Start among the Indians

John Sergeant had been a missionary at Stockbridge for eight years when David Brainerd arrived there on March 31, 1743. Eight years older than Brainerd, Sergeant had graduated from Yale in 1729 at nineteen years of age. A brilliant young man, after graduating as valedictorian of his class, he returned to serve as tutor at the college and to study theology from 1731 to 1735. In the fall of 1734 he accepted the invitation of the Boston Commissioners for the London Society for Propagating the Gospel in Foreign Parts to become a missionary to the Mahican Indians on Massachusetts' western frontier.

These natives, of Algonquian descent, had migrated eastward from the Hudson River valley in New York when Dutch settlers entered that region, resettling along the northern reaches of the Housatonic River in Massachusetts. They called themselves Mahiccondas, 'the people of the continually flowing water,' while the English called them Housatonics and later the Stockbridge Indians. White settlers found them to be friendly, generally of good moral character and receptive to Christian teaching.

In 1735 the General Court of Massachusetts set aside six square miles of land at Wnahktutook as a town for the ninety Indians of the area. Four white families were chosen to settle with the natives in the town that was incorporated as Stockbridge in May of 1739.

Sergeant's spiritual labors soon bore fruit. In 1737 he baptized the sachem Yokun and fifty of his tribesmen. By the time Brainerd arrived at Stockbridge there were 400 civilized Indians living in and around the town.

One of the original English families to settle at Stockbridge was that of Ephraim Williams, a distant cousin of Jonathan Edwards. Sergeant married Ephraim's attractive daughter, Abigail, in 1739, when she was eighteen. That same year, aided by a government grant, the missionary built an impressive home that boasted three floors and two fireplaces, handsome pine paneling and an attractive baroque doorway. A dozen native students from the missionary's school boarded in his home.[1]

Brainerd did not tarry at Stockbridge. The day after his arrival there, Friday, April 1, he pressed on to Kaunaumeek, some twenty miles northwest of Stockbridge and eighteen miles southeast of Albany, in the woods of eastern New York. The natives there lived near a mountain from which they claimed to hear a voice proclaiming *Kau-nau-meek, Kau-nau-meek*, a message meaning that deer were about and hunting prospects were good.

The Indians received him kindly and from the outset were 'seriously attentive' to his teaching efforts. Of his preaching to them the morning and afternoon of Sunday, April 10, he commented: 'They behaved soberly in general: two or three in particular appeared under some religious concern; with whom I discoursed privately; and one told me her heart had cried ever since she heard me preach first.'

Nineteen months later, in November of 1744, he wrote a letter to Ebenezer Pemberton in which he reported highlights of his first year and a half of missionary work. In that correspondence he credited John Sergeant's ministry among the Indians of that area as being largely responsible for the ready reception he received at Kaunaumeek.[2]

Serving as Brainerd's interpreter at Kaunaumeek was an intelligent young Indian from Stockbridge named John Wau-waumpequunnaunt. He had been instructed in the Christian religion by both Sergeant and Rev. Stephen Williams, the pastor at Longmeadow, Massachusetts, just south of Springfield. Stephen, who had played a key role in the founding of Stockbridge, was a brother of Solomon Williams (pastor of the First Church of Lebanon, Connecticut) and Jonathan Edwards' cousin. As a boy of eleven Stephen had been captured by Indians and held in Canada

1. Wynbeek, *Beloved Yankee*, pp. 59-60.
2. Pettit, *Life of David Brainerd*, p. 572.

for nearly two years. There he learned the Algonquian language. In adulthood he helped to educate John Wauwaumpequunnaunt, who became proficient both in speaking and writing English.[3]

The despondency that had accompanied Brainerd on his journey from Newark to Stockbridge continued and deepened at Kaunaumeek. In fact, he appears to have been plagued with marked depression, from which he had only periodic and brief seasons of relief during his first few months there. His primary grief continued to be an oppressive sense of his own spiritual unfitness. So discouraged was he during his first week at Kaunaumeek that he wrote: 'My soul was weary of my life: I longed for death, beyond measure. When I thought of any godly soul departed, my soul was ready to envy him his privilege, thinking, "Oh, when will my turn come? Must it be years first?"'

He continued to chastise himself for his rancorous spirit and conduct at college: 'Was exceedingly pressed under a sense of my pride, selfishness, bitterness, and party-spirit in times past while I attempted to promote the cause of God.' He was even tempted to question his own salvation, though in his heart he knew better:

> Wednesday, April 13. My heart was overwhelmed within me: I verily thought I was the meanest, vilest, most helpless, guilty, ignorant, benighted creature living. And yet I knew what God had done for my soul, at the same time: though sometimes I was assaulted with damping doubts and fears whether it was possible for such a wretch as I to be in a state of grace.

Despite those personal discouragements, his heart quickly began to bond to the natives to whom he was seeking to minister. Soon he started referring to them as 'my people,' as in this more hopeful sentence from his diary on April 15: 'In the afternoon, preached to my people and was a little encouraged in some hopes God might bestow mercy on their souls.'

In his depressed state, he was greatly distressed by a visit he received the next day from two godless settlers. Upon learning that he was a missionary, the Irishman and Dutchman announced their intent to stay overnight so as to hear him preach on Sunday.

3.   Wynbeek, *Beloved Yankee*, p. 62.

Confided Brainerd to his diary: '... but none can tell how I felt to hear their profane talk. ... I got into a kind of hovel, and there groaned out my complaint to God; and withal felt more sensible gratitude and thankfulness to God that He had made me to differ from these men, as I knew through grace He had.'

His measured efforts to have a positive spiritual influence on them the next day proved futile: 'In the morning was again distressed as soon as I waked, hearing much talk about the world and the things of it: ... I discoursed something about sanctifying the Sabbath, if possible, to solemnize their minds: But when they were at a little distance, they again talked freely about secular affairs.'

He devoted the following Wednesday, his twenty-fifth birth-day, to fasting and prayer. Most of the day was spent alone in the woods, thanking God for His goodness to him in the past year and requesting His enablement to live more fully to His glory in the future. He also implored the Lord to use his recent inward afflictions for the sanctifying of his soul.

The last day of that month he wrote a letter to his brother John, a freshman at Yale. In it he described his difficult living conditions:

> I live in the most lonely, melancholy desert, about 18 miles from Albany. I board with a poor Scotchman: His wife can talk scarce any English. My diet consists mostly of hasty pudding, boiled corn, and bread baked in the ashes, and sometimes a little meat and butter. My lodging [bed] is a little heap of straw, laid upon some boards, a little way from the ground: for it is a log room without any floor that I lodge in. My work is exceeding hard and difficult: I travel on foot a mile and half the worst of way, almost daily, and back again; for I live so far from my Indians. ... I have not seen any English person this month. These and many other circumstances as uncomfortable attend me; and yet my spiritual conflicts and distresses so far exceed all these that I scarce think of them, or hardly mind but that I am entertained in the most sumptuous manner. The Lord grant that I may learn to 'endure hardness, as a good soldier of Jesus Christ' (2 Tim. 2:3).[4]

---

4. Pettit, *Life of David Brainerd*, pp. 484-5.

One must appreciate his ability to speak facetiously of being entertained in a sumptuous manner. The letter continued on to relate the response of the natives to his early efforts among them:

> As to my success here, I can't say much as yet: The Indians seem generally kind and well disposed towards me, and are mostly very attentive to my instructions, and seem willing to be taught further: Two or three, I hope, are under some convictions; but there seems to be little of the special work-ings of the divine Spirit among them yet; which gives me many a heart-sinking hour.

In the first half of May he began to devote part of his time to building a small cottage for himself among the Indian wigwams. He desired to establish his residence among the natives so he would have increased opportunities to minister to them when they were at their homes.

A few days later he confided to his diary a list of the difficult trials that doubtless were contributing to his continued discouragement:

> Wednesday, May 18. My circumstances are such that I have no comfort of any kind but what I have in God. I live in the most lonesome wilderness; have but one single person to converse with, that can speak English: Most of the talk I hear is either Highland Scotch or Indian. I have no fellow Christian to whom I might unbosom myself and lay open my spiritual sorrows, and with whom I might take sweet counsel in conversation about heavenly things, and join in social prayer. I live poorly with regard to the comforts of life: most of my diet consists of boiled corn, hasty pudding, etc. I lodge on a bundle of straw, and my labor is hard and extremely difficult; and I have little appearance of success to comfort me. The Indian affairs are very difficult; having no land to live on, but what the Dutch people lay claim to, and threaten to drive them off from; they have no regard to the souls of the poor Indians; and, by what I can learn, they hate me because I come to preach to 'em. But that which makes all my difficulties grievous to be born[e] is that 'God hides His face from me' (Job 13:24).

This is the first reference in his diary to settlers threatening to drive Indians from their land as well as their opposition to his ministry to the natives. Such tensions would prove to be all too common throughout the remainder of his ministry, both at Kaunaumeek and elsewhere.

On May 30, 1743, he set out to visit the Scottish Society commissioners in New Jersey and New York. His chief purpose in making the journey was to seek their permission to establish a school for the Indians at Kaunaumeek, with his interpreter serving as the schoolmaster. After receiving their approval, he traveled to New Haven, where he attempted unsuccessfully to be reconciled with the authorities at Yale. One wishes such reconciliation could have taken place, if for no other reason than that he might have gained some relief from his distress over that earlier affair. The remainder of the week was spent visiting friends both at New Haven and along the way while journeying back to Kaunaumeek.

Unfortunately, on Saturday, June 11, he became lost in the woods between Stockbridge and Kaunaumeek and was forced to spend the night sleeping out in the open air. The next morning, however, he found his way to Kaunaumeek and preached to the Indians. The Lord was gracious to bring timely encouragement to his faithful messenger, for on that occasion he 'had greater assistance in preaching among them than ever before.'

Sometime that same month, while continuing work on his own cottage, he left the Scottish family he had been staying with and moved into one of the Indian wigwams. He had been unable to find adequate pasture for his horse nearby the Scotch dwelling, and he was not eager to continue the difficult and time-consuming daily trek to and from the native village. More importantly, by residing among the Indians he was able to take advantage of and promote more regular teaching opportunities when they were in the village, normally mornings and evenings.

His inner distresses continued largely unabated. In addition to reiterating some of his previously mentioned trials, his diary entry of July 2 added another concern:

> Of late ... my great difficulty has been a sort of carelessness, a kind of regardless temper of mind, whence I have been dis-

posed to indolence and trifling: And this temper of mind has constantly been attended with guilt and shame; so that sometimes I have been in a kind of horror to find myself so unlike the blessed God; and have thought I grew worse under all my trials; and nothing has cut and wounded my soul more than this.

Desperate to be freed from his turmoil, he returned to New Haven early that month to again seek reconciliation with the college governors. When he was once more rebuffed it appears that his patience failed and his temper flared, at least temporarily.

More than one hundred years later, Thomas Brainerd revealed that David Brainerd actually kept two separate diaries while at Kaunaumeek. The first volume, bound with parchment, contained a record of his religious experiences, and in large part was copied verbatim by Edwards. The other volume, written from May to November of 1743, included a record of his conflict with the authorities at Yale. According to Thomas Brainerd, Edwards cited 'not more than a fourth part' of that account. Thomas still had that second volume in his possession in 1865, and wrote of it: 'We may yet give it entire, just as Brainerd wrote it. It is justly severe on the college authorities; they broke his heart.'[5]

Thomas did share one telltale excerpt from Brainerd's diary at that time which Edwards chose to omit:

New Haven, July 9, 1743. I was still occupied with some business depending on certain grandees for performance. Alas! How much men may lord and tyrannize over their fellow countrymen, yet pretend that all their treatment of them is full of lenity and kindness, – that they owe them some special regard, – that they would hardly treat another with so much tenderness, and the like. Like the Holy Court of Inquisition, when they put a poor innocent to the rack, they tell him that what they do is all for the benefit of his soul! Lord, deliver my soul from this temper![6]

This quote certainly reveals the bitter feelings he wrestled with immediately after yet another disappointment at the hands of the

5. Thomas Brainerd, *Life of John Brainerd*, p. 130.
6. Thomas Brainerd, *Life of John Brainerd*, pp. 54-5.

Yale officials. He realized the inappropriateness of his response, was troubled by it and asked God to deliver him from such a spirit.

While some have criticized Edwards for concealing this portion of the diary, he almost certainly made an appropriate decision in doing so. Edwards was charitable enough toward Brainerd not to reveal to the world an extremely uncharacteristic outburst that he vented only in the privacy of his personal journal and that he himself immediately acknowledged as inappropriate. Furthermore, Edwards was doubtless being careful not to publish information that would have cast the school governors, who were still living and ministering at the time, in an unfavorable light. In addition, by the time *The Life of David Brainerd* was originally published, Brainerd's conflict with college officials had been resolved, so it would not have been appropriate to dredge up and rehash the worst, private hard feelings that had once been generated by that situation.

In the end Thomas Brainerd, like Edwards, chose not to publish that portion of the diary. Both segments of Brainerd's private journal (comprising 120 pages written in his own hand) that Thomas had in his possession in 1865 have since been lost. Apparently those were the only two sections of the diary that Thomas possessed.

He reported that around 1825 most of the writings of both David Brainerd and his brother John had been 'innocently but ... most disastrously' consigned to the flames by a relative of the family of John's son-in-law, Major John Ross. The papers of the two missionaries were burned after they had been stored for decades in the attic of a house in Mount Holly, New Jersey.[7] John Brainerd lived and ministered in Mount Holly (then Bridgetown) near the end of his career. His daughter, Mary, and his son-in-law, Major John Ross, made their home there.

7.   Thomas Brainerd, *Life of John Brainerd*, p. 442; Wynbeek, *Beloved Yankee*, p. 180.

8

Timely Encouragement and Fresh Challenges

Back at Kaunaumeek following his latest disappointment in New Haven, David Brainerd continued to experience considerable dejection. But thankfully his melancholy during that time was punctuated by 'some seasons of comfort, sweet tranquillity and resignation of mind, and frequent special assistance in public services.'

On the next to the last day of that month – July, 1743 – he was able to move into the little cottage he had been building for himself. With vastly increased privacy and quiet, he was able to pursue his devotional exercises and studies much more fully and undistractedly. Immediately he began to sense the personal spiritual benefit of that new arrangement:

> Lord's Day, July 31. Felt more comfortably than some days past. Blessed be the Lord that has now given me a place of retirement. Oh, that I might 'find God' (Deut. 4:29; Jer. 29:13) in it, and that He would dwell with me forever.

> Thursday, August 4. Was enabled to pray much, through the whole day; and through divine goodness found some intenseness of soul in the duty, as I used to do, and some ability to persevere in my supplications: Had some apprehensions of divine things that were engaging, and that gave me some courage and resolution. 'Tis good, I find, to persevere in attempts to pray, if I can't 'pray with perseverance' (Eph. 6:18), i.e. continue long in my addresses to the divine being. I have generally found that the more

I do in secret prayer, the more I have delighted to do, and have enjoyed more of a spirit of prayer: and frequently have found the contrary, when with journeying or otherwise, I have been much deprived of retirement. A seasonable steady performance of secret duties in their proper hours, and a careful improvement of all time, filling up every hour with some profitable labor, either of heart, head, or hands, are excellent means of spiritual peace and boldness before God.

He continued in a grateful, joyous devotional frame throughout the entire week to follow. On Saturday, August 13, he was even able to write, 'All my past sorrows seemed kindly to disappear, and I remembered no more the "sorrow, for joy" (John 16:20-21).'

The improvement in his outlook at that time was quite remarkable. After four very dark, discouraging and distressing months, the clouds suddenly dissipated. While he would experience further significant trials and discouragements in the months to come, his overall outlook throughout the remainder of his ministry at Kaunaumeek was noticeably improved.

The very next week was not without its marked challenges. In addition to finding it hard to locate an adequate food supply for himself and his horse, he was hampered by ill health.

Monday, August 15. Spent most of the day in labor to procure something to keep my horse on in the winter. ... Was very weak in body through the day, and thought this frail body would soon drop into the dust: Had some very realizing apprehensions of a speedy entrance into another world. And in this weak state of body, was not a little distressed for want of suitable food. Had no bread, nor could I get any. I am forced to go or send ten or fifteen miles for all the bread I eat; and sometimes 'tis moldy and sour before I eat it, if I get any considerable quantity: And then again I have none for some days together, for want of an opportunity to send for it, and can't find my horse in the woods to go myself; and this was my case now: But through divine goodness I had some Indian meal, of which I made little cakes and fried them. Yet felt contented with my circumstances, and sweetly resigned to God. In prayer I enjoyed great freedom; and blessed God as much for my present circumstances as if I had been a king; and thought I found a disposition to be contented in any circumstances: Blessed be God!

Throughout the remainder of the week his efforts to study and to procure fodder for his horse were repeatedly interrupted by spells of great bodily weakness, sharp pains in his face and teeth, and considerable mental confusion. Though his health improved the following week, he had thoughts of dying and going to heaven that were an attractive prospect to him:

> Tuesday, August 23. . . . Towards night, was very weary and tired of this world of sorrow: The thoughts of death and immortality appeared very desirable, and even refreshed my soul. Those lines turned in my mind with pleasure,
>
>> Come, Death, shake hands; I'll kiss thy bands:
>> 'Tis happiness for me to die.
>> What! Dost thou think, that I will shrink?
>> I'll go to immortality.
>
> Wednesday, August 24. ... Towards night, found a little time for some particular studies. I thought if God should say, 'Cease making any provision for this life, for you shall in a few days go out of time into eternity,' my soul would leap for joy. Oh, that I may both 'desire to be dissolved to be with Christ' (2 Cor. 5:1,8; Phil. 1:23), and likewise 'wait patiently all the days of my appointed time till my change come' (Job 14:14).

At the same time, he was concerned and determined to fill up whatever time he had on the earth with active service for the Lord: 'Thursday, August 25. ... I find 'tis impossible to enjoy peace and tranquillity of mind without a careful improvement of time. This is really an imitation of God and Christ Jesus: "My Father worketh hitherto, and I work" (John 5:17), says our Lord. But still, if we would be like God, we must see that we fill up our time for Him.'

In the week that followed he rode to New York, making stops at Bethlehem and Danbury, Connecticut, along the way. After spending two or three days in New York, presumably conferring with the Scottish Society commissioners, he set out for New Haven, intending to be there at the time of Yale's commencement. On Saturday and Sunday, September 9-10, he preached at Stanwich and Horseneck, in the southwest corner of Connecticut, attempting to help the believers in those locations avoid unhealthy spiritual extremes: 'Endeavored much ... to establish holiness, humility, meekness, etc. as the essence of true religion; and to moderate some noisy sort of persons that appeared to me to be acted [animated] by unseen spiritual pride.'

Considerable religious agitation continued to stir in the churches in that part of the colony. Just one week earlier, tensions had again come to a head in New Haven, this time involving prominent and influential James Pierrepont. James bore the name of his father who had served as New Haven's first minister from 1685 until his death in 1714. James, Jr., a 1718 graduate of Yale, was a brother-in-law of both Joseph Noyes, the present pastor of New Haven's First Church, and Jonathan Edwards. A committed New Light, he had not only helped to organize the town's Second Church, but had also opened his house for preaching.

Very recently, Pierrepont had invited an Irish Presbyterian preacher, Samuel Finley, to speak in his home. But on his way to the meeting, on September 5, the guest evangelist was arrested by the constable. After Finley was confined for several days, the Grand Jury determined he should be transferred from constable to constable and town to town until he was placed beyond the colony's borders.[1] Those events transpired just before Brainerd arrived in New Haven for commencement.

For a long time he had felt apprehensive about this particular commencement when his fellow classmates would receive their degrees. But when the actual day came he found himself much more comforted by God and resigned to His will than he had anticipated:

---

1. Wynbeek, *Beloved Yankee*, p. 70.

Wednesday, September 14. This day I ought to have taken my degree; but God sees fit to deny it me. And though I was greatly afraid of being overwhelmed with perplexity and confusion, when I should see my classmates take theirs; yet, in the very season of it, God enabled me with calmness and resignation to say, 'The will of the Lord be done' (Acts 21:14). Indeed, through divine goodness, I have scarcely felt my mind so calm, sedate, and comfortable for some time. I have long feared this season, and expected my humility, meekness, patience and resignation would be much tried: but found much more pleasure and divine comfort than I expected. Felt spiritually serious, tender and affectionate in private prayer with a dear Christian friend today.

He still desired to have his record cleared with regard to his earlier conflict with school officials and, if possible, to be granted his college degree. During that visit to New Haven he sought guidance about those matters from Jonathan Edwards (whom he met for the first time that week), Aaron Burr and other friends. Following their advice, on Thursday evening he submitted a full written apology to Rector Clap and the college trustees for any wrongdoing he had committed against them.

Whereas I have said before several persons, concerning Mr Whittelsey, one of the tutors of Yale College, that I did not believe he had any more grace than the chair I then leaned upon; I humbly confess that herein I have sinned against God, and acted contrary to the rules of His Word, and have injured Mr Whittelsey. I had no right to make thus free with his character; and had no just reason to say as I did concerning him. My fault herein was the more aggravated, in that I said this concerning one that was so much my superior, and one that I was obliged to treat with special respect and honor, by reason of the relation I stood in to him in the college. Such a manner of behavior, I confess, did not become a Christian; it was taking too much upon me, and did not savor of that humble respect that I ought to have expressed towards Mr Whittelsey. I have long since been convinced of the falseness of those apprehensions by which I then justified such a conduct. I have often reflected on this act with grief; I hope, on account of the sin of it: and am willing to lie low and be abased before God and man for it. And humbly ask the forgiveness of the governors of the college, and of the whole society; but of Mr Whittelsey in particular.

And whereas I have been accused by one person of saying concerning the Rev. Rector of Yale College that I wondered he did not expect to drop down dead for fining the scholars that followed Mr Tennent to Milford; I seriously profess that I don't remember my saying anything to this purpose. But if I did, which I am not certain I did not, I utterly condemn it, and detest all such kind of behavior; and especially in an undergraduate towards the Rector. And I now appear to judge and condemn myself for going once to the Separate meeting in New Haven, a little before I was expelled, though the Rector had refused to give me leave. For this I humbly ask the Rector's forgiveness. And whether the governors of the college shall ever see cause to remove the academical censure I lie under, or no, or to admit me to the privileges I desire; yet I am willing to appear, if they think fit, openly to own and to humble myself for those things I have herein confessed.

According to Brainerd's record in his diary, these apologies were 'for substance the same that I had freely offered to the Rector before, and entreated him to accept.'

Edwards testified of Brainerd's spirit and conduct during that difficult week:

I was witness to the very Christian spirit Mr Brainerd showed at that time, being then at New Haven, and being one that he saw fit to consult on that occasion. (This was the first time that ever I had opportunity of personal acquaintance with him.) There truly appeared in him a great degree of calmness and humility; without the least appearance of rising of spirit for any ill treatment he supposed he had suffered, or the least backwardness to abase himself before them who he thought had wronged him. What he did was without any objection or appearance of reluctance, even in private to his friends, that he freely opened himself to. ... He desired his degree, as he thought it would tend to his being more extensively useful; but still when he was denied it, he manifested no disappointment or resentment.

The Scottish Society commissioners had sent Aaron Burr as their representative to appeal once again with Yale officials on Brainerd's behalf. According to Edwards, Burr used 'many arguments' in making 'earnest application' that Brainerd would be granted a degree at that time. Being satisfied with the genuineness of his written apology, the governors were willing to readmit him as a student. But they were not willing to grant him a degree until he completed another year of studies at the college.

That proposal ran contrary to the collective conviction of the Scottish Society commissioners, so Brainerd did not consent to it. Apparently the commissioners thought he ought not to leave the missionary enterprise to which God had called him in order to return to school.

Brainerd never graduated or received a degree from Yale. Yet the institution has honored him by erecting The Brainerd House in the Yale Divinity School Quadrangle. An oval bronze plaque on the front of the building reads, 'David Brainerd, Class of 1743.'

After the events of that commencement week, he did seem to find a good degree of closure to his distressing history at Yale. Likely he felt at peace over having done all he could to right any wrongs he had committed in the affair. Doubtless he was relieved that the college officials had finally accepted his confession and efforts at reconciliation, thus effectively clearing his reputation. Probably, too, he was comforted by the fact that in the end his devotion to duty in serving Christ rather than his past transgressions was what prevented him from completing his college course.

He left New Haven on Friday, September 16, traveling first to Derby, then to Southbury where he spent the Lord's Day. The next day he continued on to Bethlehem where he preached at

Bellamy's church. Tuesday evening he came down with a serious fever that, along with pains throughout his body, lasted for three full days. When the fever finally broke that Friday night, he was left exceedingly weak. Gratefully he wrote in his diary: 'I had a sense of the divine goodness in appointing this to be the place of my sickness, viz. Among my friends that were very kind to me ... Here I saw was mercy in the midst of affliction.'

He was able to resume his journey the following Tuesday, but it was not until a full week later that he arrived back in Kaunaumeek. Thanksgiving welled up in his heart for God's protection of him not only in his recent journey, but also throughout the past year:

> Tuesday, October 4. This day rode home to my own house and people. The poor Indians appeared very glad of my return. Found my house and all things in safety. I presently fell on my knees and blessed God for my safe return after a long and tedious journey, and a season of sickness in several places where I had been, and after I had been sick myself. God has renewed His kindness to me, in preserving me one journey more. I have taken many considerable journeys since this time last year, and yet God has never suffered one of my bones to be broken, or any distressing calamity to befall me, excepting the ill turn I had in my last journey; though I have been often exposed to cold and hunger in the wilderness, where the comforts of life were not to be had; have frequently been lost in the woods; and sometimes obliged to ride much of the night; and once lay out in the woods all night. Blessed be God that has preserved me.

Throughout his entire time of ministry at Kaunaumeek, Brainerd faithfully sought to teach the Indians, on a daily basis whenever possible. At first he shared the simplest and clearest truths of Christianity, especially those he thought most likely to help lead the natives to a speedy conversion to God. In keeping with Puritan evangelistic emphases, he laid great stress on two main themes:

> First, the sinfulness and misery of the estate they were naturally in: the evil of their hearts, the pollution of their na-

tures, the heavy guilt they were under, and their exposedness to everlasting punishment; as also their utter inability to save themselves either from their sins or from those miseries which are the just punishment of them; and their unworthiness of any mercy at the hand of God on account of anything they themselves could do to procure His favor, and consequently their extreme need of Christ to save them.

And secondly, I frequently endeavored to open to them the fullness, all-sufficiency, and freeness of that redemption which the Son of God has wrought out by His obedience and sufferings for perishing sinners; how this provision He had made was suited to all their wants, and how He called and invited them to accept of everlasting life freely, notwithstanding all their sinfulness, inability, unworthiness, etc.[2]

After he had been at Kaunaumeek a few months, he composed various prayers relating to the Indians' circumstances of life and, with the help of his interpreter, translated them into Algonquian. He soon learned to pronounce the natives' words so he could pray with them in their own tongue. He also translated sundry Psalms into their language, which they were soon able to sing in worship of God.

After that initial foundation was laid, he provided the Indians with a historical overview of God's dealings with His ancient people, the Jews. He explained some of the Jewish sacrifices and ceremonies (along with what they signified spiritually), shared the surprising miracles God wrought on behalf of His people when they trusted in Him, and also related the punishments He sometimes brought upon them when they forsook and sinned against Him. Continuing on in survey fashion, he next provided a summary of Christ's birth, earthly life, miracles, sufferings, death, resurrection, ascension and subsequent sending of the Holy Spirit. Having completed that survey, he began to read and expound the Gospel of Matthew, a paragraph at a time. Whenever he was home at Kaunaumeek, nearly every evening was given over to those expositions.

2.   Pettit, *Life of David Brainerd* , pp. 572-3.

In addition, John Wauwaumpequunnaunt held school daily for the native children, teaching them to read and write in English. Brainerd frequently visited the school in order to give the young children and teens 'some proper instructions and serious exhortations suited to their age.' Some of the children exhibited considerable proficiency in their learning.

On the evening of Sunday, October 16, 1743, twelve days after his return from his most recent journey, Brainerd was meeting with his Indians, teaching them Psalm tunes. Suddenly, a messenger arrived from Stockbridge. The fact that the messenger had been dispatched on the Christian Sabbath made his communiqué seem all the more urgent. It read:

> Sir, Just now we received advices from Col. Stoddard, that there is the utmost danger of a rupture with France. He has received the same from His Excellency our governor, ordering him to give notice to all the exposed places, that they may secure themselves the best they can against any sudden invasion. We thought best to send directly to Kaunaumeek, that you may take the prudentest measures for your safety that dwell there. I am, Sir, etc.

Colonel John Stoddard, Jonathan Edwards' uncle, lived in Northampton. He served as commander-in-chief of the militia of the western Massachusetts frontier. Tensions had existed for years between France and Britain over competing claims in the New World, and were threatening to erupt into armed conflict. Native American tribes ended up being divided in their loyalties to those two foreign powers.

For no particular reason that he was aware of, earlier that same day Brainerd had contemplated whether he could be resigned if God allowed the 'French Indians' to attack and capture him or even take his life. So now when he received the message of warning:

> I thought, upon reading the contents, it came in a good season; for my heart seemed something fixed on God, and therefore I was not much surprised: But this news only

made me more serious, and taught me that I must not please myself with any of the comforts of life which I had been preparing in my support.

Two days later he rode to Stockbridge, perhaps to learn more from John Sergeant about the existing threat. On the last day of October he rode fifteen miles southwest of Kaunaumeek to Kinderhook, probably to purchase supplies. While returning home in the chilly air that same evening he caught a bad cold, and for the next two days suffered considerable pain.

All of Thursday, November 3, was devoted to private prayer and fasting, and proved to be a time of great spiritual blessing to him. In addition to spending periods in prayer, he meditated on a number of Old Testament passages that had to do with God's mighty undertakings for various of His servants: Abraham and Joseph in Genesis, Moses in Exodus, and Elijah and Elisha in 1 and 2 Kings. As a result of those meditations:

> Was enabled to wrestle with God by prayer in a more affectionate, fervent, humble, intense, and importunate manner than I have for many months past. Nothing seemed too hard for God to perform; nothing too great for me to hope for from Him. I had for many months entirely lost all hopes of being made instrumental of doing any special service for God in the world; It has appeared entirely impossible that one so black and vile should be thus improved for God! But at this time God was pleased to revive this hope.

He returned to Kinderhook the next day to carry out further business, and once more pushed to get back home that same night. 'I had rather ride hard, and fatigue myself to get home,' he commented in his diary, 'than to spend the evening and night amongst those that have no regard for God.' But again he overtaxed his strength, and in the week that followed he experienced illness and pain.

Thursday, November 10, was again given over to secret fasting, prayer and Scripture meditation. He especially resonated with King David's exemplary response to his foes in the midst of his trials: 'Was afterwards refreshed, observing the blessed temper that was wrought in David by his trials: All bitterness and desire of revenge seemed wholly taken away; so that he mourned for the death of his enemies; 2 Sam. 1:17, and 4:9, ad fin. Was enabled to bless God that He had given me something of this divine temper, that my soul freely forgives and heartily "loves my enemies" (Matt. 5:44).'

His ill health stretched out for two more weeks. Toward the end of the month he received further encouragement to continue on faithfully in his service to the Lord:

Lord's Day, November 27. In the evening, was greatly affected in reading an account of the very joyful death of a pious gentleman; which seemed to invigorate my soul in God's ways: I felt courageously engaged to pursue a life of holiness and self-denial as long as I live; and poured out my soul to God for His help and assistance in order thereto. Eternity then seemed near, and my soul rejoiced and longed to meet it. Oh, I trust, that will be a blessed day that finishes my toil here!

9

Wintertime Studies and Reflections

The Scottish Society commissioners had instructed Brainerd to spend much time that winter with John Sergeant in Stockbridge, learning the Algonquian language. Likely they thought it would also do him good to have opportunities for Christian fellowship and social interaction with the Sergeants and others at Stockbridge rather than being entirely isolated from European settlers throughout the long winter. Accordingly, the last week of November he traveled to Stockbridge to begin his language studies. His initial perspectives about being there were not positive:

> Monday, November 28. In the evening, was obliged to spend time in company and conversation that was unprofitable. Nothing lies heavier upon me than the misimprovement of time.

> Wednesday, November 30. Pursued my study of Indian: But was very weak and disordered in body, and was troubled in mind at the barrenness of the day, that I had done so little for God. I had some enlargement in prayer at night. Oh, a barn, or stable, hedge, or any other place, is truly desirable if God is there!

When he returned to Stockbridge early the following week, he continued to pour out his private distresses in his diary. He was burdened to see his days slip away with seemingly 'but little done for God.' He was perplexed to observe 'the vanity and levity of professed Christians.' He wrestled with a sense of 'guilty indolence' and negligence because he was not 'engaged in my work and business to the utmost extent of my strength and ability.'

Then came a day of marked spiritual struggle with a temptation he had experienced in the past:

> Thursday, December 8. My mind was much distracted with different affections. Seemed to be at an amazing distance from God: and looking round in the world, to see if there was not some happiness to be derived from it, God, and some certain objects in the world, seemed each to invite my heart and affections; and my soul seemed to be distracted between them. I have not been so much beset with the world for a long time; and that with relation to some particular objects which I thought myself most dead to. But even while I was desiring to please myself with anything below, guilt, sorrow, and perplexity attended the first motions of desire. Indeed, I can't see the appearance of pleasure and happiness in the world, as I used to do: And blessed be God for any habitual deadness to the world. I found no peace or deliverance from this distraction and perplexity of mind 'till I found access to the throne of grace: And as soon as I had any sense of God and things divine, the allurements of the world vanished, and my heart was determined for God. But my soul mourned over my folly, that I should desire any pleasure but only in God. God forgive my spiritual idolatry.

One can only speculate what specific worldly attractions he had in mind when he referred to 'some particular objects which I thought myself most dead to.' Perhaps they were things, not wrong in and of themselves, that he saw John Sergeant enjoying in Stockbridge: a wife and children, a large and comfortable home, a flourishing ministry and the honor that accompanies it. What is clear is that he was determined to continue finding his happiness in God rather than in what the world had to offer him.

His trip to Stockbridge on Monday, December 26, proved especially trying. Along the way he lost his footing or was unseated from his horse and plunged into an icy river. He had to finish the journey drenching wet and terribly exposed in the frigid air.

The next day he penned a letter to his brother, John, at Yale. The correspondence honestly portrays his outlook on life following the challenges of recent months. While thoroughly sober in nature, it is not without consolation, especially in light of his steadfast hope of eternal life and rest:

Dear Brother,

I long to see you and know how you fare in your journey through a world of inexpressible sorrow, where we are compassed about with vanity, confusion, and vexation of spirit. I am more weary of life, I think, than ever I was. The whole world appears to me like a huge vacuum, a vast empty space, whence nothing desirable, or at least satisfactory, can possibly be derived; and I long daily to die more and more to it; even though I obtain not that comfort from spiritual things which I earnestly desire. Worldly pleasures such as flow from greatness, riches, honors, and sensual gratifications, are infinitely worse than none. May the Lord deliver us more and more from these vanities. I have spent most of the fall and winter hitherto in a very weak state of body; and sometimes under pressing inward trials and spiritual conflicts: but 'having obtained help from God, I continue to this day' (Acts 26:22); and am now something better in health than I was some time ago. I find nothing more conducive to a life of Christianity than a diligent, industrious, and faithful improvement of precious time. Let us then faithfully perform that business, which is allotted to us by divine Providence, to the utmost of our bodily strength and mental vigor. Why should we sink and grow discouraged with any particular trials and perplexities we are called to encounter in the world? Death and eternity are just before us; a few tossing billows more will waft us into the world of spirits, and, we hope (through infinite grace), into endless pleasures and uninterrupted rest and peace. Let us then 'run with patience the race set before us' (Heb. 12:1). ...[1]

---

1. Pettit, *Life of David Brainerd*, p. 486.

The following day he rode to Sheffield, twelve miles south of Stockbridge, for the ordination service of Samuel Hopkins. It will be recalled, Brainerd had played a key role in Hopkins' conversion while they were students at Yale. Hopkins had recently accepted the call to pastor the new church at Sheffield, despite the fact that the work there would likely prove exceptionally difficult. Hopkins described the community as a place of taverns and very wicked people where there seemed to be no religion. The church had only five communicant members.

The service itself made a positive impact on Brainerd: 'In the season of the solemnity was somewhat affected with a sense of the greatness and importance of the work of a minister of Christ.' He was not pleased, however, with the conduct or the temporal focus of the assembled guests following the service: 'Afterwards was grieved to see the vanity of the multitude.' Nor did he find the social interaction afforded the next day to be satisfactory: 'Spent the day mainly in conversing with friends; yet enjoyed little satisfaction, because I could find but few disposed to converse of divine and heavenly things.'

That evening he traveled back to Stockbridge and two days later, on the last day of the year, he returned to Kaunaumeek. The weather for the latter trip was dangerously cold: 'The air was clear and calm, but as cold as ever I felt it in the world, or near. I was in great danger of perishing by the extremity of the season.'

New Year's Day, 1744, fell on a Sunday. In addition to ministering to the Indians, he enjoyed a season of prayer and spent some time reflecting on God's goodness in protecting and providing for him in the past year:

> Of a truth God has been kind and gracious to me, though He has caused me to pass through many sorrows; He has provided for me bountifully, so that I have been enabled, in about 15 months past, to bestow to charitable uses about an hundred pounds New England money, that I can now remember. Blessed be the Lord, that has so far used me as 'His steward' (Matt. 20:8), to distribute a 'portion of His goods' (Luke 15:12). May I always remember that all I have

comes from God. Blessed be the Lord that has carried me through all the toils, fatigues, and hardships of the year past, as well as the spiritual sorrows and conflicts that have attended it. Oh, that I could begin this year with God, and spend the whole of it to His glory, either in life or death!

Throughout the opening weeks of 1744 he remained intensely focused on the theme of finding his satisfaction wholly in God rather than in the world's vain allurements. On Friday, January 6, he observed a strict day of fasting and prayer, eating and drinking nothing for twenty-four hours. During that time of reconsecration: 'I solemnly renewed my dedication of myself to God, and longed for grace to enable me always to keep covenant with Him. Time appeared very short, eternity near; and a great name, either in or after life, together with all earthly pleasures and profits, but an empty bubble, a deluding dream.'

Nine days later, on Monday, January 16, he again rode to Stockbridge in the bitter cold. After spending four days there quite ill, he traveled on to visit Samuel Hopkins at Sheffield on that Friday evening. Saturday he rode twelve miles south to Solsbury (later Salisbury), Connecticut, where he spent the Lord's Day. While there he wrote a lengthy letter to his brother Israel in Haddam. The correspondence not only manifests his earnest concern for the spiritual welfare of his youngest sibling, but also delineates the fundamental principles that guided his own Christian service:

January 21, 1744

My Dear Brother,

There is but one thing that deserves our highest care and most ardent desires; and that is that we may answer the great end for which we were made; viz., to glorify that God who has given us our beings and all our comforts, and do all the good we possibly can to our fellow men while we live in the world: And verily life is not worth the having if it be not improved for this noble end and purpose. Yet, alas, how little is this thought of among mankind! Most men seem to 'live to themselves' (2 Cor. 5:15) without much regard to the glory of God or the good of their fellow creatures; they earnestly desire and eagerly pursue after the riches, the honors, and the pleasures of life, as if they really supposed that wealth, or greatness, or merriment, could make their immortal souls happy. But alas, what false and delusive dreams are these! ...

Oh, may you never fall into the tempers and vanities, the sensuality and folly, of the present world! You are, by divine Providence, left as it were alone in a wide world to act for yourself: Be sure, then, to remember 'tis a world of temptation. You have no earthly parents to be the means of forming your youth to piety and virtue by their pious examples and seasonable counsels; let this, then, excite you with greater diligence and fervency to look up to the 'Father of mercies' (2 Cor. 1:3) for grace and assistance against all the vanities of the world. And if you would glorify God, answer His just expectations from you, and make your own soul happy in this and the coming world, observe these few directions; though not from a father, yet from a brother who is touched with a tender concern for your present and future happiness.

First, resolve upon and daily endeavor to practice a life of seriousness and strict sobriety. The wise man will tell you the great advantage of such a life, Eccles. 7:3. Think of the life of Christ; and when you can find that *He* was pleased with jesting and vain merriment, then you may indulge in it yourself.

Again, be careful to make a good improvement of precious time. When you cease from labor, fill up your time in reading, meditation, and prayer: And while your hands are laboring, let your heart be employed as much as possible in divine thoughts.

Further, take heed that you faithfully perform the business you have to do in the world from a regard to the commands of God; and not from an ambitious desire of being esteemed better than others. We should always look upon ourselves as God's servants, placed in God's world to do His work; and accordingly labor faithfully for Him; not with a design to grow rich and great, but to glorify God and do all the good we possibly can.

Again, never expect any satisfaction or happiness from the world. If you hope for happiness *in* the world, hope for it from God and not *from* the world. Don't think you shall be more happy if you live to such or such a state of life, if you live to be for yourself, to be settled in the world, or if you should gain an estate in it: but look upon it that you shall then be happy when you can be constantly employed for God and not for yourself; and desire to live in this world only to do and suffer what God allots to you. When you can be of the spirit and temper of angels, who are willing to come down into this lower world to perform what God commands them, though their desires are heavenly and not in the least set on earthly things, then you will be of that temper that you ought to have, Col. 3:2.

Once more, never think that you can live to God by your own power or strength; but always look to, and rely on, Him for assistance, yea, for all strength and grace. There is no greater truth than this, 'that we can do nothing of ourselves' (John 15:5 and 2 Cor. 3:5). Yet nothing but our own experience can effectually teach it [that truth] to us. Indeed, we are a long time in learning that all our strength and salvation is in God. This is a life that I think no unconverted man can possibly live; and yet it is a life that every godly soul is pressing after in some good measure. ...[2]

Traveling back to Kaunaumeek the next week in cold, stormy weather left him physically ill and spiritually depressed. For several days he was filled with shame and self-loathing not only due to his spiritual sluggishness, but also because of inner corruption he found at work in his heart. As a result, he devoted Thursday, February 2, to fasting and prayer, earnestly seeking God's help 'to overcome all my corruptions and spiritual enemies.'

The next day he began to compose a detailed spiritual allegory, which he entitled 'A scheme of a dialogue between the various

2.   Pettit, *Life of David Brainerd*, pp. 487-8.

powers and affections of the mind, as they are found alternately whispering in the godly soul.' In the allegory different aspects of the committed Christian's heart – Understanding, Will, Ardent Love, Holy Desire, Tender Conscience and others – are portrayed as separate characters who verbalize a wide variety of thoughts about devotedly loving and living for God. The overarching theme of the allegory is that the human heart cannot find sublime pleasure, satisfaction and happiness among created beings, but only in God Himself. It appears he composed the allegory over a period of a few days, for in his diary he referred to working on it Friday, February 3, and again the following Tuesday. When completed, the composition ran several pages (some 2,300 words) in length.[3]

Such devotional reflection proved extremely enjoyable and beneficial to him. 'Enjoyed more freedom and comfort than of late,' he wrote in his diary on that first Friday of February. 'Was intensely engaged in meditation upon the different whispers of the various powers and affections of a pious mind, ... and could not but write as well as meditate on so entertaining a subject.' The benefit continued to be felt in the days that followed:

> Lord's Day, February 5. ... Thought myself, after the season of weakness, temptation, and desertion I endured the last week, to be somewhat like Samson when his locks began to grow again. Was enabled to preach to my people with more life and warmth than I have for some weeks past.
>
> Monday, February 6. ... Spent most of the day in reading God's word, in writing, and prayer. Enjoyed repeated and frequent comfort and intenseness of soul in prayer through the day. In the evening spent some hours in private conversation with my people: And afterwards, felt some warmth in secret prayer.

As he returned to (and likely concluded) the composition of his spiritual allegory on Tuesday, his heart overflowed as he expressed his devotion to the Lord through the character Spiritual Sensation:

3.   The allegory in its entirety is recorded in Pettit, *Life of David Brainerd*, pp. 477-82.

'Whom have I in heaven but Thee? And there is none upon earth that I desire besides this blessed portion' (Ps. 73:25-26). Oh, I feel 'tis heaven to please Him, and to be just what He would have me to be! Oh, that my soul were 'holy, as He is holy' (Lev. 19:2; 1 Pet. 1:16)! Oh, that it were 'pure even as Christ is pure' (1 John 3:3): and 'perfect, as my Father in heaven is perfect' (Matt. 5:48)! These, I feel are the sweetest commands in God's Book, comprising all others. ... How shall I yield ten thousand times more honor to Him? What shall I do to glorify and worship this best of beings? Oh, that I could consecrate myself, soul and body, to His service forever! Oh, that I could give up myself to Him so as never more to attempt to be my own, or to have any will or affections that are not perfectly conformed to Him. But, alas, alas, I find I can't be thus entirely devoted to God: I can't live and not sin. Oh, ye angels, do ye glorify Him incessantly; and if possible, prostrate yourselves lower before the blessed King of heaven. I long to bear a part with you; and, if it were possible, to help you. Oh, when we have done all that we can, to all eternity, we shall not be able to offer the ten thousandth part of the homage that the glorious God deserves!

Inevitably, he found that he was not able to sustain such an intense spirit of devotion. 'I find that both mind and body are quickly tired with intenseness and fervor in the things of God,' he lamented in his diary the next day. 'Oh, that I could be as incessant as angels in devotion and spiritual fervor!' As was often the case, he devoted Thursday of that week to fasting and prayer, only to find, 'in the general, was more dry and barren than I have usually been of late upon such occasions.'

A discourse he heard in Stockbridge six days later pricked his sensitive conscience and brought back the ghosts of his past transgressions to haunt him. For more than a week afterward he was again cast into a melancholy gloom, making it difficult to study. He even began impugning his own motives with regard to his studies:

Friday, February 24. ... I could not compose my mind to any profitable studies, by reason of this pressure. And the reason, I judge, why I am not allowed to study, a great part of my time, is because I am endeavoring to lay in such a stock of knowledge as shall be a self-sufficiency. I know it to be my indispensable duty to study and qualify myself in the best manner I can for public service: But this is my misery, I naturally study and prepare that I may 'consume it upon my lusts' (James 4:3) of pride and self-confidence.

Gratefully, however, by the following week, his despondency had once again lifted, and in its place was a spirit of exceptional benevolence:

Friday, March 2. ... But in the evening, God was pleased to grant me a divine sweetness in prayer; especially in the duty of intercession. I think I never felt so much kindness and love to those who I have reason to think are my enemies (though at that time I found such a disposition to think the best of all, that I scarce knew how to think that any such thing as enmity and hatred lodged in any soul; it seemed as if all the world must needs be friends), and never prayed with more freedom and delight, for myself, or dearest friend, than I did now for my enemies.

10

'RESOLVED TO GO ON STILL WITH THE INDIAN AFFAIR'

As the spring of 1744 drew near, Brainerd informed the Indians at Kaunaumeek he likely would soon be leaving in order to be sent to another tribe of Indians far from them. The Kaunaumeek natives were greatly saddened at this news, and some of them tried to dissuade him: 'Now that we have heard so much about our soul's concerns, we could never again be willing to live as we have in the past, without a minister and further instructions in the way of heaven.'

Gently he told them, 'But you ought to be willing that others also should hear about their souls' concerns, seeing that they need it as much as yourselves.'

'Those Indians to whom you're thinking of going are not willing to become Christians as we are,' the Kaunaumeekians predicted. 'Therefore you should tarry with us.'

'You may receive further instruction without me,' he pointed out, 'but the Indians to whom I expect to be sent cannot, since there is no minister near to teach them.' After that he advised them, should he be sent away to minister elsewhere, to relocate to Stockbridge. There they would be supplied with land and have the benefit of being under the care of John Sergeant. The Indians seemed favorably disposed to that proposal.

The factor that had most encouraged Brainerd in his ministry to the natives was that sometimes the proclamation of the truths of Scripture seemed to be accompanied by convicting power upon the consciences of his hearers. A few individuals appeared to be awakened to their spiritually lost state and desirous of being delivered from it. Several Indians had come of their own accord to visit him about their spiritual concerns and, in some cases, had inquired with tears what they needed to do to be saved. Some wondered if the Christians' God would be merciful to them since they had been frequently drunk.

In the end, however, he had to content himself with the hope that God was preparing their hearts for salvation rather than bringing about actual conversions at that time. He was also encouraged by some reformation in their outward conduct and customs:

> Their idolatrous sacrifices (of which there was but one or two that I know of after my coming among them) were wholly laid aside. And their heathenish custom of dancing, hallowing, etc., they seemed in a considerable measure broken off from. And I could not but hope that they were reformed in some measure from the sin of drunkenness. They likewise manifested a regard to the Lord's Day, and not only behaved soberly themselves, but took care also to keep their children in order.[1]

On Sunday, March 11, he preached his final sermons at Kaunaumeek, speaking both morning and evening on the parable of the sower in Matthew 13. He had so much he wanted to communicate to them in those final discourses that he hardly knew how to leave off speaking.

The next day he worked hard making preparations for a journey that eventually would take him to New Jersey for a meeting with the Scottish Society commissioners. He devoted Tuesday evening to prayer, asking that God's evident presence would attend him everywhere the business of his journey led him.

A surprise awaited him in Sheffield when he arrived there two days later. A messenger from East Hampton on Long Island intercepted him with the news that the people of that large town had voted unanimously to invite him to come and settle

1. Pettit, *Life of David Brainerd*, pp. 574-5.

as their permanent pastor. While ministering at East Hampton previously, he had been 'frequently' invited to become the pastor of that parish.

From a human perspective this would have been an extremely attractive invitation. Jonathan Edwards described East Hampton as 'the fairest, pleasantest town on the whole island, and one of its largest and most wealthy parishes.' The people there eagerly desired Brainerd to come as their pastor. In addition, he seemed ideally suited to shepherd them through some of the challenging issues they still faced as a congregation.

He did not know how to respond appropriately to the invitation, so determined to make it a matter of prayer: 'Seemed more at a loss what was my duty, than before; when I heard of the great difficulties of that place, I was much concerned and grieved, and felt some desires to comply with their request; but knew not what to do: Endeavored to commit the case to God.'

Friday he traveled to Salisbury, Connecticut, where he was detained by heavy rains. Despite the fact that on Sunday he felt very weak and somewhat faint, he was greatly strengthened by God to preach with considerable clarity and fervency: 'I have not had the like assistance in preaching to sinners for many months past.'

While in Salisbury he was met by another messenger, this one from Millington, about eight miles east of his hometown of Haddam. The congregation there had extended him a unanimous call to come as its pastor for a probationary period with a view to becoming the permanent minister. That invitation would have had the appeal of allowing him to settle back in his home area, not far from relatives.

He continued to make his way slowly toward New Jersey. Despite ongoing poor health, at the urging of friends he preached several times along the way and experienced considerable divine assistance in those undertakings. On the last day of March he arrived in Elizabethtown. The following Thursday, April 5, he met with the Scottish Society commissioners. They determined that the time was right for him to begin a ministry among Indians along the Delaware River in Pennsylvania and encouraged him to go there as soon as was convenient.

He accepted this direction as the Lord's will for his life. Of the decision he wrote in his diary: 'Resolved to go on still with the Indian affair, if divine providence permitted; although I had before felt some inclination to go to East Hampton, where I was solicited to go.'

Due to lingering illness, he remained in New Jersey for two or three days after his meeting with the commissioners. Then he made his way to Haddam, arriving on Saturday, April 14. After visiting several ministerial acquaintances in Connecticut, he traveled back to Stockbridge toward the end of the month.

Most of the Kaunaumeek Indians had moved there by that time, so he spent two days visiting and counseling them. 'They appeared very glad to see me, after a season of absence from them,' he reported, 'and very attentive to, and thankful for my advice.' On Sunday, April 29, he preached in both services at Stockbridge from Revelation 14:4. Of the final farewell to his Indians that day, he revealed, 'Was affected at parting with those that I had spent so much time, and pains, to instruct; and observed some affection.'

The next day he returned one last time to Kaunaumeek. Gathering his belongings, he set out for the Delaware River on May 1, disposing of his goods along the way, presumably at Kinderhook. Still seriously ill, however, he was forced to abandon his plan to press on toward the Delaware and, instead, returned to Stockbridge. It proved to be a brutal day of travel that he completed just at nightfall: 'Rode several hours in the rain through the howling wilderness, although I was so disordered in body that little or nothing but blood came from me.' This was an ominous manifestation of the tuberculosis that would eventually take his life.

Over the course of the next few days he slowly made his way south through Sheffield, Salisbury and Sharon. On Tuesday, May 8, he left Sharon and rode about forty-five miles southwest to Fishkill ('fish creek,' part of modern Beacon, New York), on the east bank of the Hudson River. As he rode that day:

> My heart sometimes was ready to sink with the thoughts
> of my work, and going alone in the wilderness, I knew not

where: But still it was comfortable to think that others of God's children had 'wandered about in caves and dens of the earth' (Heb. 11:38); and Abraham, when he was called to go forth, 'went out not knowing whither he went' (Heb. 11:8). Oh, that I might follow after God!

Crossing the Hudson on Wednesday, he ventured twenty miles to Goshen. Thursday brought him another score of miles west, to Minisink. That ancient Indian town was on the eastern side of the Delaware, near present-day Montague, in the far northwest corner of New Jersey. The natives who lived there at that time were remnants of various tribes commonly known as Munsees.

The next day he tried to strike up a friendly conversation with the Indians' chief. But when he shared his desire to instruct them in Christian teaching for their benefit and happiness, the native leader just laughed, turned his back on him and walked away. Not to be put off, the missionary addressed another 'principal man' who indicated a willingness to hear what he had to say. After a time Brainerd followed the original chief into his house and attempted to renew his discourse with him, but the tribal leader refused to talk to him and left the matter to one of his officials to consider.

That man conversed with him for about a quarter of an hour. Somewhat angrily he demanded: 'Why do you desire the Indians to become Christians, seeing the Christians are so much worse than the Indians are in their present state. The Christians lie, steal and drink worse than the Indians. 'Twas they who first taught the Indians to be drunk. And they stole from one another to the degree that their rulers were obliged to hang them for it. And that was not enough to deter others from doing the same thing. None of the Indians have ever been hanged for stealing, and yet they do not steal half so much as the Christians do. I suppose that if the Indians should become Christians they would then be as bad as these. We will live as our fathers lived and go where our fathers are when we die.'

'I then freely owned, lamented, and joined with him in condemning the ill conduct of some who are called Christians,'

Brainerd later reported. 'These are not Christians in heart,' he told the official. 'I hate such wicked practices, and do not desire the Indians to become such as these.' His words appeared to have a calming effect on the native, so he asked, 'Are you willing that I would come and see your people again?'

'I would be willing to see you again as a friend,' the man stated frankly, 'if you would not desire us to become Christians.'

Bidding them farewell, Brainerd continued on the next day. It is not known with certainty which route he took as he made his way south and west. But by the end of that Saturday, May 12, he arrived at Hunter's Settlement, twelve miles above the Forks of the Delaware. The Forks, the area where modern Easton, Pennsylvania, is located, was at the confluence of the Delaware and Lehigh Rivers. The Lehigh used to be called the West Branch of the Delaware. The local natives called the area Lakhauwotung, which means 'the forks of a stream' or 'the mouth of a creek where someone resides.'

Edwards described the hundred miles of wooded territory that Brainerd had traveled between the Hudson and Delaware Rivers as being 'a desolate and hideous country' with very few settlements. He also states that the missionary 'suffered much fatigue and hardship' on the journey and 'was considerably melancholy and disconsolate, being alone in a strange wilderness.'

Hunter's Settlement had been established fifteen years earlier by a group of thirty Scotch-Irish families under the leadership of Alexander Hunter. A well-educated and pious individual who became one of the first magistrates of Northampton County, Hunter owned 300 acres of land and operated a ferry across the Delaware directly east of present-day Richmond, Pennsylvania. His settlement had also become home to a number of Palatinate Germans who had immigrated into the region from their original Hudson River settlements. Brainerd took lodgings in Hunter's house soon after arriving at the Forks.[2]

His first full day at this new location began quite bleakly, but the Lord provided him with support and encouragement as it unfolded:

2. Wynbeek, *Beloved Yankee*, pp. 88, 103.

Lord's Day, May 13. Rose early: Felt very poorly after my long journey, and after being very wet and fatigued. Was very melancholy; have scarce ever seen such a gloomy morning in my life; there appeared to be no Sabbath; the children were all at play; I a stranger in the wilderness, and knew not where to go; and all circumstances seemed to conspire to render my affairs dark and discouraging. Was disappointed respecting an interpreter, and heard that the Indians were much scattered, etc. ... Rode about three or four miles to the Irish people, where I found some that appeared sober and concerned about religion. My heart then began to be a little encouraged: Went and preached, first to the Irish and then to the Indians: And in the evening, was a little comforted; my soul seemed to rest on God and take courage.

Although Hunter's Settlement had no church building, it had profited through the years from the services of a number of supply ministers. Among those who had served there in the past were Eleazar Wales, the first settled pastor at the Forks of the Delaware (from 1731 to 1734), Gilbert Tennent, Charles Beatty, Azariah Horton and Charles McKnight. Brainerd had differing degrees of contact with each of those men during his lifetime.

His diary reveals that his initial week at the Forks was not without a significant degree of inner struggle. Monday: 'Seemed something lonesome and disconsolate, as if I was banished from all mankind and bereaved of all that is called pleasurable in the world.' Saturday: 'Was, some part of the time, greatly oppressed with the weight and burden of my work: It seemed impossible for me ever to go through with the business I had undertaken.'

Thursday of that week he met with the Indians of the area by appointment and preached to them. Either that day or the previous Sunday was the occasion he later wrote about to the Scottish Society commissioners, describing his initial interaction with the natives at the Forks:

Here also when I came to the Indians I saluted their King and others in a manner I thought most engaging, and soon after informed the King of my desire to instruct them in the

Christian religion. After he had consulted a few minutes with two or three old men, he told me he was willing to hear. I then preached to those few that were present, who appeared very attentive and well disposed. And the King in particular seemed both to wonder and at the same time to be well pleased with what I taught them respecting the Divine Being, etc.[3]

So pleased was the chief with what Brainerd had to share that he gave him permission to preach in his house whenever he saw fit. The missionary regularly took advantage of that opportunity in the months that followed. The chief 's house was probably part of the native village Brainerd regularly referred to in his diary as being located three miles downriver from Hunter's settlement. Count Zinzendorf, the Moravian leader, had visited the Indian village not quite two years earlier, in August of 1742. He reported its name as being Clistonwackin, meaning 'fine land.'

Brainerd revealed that the number of Indians left in the area at that time was small, most of the native population having already migrated further westward into the Pennsylvania wilderness. Only about ten Indian families still had their homes in the region, and some of them were separated from each other by a distance of several miles. So during his initial preaching opportunities to the natives of the area he spoke to audiences of not more than twenty to twenty-five people.

These Delawares or, as they called themselves, Lenni-Lenapes, 'the original people,' had once had as their home most of New Jersey and the Delaware River valleys. They were the even-tempered Algonquians who made the famous peace treaty with William Penn as he sought to establish the colony that would come to bear his name. At that time they lived in thriving communities of hundreds of people, with related familial households living together in bark long-houses.

Through a century of contact with ever-increasing numbers of settlers, the Delawares' cultural and communal life had largely disintegrated. Many of them adopted the white man's ways and

3. Pettit, *Life of David Brainerd*, pp. 576-7.

clothes and inherited his liquor and diseases. Some moved west in an attempt to preserve their ancient customs and beliefs.

Up until a few years before Brainerd's arrival at the Forks, a goodly number of Delawares had continued to live in that choice agricultural area. The infamous Walking Purchase of 1737, however, stripped the natives of nearly all their lands and homes in the Forks of the Delaware triangle. As a result of that dubious transaction, the Delawares lost 1,200 square miles of land. Of that vast tract, only ten square miles were allowed for all the Indians living in the entire Forks region. In the seven years that followed, leading up to the time of Brainerd's arrival at the Forks, hundreds of white families settled in the area.

To make matters worse for the Delawares, when they appealed to their Iroquois 'cousins,' the powerful Five Nations Confederacy of New York State, they received rebuke and ridicule rather than assistance. At the Great Treaty held with the Five Nations Confederacy at Philadelphia in July of 1742, the Iroquois mercilessly upbraided the Delawares for losing their lands to the whites, scorned them as 'weak women' and ordered them to remove westward to the region of the Susquehanna River.[4]

On his second Sunday at the Forks, Brainerd again preached to both natives and settlers. He attended a native funeral the following Sunday. 'Was affected to see their heathenish practices,' he commented afterwards. Following the funeral he was able to preach a sermon to a considerable number of them and observed that they were very attentive. He then preached with power to the settlers. 'Several people seemed much concerned for their souls,' he related, 'especially one who had been educated a Roman Catholic.'

Having been at the Forks only two weeks, he set out on a journey back to Newark, New Jersey, on Monday, May 28. There he was to undergo his ordination examination. His first day out he rode through the wooded New Jersey wilderness to Black River (modern Chester), becoming quite fatigued in the late spring heat. He finished the seventy-mile journey to Newark the next day.

4.   Wynbeek, *Beloved Yankee*, pp. 97-9.

Wednesday he rode the few miles to Jonathan Dickinson's home in Elizabethtown where he was invited to stay for several days as he finalized his preparations for the examination. His week of studies there was prosecuted 'in a very weak state of body.'

When the New York Presbytery gathered in Newark on Monday, June 11, to begin the examination, Brainerd revealed of himself: 'Was very weak and disordered in body, yet endeavored to repose my confidence in God.' After spending most of the morning alone in private prayer and reflection, he preached his probation sermon at three in the afternoon on the text that had been assigned to him for the occasion, Acts 26:17-18: 'Delivering thee from the people, and from the Gentiles, unto whom now I send thee, to open their eyes, and to turn them from darkness to light, and from the power of Satan unto God, that they may receive forgiveness of sins, and inheritance among them which are sanctified by faith that is in me.'

Following the sermon he underwent an initial verbal examination, likely having to do with his understanding of Christian doctrine, before the presbytery. That evening, though very tired, he was unable to sleep: 'Was much tired, and my mind burdened with the greatness of that charge I was in the most solemn manner about to take upon me: My mind was so pressed with the weight of the work incumbent upon me that I could not sleep this night, though very weary and in great need of rest.'

The next morning he was examined further, this time with regard to his 'experimental acquaintance with Christianity' – probably including both his personal spiritual life and his Christian service experience. Having satisfactorily passed all the examinations, his ordination service was held at ten o'clock that morning. Ebenezer Pemberton preached from Luke 14:23: 'And the lord said unto the servant, Go out into the highways and hedges, and compel them to come in, that my house may be filled.'[5]

Brainerd responded to this charge in his typical sober fashion:

5. The complete sermon Pemberton preached at Brainerd's ordination service is recorded in Sereno Edwards Dwight, *Memoirs of the Rev. David Brainerd* (New Haven: Converse, 1822), pp. 13-28.

At this time I was affected with a sense of the important trust committed to me; yet was composed and solemn, without distraction: And I hope I then (as many times before) gave myself up to God, to be for Him and not for another. Oh, that I might always be engaged in the service of God, and duly remember the solemn charge I have received, in the presence of God, angels, and men; Amen!

11

SUMMER AT THE FORKS

Brainerd spent the day after his ordination back at Jonathan Dickinson's home in Elizabethtown, working on a written account he was preparing for the Scottish Society of his missionary endeavors to date. He had hoped to depart for the Forks of the Delaware the following afternoon, but a severe headache forced him, instead, to take to a bed.

He doubtless received excellent care from his host, for in addition to being an outstanding pastor, Dickinson excelled in the practice of medicine. In fact, in 1740 he had published one of the first American documents on the subject of sinus infection, *Observations of that terrible disease, vulgarly called throat distemper*. For this fortuitous, providential ordering of affairs, Brainerd wrote with gratitude: 'I often admired the goodness of God, that He did not suffer me to proceed on my journey from this place where I was so tenderly used [treated], and to be sick by the way among strangers. God is very gracious to me, both in health and sickness, and intermingles much mercy with all my afflictions and toils.'

That Saturday, June 16, he received some relief from his physical distress through the administration of an emetic. He left for the Forks of the Delaware the following Tuesday and completed the seventy-mile journey in three days. His first Sunday back at the Forks, despite being 'extremely feeble' and 'scarce able to walk,' he visited the Indians. He took special pains to instruct some who were disaffected to Christianity. Even as he taught the natives, he privately implored God to do a work among them: 'My mind was much burdened with the weight and difficulty of my work.

My whole dependence and hope of success seemed to be on God; who alone I saw could make them willing to receive instruction. My heart was much engaged in prayer, sending up silent requests to God even while I was speaking to them.'

Most of Tuesday was spent translating prayers into the Indians' native tongue. As the Mahican dialect he had learned at Kaunaumeek and Stockbridge was useless among the Delawares at the Forks, this translating was done with the help of a native interpreter named Moses Tattamy. (His actual name was Moses Tinda Tautamy, but he came to be known more commonly in historical accounts as Moses Tattamy.)

About fifty years old when Brainerd first met him, Tattamy had earlier served as a messenger and translator for the Penn government during various negotiations with area Indians. For those services he received a grant of some 200 acres of land near present-day Stockertown and Tatamy. He encouraged his fellow natives to adopt the white man's customs and way of living. He had received a small amount of Christian instruction and professed his willingness to embrace that religion and English laws. For these reasons he had been permitted to retain his land when most of his fellow Delawares were forced to leave the Forks.

Tattamy had hosted a delegation of fifteen Moravians, led by Count Zinzendorf, when the group visited his 'plantation' two summers earlier, in July of 1742. Moravian historian John Heckewelder described Tattamy as the Delawares' 'good and highly respected chief Tademi, a man of such an easy and friendly address, that he could not but be loved by all who knew him.'[1]

While Tattamy had obvious qualities and accomplishments to commend him, his acquaintance with spiritual matters was practically nil. Of the original attempt at translating prayers into the Delaware tongue, Brainerd wrote, 'Met with great difficulty by reason that my interpreter was altogether unacquainted with the business.'

That initial struggle with translation work left the missionary feeling quite discouraged. But that evening the Lord brought him timely encouragement through prayer and meditation on a pair of relevant scriptural examples:

1. Wynbeek, *Beloved Yankee*, p. 99.

In prayer my soul was enlarged, and my faith drawn into sensible exercise; was enabled to cry to God for my poor Indians; and though the work of their conversion appeared 'impossible with man,' yet 'with God' I saw 'all things were possible' (Luke 18:27). My faith was much strengthened by observing the wonderful assistance God afforded his servants Nehemiah and Ezra in reforming his people and re-establishing his ancient church.

As he rode to preach to the Indians about noon that Thursday, June 28, he prayerfully sought God's blessing on them for the Lord's glory rather than his own honor: 'Could freely tell God He knew that the cause was not mine, which I was engaged in; but it was His own cause, and it would be for His own glory to convert the poor Indians: And blessed be God, I felt no desire of their conversion that I might receive honor from the world, as being the instrument of it.'

He was 'much solemnized' on Saturday by reading Daniel 9, where the prophet earnestly prayed for the restoration of God's people to their homeland following seventy years of captivity in Babylon. 'I saw how God had called out his servants to prayer,' he wrote, 'and made them wrestle with Him when He designed to bestow any great mercy on His church.' As a result, right then and again later that day he spent time fervently petitioning the Lord for the building up of Zion, His Church.

But the very next morning he was grieved by wandering, vain thoughts and preached 'without any heart.' In his afternoon discourse, however, he began to feel within himself a spirit of love, warmth and power with which to address his audience. He sensed the Lord's assistance as he pleaded with the natives from Jeremiah 10:2, 3 and 10 to turn from all the vanities of the heathen to the living God. He was also sure that God had touched their consciences, because they suddenly became more attentive than he had ever seen them before.

As he returned to Hunter's Settlement that afternoon his fingers became very weak and somewhat numb so that he had difficulty straightening them. When he dismounted at his residence, he could hardly walk. 'My joints seemed all to be loosed.' Yet he summoned enough strength to preach to the settlers that evening. Some of the

Indians had been so moved at the afternoon meeting that they attended the service at the settlement as well. One native appeared to be under considerable spiritual concern.

Brainerd's physical weakness continued throughout the days that followed and likely contributed to some feelings of spiritual barrenness and vileness that he wrestled with that week. On Friday, July 6, after earnestly praying that his soul might be 'washed from its exceeding pollution and defilement,' he recorded a significant shift he detected in his more recent desires for personal holiness and ministry:

> I am, of late, most of all concerned for ministerial qualifications and the conversion of the heathen: Last year I longed to be prepared for a world of glory, and speedily to depart out of this world; but of late all my concern almost is for the conversion of the heathen; and for that end I long to live. But blessed be God, I have less desire to live for any of the pleasures of the world, than ever I had: I long and love to be a pilgrim; and want grace to imitate the life, labors, and sufferings of St Paul among the heathen. And when I long for holiness now, it is not so much for myself as formerly; but rather that thereby I may become an 'able minister of the New Testament' (2 Cor. 3:6), especially to the heathen.

The next day he was 'refreshed and invigorated' by reading the biblical account of Elijah's translation to heaven. Comparing his diary entry of Sunday evening to what he had written just two days earlier reveals that he must have been experiencing mixed desires with regard to continuing his earthly ministry or going to be with the Lord, just as the Apostle Paul did in Philippians 1:23-24. At the end of that Lord's Day he wrote: 'Longed to "depart and be with Christ" (Phil. 1:23), more than at any time of late. My soul was exceedingly united to the saints of ancient times, as well as those now living; especially my soul melted for the society of Elijah and Elisha.'

Nearly two weeks later, on Saturday, July 21, he became deeply distressed when he learned the Indians were planning to meet the next day for an idolatrous feast and dance. He thought that in good conscience he must go and attempt to dissuade them from their intended activities, but was unsure how to go about it. So he turned to mighty prevailing prayer:

> I withdrew for prayer, hoping for strength from above. And in prayer I was exceedingly enlarged, and my soul was as much drawn out as ever I remember it to have been in my life, or near. I was in such anguish, and pleaded with so much earnestness and importunity, that when I rose from my knees I felt extremely weak and overcome; I could scarcely walk straight, my joints were loosed, the sweat ran down my face and body, and nature seemed as if it would dissolve. So far as I could judge, I was wholly free from selfish ends in my fervent supplications for the poor Indians. I knew they were met together to worship devils, and not God; and this made me cry earnestly, that God would now appear and help me in my attempts to break up this idolatrous meeting. ... And thus I spent the evening, praying incessantly for divine assistance, and that I might not be self-dependent, but still have my whole dependence upon God.

He slept restlessly that night, dreaming about the troubling situation and waking frequently. Each time he awoke, 'the first thing I thought of was this great work of pleading for God against Satan.' As soon as he was dressed the next morning he withdrew into the woods to again pour out his burdened soul to the Lord. As he rode the three miles to where the Indians were meeting, he continually asked God for His presence and assistance. He began 'hoping and almost expecting' that God would make that the day when He would show His spiritual power and grace among the Indians in a remarkable fashion.

'When I came to them,' he afterward reported, 'I found them engaged in their frolic, but through divine goodness I got them to break up and attend to my preaching.' Both that morning and afternoon the natives listened to his sermons, but there was no evidence of any special working of God's power among them. Consequently, later that evening: 'Satan took occasion to tempt and buffet me with these cursed suggestions, "There is no God" (Ps. 14:1), or if there be, He is not able to convert the Indians before they had more knowledge, etc.'

The next day, Monday, July 23, he rode fifteen miles southwest to a settlement of Irish families near the Lehigh River. The community, located about three miles north of contemporary Catasauqua, was named Craig's Settlement after its two unrelated founders, Thomas and James Craig. The Craigs had led a group of sixteen families that settled as squatters at the location in 1728. Brainerd's first sermon at that settlement was on Matthew 5:3, 'Blessed are the poor in spirit: for theirs is the kingdom of heaven.' As the settlement did not have a church building, he may have preached at the home of James Craig, the usual lodging place for visiting ministers. [2]

He ventured seventeen miles further west on Tuesday to visit a group of Indians who were camped temporarily at a place called Kauksesauchung, near present Cherryville. In order to get there he needed to cross 'a hideous mountain,' the easternmost range of the Appalachian chain. Some 1,500 feet high, it was rough, rocky and very steep.

The group of thirteen natives camping there readily accepted his offer to preach to them that evening and the next morning. They listened attentively and were somewhat surprised at what he had to say, having never heard Christian teaching before. Two or three of the Indians were suspicious of him. Pointing out that settlers had abused them and seized their lands, they could not believe that he, a white man, was truly concerned for their happiness. On the contrary, they feared that the whites intended to make them slaves or even to take them on board their ships and compel them to fight with 'the people over the water' (their designation of the French and Spanish).

Most in the group, however, were very friendly toward him. They informed him that they were soon departing for their home on the Susquehanna and encouraged him to come visit them there. They indicated considerable desire to receive further Christian instruction.

Returning to Craig's Settlement on Wednesday, he preached to a sizable congregation and noted a considerable appearance of

2. Wynbeek, *Beloved Yankee*, pp. 103-4.

spiritual awakening in the audience as he spoke. That was likely the particular occasion he would write about in his Journal nearly a year later as being when a definite spiritual impression was made on the heart of his interpreter, Moses Tattamy. Brainerd wrote in retrospect of Tattamy on July 21, 1745:

> But he seemed to have little or no impression of religion upon his mind, and in that respect was very unfit for his work [of translating], being incapable of understanding and communicating to others many things of importance; so that I labored under great disadvantages in addressing the Indians, for want of his having an experimental, as well as more doctrinal acquaintance with divine truths; and, at times, my spirits sank, and were much discouraged under this difficulty, especially when I observed that divine truths made little or no impressions upon his mind for many weeks together. ...
>
> Near the latter end of July, 1744, I preached to an assembly of white people, with more freedom and fervency than I could possibly address the Indians with, without their having first attained a greater measure of doctrinal knowledge. At this time he was present, and was somewhat awakened to a concern for his soul; so that the next day he discoursed freely with me about his spiritual concerns, and gave me an opportunity to use further endeavors to fasten the impressions of his perishing state upon his mind. I could plainly perceive for some time after this, that he addressed the Indians with more concern and fervency than he had formerly done.

Brainerd arrived back at Hunter's Settlement on Thursday, July 26, thoroughly worn out. There he suddenly fell very ill, so much so that on Sunday he was unable to preach. Throughout the week that followed he was extremely weak and faint as well as sick to his stomach.

On the last day of July he did manage to write a letter to an unidentified individual. When Edwards published his account of Brainerd's life, he appended a sampling of letters the missionary had written to various people between the years

1743 and 1747. This one, of July 31, 1744, Edwards states, was written 'to a special friend.' Some have postulated that Edwards intentionally concealed the identity of the recipient of this particular letter because this 'special friend' was a young woman, most likely Edwards' own daughter, Jerusha. As will be seen in later chapters, a close but non-romantic friendship did develop between Brainerd and Jerusha near the end of his life. But four considerations render the unfounded speculation that he wrote her a letter from the Forks of the Delaware in the summer of 1744 virtually untenable.

First of all, Edwards used very similar friendship terminology to designate, again quite anonymously, two male acquaintances to whom Brainerd later wrote. According to Edwards, Brainerd's letter of December 24, 1744, was written 'to a special friend, a minister of the Gospel in New Jersey,' while the missionary's correspondence during the summer of 1747 was penned 'to a young gentleman, a candidate for the work of the ministry, for whom he had a special friendship.'

In the second place, there is simply no clear evidence that Brainerd ever met Jerusha Edwards till the closing months of his life. Without a shred of verifying evidence some have suggested that he first met Jerusha at Yale's commencement in September of 1743, when Jonathan Edwards advised him about apologizing to the school officials. It is known that one or another of Edwards' daughters sometimes accompanied him on his journeys. But by no means was that always the case, and there is no record of a daughter being with him on that occasion.

Thirdly, and even more telling, it seems nearly impossible to believe that Brainerd would have written some of the following remarks, from the second half of the letter of July 31, 1744, to Jerusha:

> I am in a very poor state of health; I think, scarce ever poorer:
> But, through divine goodness, I am not discontented under
> my weakness and confinement to this wilderness: I bless
> God for the retirement: I never was more thankful for
> anything than I have been of late for the necessity I am under
> of self denial in many respects: I love to be a 'pilgrim' and

'stranger' (Heb. 11:13) in this wilderness: ... I feel as if my all was lost and I was undone for this world if the poor heathen mayn't be converted. I feel, in general, different from what I did when I saw you last; at least more crucified to all the enjoyments of life. It would be very refreshing to me to see you here in this desert; especially in my weak, disconsolate hours: But I think I could be content never to see you, or any of my friends again in this world, if God would bless my labors here to the conversion of the poor Indians.

It strains credulity to suggest that he would have written such perspectives on self-denial and being crucified to the enjoyments of life to a young lady with whom he hoped to cultivate a romantic relationship. Nor does it seem at all believable that he would even suggest the possibility of a fifteen-year-old girl (Jerusha's age at the time) refreshing him by coming from a great distance to visit him in the frontier wilderness. To even make such a suggestion to a young lady would have doubtless been viewed as toying with her emotions and the height of impropriety.

Finally, less than a month after Brainerd penned this letter, he received an uplifting personal visit from some of his ministerial colleagues. Very likely one of those fellow ministers was the recipient of his correspondence and arranged a collective response to it.

His debilitating illness continued throughout the days that followed the writing of the letter. His consequent inactivity caused him considerable inner distress, as he related in his diary on August 10:

And thus I have continued much in the same state that I was in last week, through the most of this (it being now Friday) unable to engage in any business; frequently unable to pray in the family [presumably in Alexander Hunter's home]. I am obliged to let all my thoughts and concerns run at random; for I have neither strength to read, meditate, or pray: And this naturally perplexes my mind. I seem to myself like a man that has all his estate embarked in one small boat, unhappily going adrift down a swift torrent. The poor owner stands on the shore and looks, and laments his loss. But alas, though my all seems to be adrift, and I stand and see it, I dare not lament; for this sinks my spirits more, and aggravates my bodily disorders! I am forced therefore to divert myself with trifles; although at the same time I am afraid, and often feel as if I was guilty of the misimprovement of time. And oftentimes my conscience is so exercised with this miserable way of spending time, that I have no peace; though I have no strength of mind or body to improve it to better purpose. Oh, that God would pity my distressed state!

Thankfully, his health improved somewhat in the three weeks that followed. He was able to resume regular ministry to the Indians and was heartened to see an increased level of spiritual concern developing among them. When he had first arrived at the Forks of the Delaware, his native audiences consisted of twenty to twenty-five people. Now he frequently preached to forty or more, and often most of the Indians who were still in that region came together to hear him speak.

He was also greatly encouraged toward the end of August by the aforementioned visit from a group of his fellow ministers. Almost certainly that delegation came in response to his letter of July 31. Regrettably, the identities of those ministerial colleagues were not preserved.

The first Sunday in September, he observed that some of the Indians were fearful of considering and embracing Christianity lest they would be 'enchanted and poisoned' by one or another of their medicine men. Throwing down the gauntlet, he issued a challenge: 'But I was enabled to plead with them not to fear these; and confiding in God for safety and deliverance, I bid a challenge to all these "powers of darkness" (Eph. 6:12; Col. 1:13) to do their worst upon *me* first: I told my people I was a Christian, and asked them why the powwows did not bewitch and poison me.'

In issuing this challenge he took a bold and potentially dangerous step. These conjurers held great power among the Indians and jealously guarded their prestige. For defying them he easily could have become the object of their serious retaliation, even to the point of his very life being threatened. But God's providential hand of protection was upon him, and no harm came to him.

12

First Susquehanna Journey

In September, 1744, perhaps at the urging of the ministerial colleagues who had visited him the previous month, Brainerd took a three-week journey into New England. Jonathan Edwards, who summarized the journey in a single paragraph, did not preserve any of the specific locations he visited on the trip. Perhaps he attended Yale's Commencement the middle of that month. He may have been able to visit his relatives around Haddam. Very likely he stopped to confer with the Scottish Society commissioners, because with their approval he undertook an itineration to a group of Indians at the Susquehanna River region just days after returning from New England.

Edwards did reveal that Brainerd was feeble through much of the New England journey, but toward its end his strength and health were greatly restored. After returning to the Forks on September 26, he wrote with gratitude: 'What reason have I to bless God, who has preserved me in riding more than 420 miles, and has "kept all my bones, that not one of them has been broken" (Ps. 34:20). My health likewise is greatly recovered. Oh, that I could dedicate my all to God! This is all the return I can make to Him.'

On Monday, the first day of October, he made preparations for the ministry foray to the Susquehanna. Those preparations included intense spiritual ones: 'Withdrew several times to the woods for secret duties, and endeavored to plead for the divine presence to go with me to the poor pagans, to whom I was going to preach the Gospel.'

That evening he rode his horse out a few miles to meet a fellow minister, Eliab Byram, whom he had invited to join him on the Susquehanna trip. Byram, a 1740 graduate of Harvard, was minister of the Presbyterian Church in Rockciticus (modern Mendham), New Jersey, some twenty-seven miles east of Hunter's Settlement. He had become the congregation's settled pastor just five months earlier, in May of 1744, and would go on to serve in that capacity for nearly a decade.[1]

The following day Brainerd and Byram, accompanied by Tattamy and 'two chief Indians from the Forks of the Delaware,' set out and traveled about twenty-five miles in a westerly, then northwesterly direction. That night they lodged at one of the last houses along that road before entering what Brainerd called 'a hideous and howling wilderness.'

'We went on our way into the wilderness,' he reported of the next day's journey, 'and found the most difficult and dangerous travelling, by far, that ever any of us had seen; we had scarce anything else but lofty mountains, deep valleys and hideous rocks, to make our way through.' Count Zinzendorf, having earlier traversed the same pass with a group of his fellow Moravians, similarly described it as the wildest he had ever seen and in places so steep that the members of his party roped themselves to each other to keep from falling over the cliffs.[2]

Late in the afternoon Brainerd's horse suddenly caught one of its legs in the rocks and fell under him. He was not hurt but one of the horse's legs was broken. In that rugged locale nearly thirty miles from the closest house, he realized there was nothing that could be done to rescue the animal. In order to deliver the horse from its suffering he was forced to kill it, likely shooting it with a rifle. While he revealed no personal feelings about the incident in his journal, doubtless it grieved him to see the life of his faithful mare, which had carried him four or five thousand miles, come to an end in that way.

As darkness fell the men kindled a fire, cut up a few bushes and constructed a simple shelter to shield themselves from the

1.   Pettit, *Life of David Brainerd*, p. 267.
2.   Wynbeek, *Beloved Yankee*, p. 113.

heavy frost that formed that night. Lying down on the ground, the weary travelers slept peacefully through the night. After traveling through and sleeping in the forest again on Thursday, the party arrived at an Indian settlement named Opeholhaupung on Friday, October 5. Located on the east bank of the North Branch of the Susquehanna, a few miles north of present-day Berwick, the village was comprised of about seventy Indians living in a dozen native houses.

Brainerd greeted the local chief in friendly fashion and shared his desire to teach the Indians Christianity. After holding a consultation, the natives gathered and he was able to preach to them twice that day. He addressed them again the next day about noon, and that afternoon visited them in their homes. All the men of the village except one came to listen to his sermons. The women, supposing the meetings concerned public matters normally considered only by the men, could hardly be persuaded to attend the gatherings.

The men had been planning to leave immediately on a hunting expedition, but agreed to delay it another day in order to hear more of his teaching on Sunday. He was able to preach twice to the Indians that day, and both times did so with a degree of freedom and power. Afterwards, however, he was discouraged by the objections his hearers raised against Christianity.

The next morning he gladly complied with the Indians' unexpected request that he preach to them once more before they departed on their hunting venture. In addition to preaching a Gospel message, he also sought to answer their objections to Christianity. As a result:

> I then asked the King if he was willing I should visit and preach to them again, if I should live to the next spring: He replied he should be heartily willing for his own part, and added he wished the young people would learn, etc. I then put the same question to the rest: Some answered they should be very glad, and none manifested any dislike to it.[3]

3. Pettit, *Life of David Brainerd*, p. 579.

125

In the written report he submitted the following month to the Scottish Society, he shed further light on several significant factors that stood in the way of the Indians turning to Christianity:

> In the first place, their minds are filled with prejudices against Christianity, on account of the vicious lives and unchristian behavior of some that are called Christians. These not only set before them the worst examples, but some of them take pains, expressly in words, to dissuade them from becoming Christians; foreseeing that if these should be converted to God the hope of their unlawful gain would thereby be lost.
>
> Again, these poor heathens are extremely attached to the customs, traditions, and fabulous notions of their fathers. And this one seems to be the foundation of all their other notions, viz., that 'twas not the same God made them who made the white people, but another who commanded them to live by hunting, etc., and not conform to the customs of the white people. Hence when they are desired to become Christians they frequently reply that they will live as their fathers lived and go to their fathers when they die. And if the miracles of Christ and his apostles be mentioned to prove the truth of Christianity, they also mention sundry miracles which their fathers have told them were anciently wrought among the Indians, and which Satan makes them believe were so. They are much attached to idolatry, frequently making feasts, which they eat in honor to some unknown beings, who, they suppose, speak to them in dreams, promising them success in hunting and other affairs, in case they will sacrifice to them. They oftentimes also offer their sacrifices to the spirits of the dead, who, they suppose, stand in need of favors from the living, and yet are in such a state as they can well reward all the offices of kindness that are shown to them. And they impute all their calamities to the neglect of these sacrifices.
>
> Furthermore, they are much awed by those among themselves who are called Powwows, who are supposed to have a power of enchanting, or poisoning them to death, or

at least in a very distressing manner. And they apprehend it would be their sad fate to be thus enchanted, in case they should become Christians.

Lastly, the manner of their living is likewise a great disadvantage to the design of their being Christianized. They are almost continually roving from place to place; and 'tis but rare that an opportunity can be had with some of them for their instruction. There is scarce any time of the year wherein the men can be found generally at home, except about six weeks before, and in the season of planting their corn, and about two months in the latter part of summer, from the time they begin to roast their corn until 'tis fit to gather in.[4]

The Opeholhaupung natives left on their hunting expedition the afternoon of Monday, October 8. Brainerd and his companions set out at five the next morning on their return trip home. That evening they erected a simple bark shelter in which to sleep. 'In the night, the wolves howled around us,' he reported, 'but God preserved us.' Wednesday they stopped at Craig's Settlement where, the next day, both Brainerd and Byram had the opportunity to preach. There, too, Brainerd was supplied with a replacement horse.

Upon arriving back at Hunter's Settlement, his heart over-flowed with thanksgiving:

Friday, October 12. Rode home to my lodging; where I poured out my soul to God in secret prayer, and endeavored to bless Him for His abundant goodness to me in my late journey. I scarce ever enjoyed more health; at least, of later years; and God marvelously, and almost miraculously, supported me under the fatigues of the way, and travelling on foot. Blessed be the Lord, that continually preserves me in all my ways.

But in the closing days of that month he again began to experience 'much disorder and pain of body' along with 'a degree of melancholy

4.   Pettit, *Life of David Brainerd*, pp. 579-80.

and gloominess of mind.' Those produced bitter complaints of his spiritual 'deadness and unprofitableness.' That, in turn, renewed his longing for death, so that he might be eternally released from such periods of deadness:

> Wednesday, October 31. Was sensible of my barrenness and decays in the things of God: My soul failed when I remembered the fervency I had enjoyed at the throne of grace. Oh (I thought), if I could but be spiritual, warm, heavenly-minded, and affectionately breathing after God, this would be better than life to me! My soul longed exceedingly for death, to be loosed from this dullness and barrenness, and made forever active in the service of God. I seemed to live for nothing and to do no good: And oh, the burden of such a life! Oh, death, death, my kind friend, hasten and deliver me from dull mortality, and make me spiritual and vigorous to eternity!

Five days later he set out for a meeting of the New York Presbytery. He carried with him a written report, completed just that morning, for the Scottish Society commissioners, describing his missionary activities during the past year and a half. Of the promising results of his first several months of ministry at the Forks he wrote:

> The effects which the truths of God's Word have had upon some of the Indians in this place are somewhat encouraging. Sundry of them are brought to renounce idolatry and to decline partaking of those feasts which they used to offer in sacrifice to certain supposed unknown powers. And some few instances among them have for a considerable time manifested a serious concern for their souls' eternal welfare, and still continue to 'inquire the way to Zion' (Jer. 50:5) with such diligence, affection, and becoming solicitude as gives me reason to hope that 'God who (I trust) has begun this work in them' (Phil. 1:6) will carry it on until it shall issue in their saving conversion to Himself. These not only detest their old idolatrous notions, but strive also to bring their friends off from them. And as they are seeking salvation

for their own souls, so they seem desirous, and some of them take pains, that others might be excited to do the like.[5]

During the journey to New York he was greatly exposed to cold and stormy weather. By the time he traveled from the presbytery meeting to Aaron Burr's home in Newark, New Jersey, on Friday, he had become very ill. After spending nearly two weeks recuperating there, he rode through the bitter cold to Morristown, near Rockciticus, on Wednesday, November 21.

There he enjoyed the company of Timothy Johnes, a 1737 graduate of Yale and the Morristown minister since 1743. Johnes would have a long and distinguished career at Morristown. His ministry there was blessed with several extensive revivals that added 420 members to his church before his death in 1794 at age seventy-eight.[6] Of his visit with Johnes, Brainerd wrote: 'Enjoyed some sweetness in conversation with dear Mr Johnes, while I dined with him: My soul loves the people of God, and especially the ministers of Jesus Christ, who feel the same trials that I do.'

While trying to reach his home the next day, Thursday, he lost his way in the woods at nightfall and spent three hours wandering over rocky, perilous steeps and through swamps. 'Was much pinched with cold,' he reported afterwards, 'and distressed with an extreme pain in my head, attended with sickness at my stomach; so that every step I took was distressing to me.' He supposed he would likely have to suffer exposure out in the woods all night. But then: 'about nine o'clock I found a house, through the abundant goodness of God, and was kindly entertained.'

About such trials he was philosophical and determined to maintain a spiritual perspective:

> Such fatigues and hardships as these serve to wean me more
> from the earth; and, I trust, will make heaven the sweeter.
> Formerly, when I was thus exposed to cold, rain, etc., I was
> ready to please myself with the thoughts of enjoying a com-
> fortable house, a warm fire, and other outward comforts; but
> now these have less place in my heart (through the grace of

5. Pettit, *Life of David Brainerd*, p. 577.
6. Wynbeek, *Beloved Yankee*, p. 117.

God) and my eye is more to God for comfort. In this world I expect tribulation; and it does not now, as formerly, appear strange to me; I don't in such seasons of difficulty flatter myself that it will be better hereafter; but rather think how much worse it might be; how much greater trials others of God's children have endured; and how much greater are yet perhaps reserved for me. Blessed be God that He makes the comfort to me, under my sharpest trials; and scarce ever lets these thoughts be attended with terror or melancholy; but they are attended frequently with great joy.

The next morning, either before or while continuing his journey, he visited and prayed with a sick man. He also paid a visit to another house where a person had just died. He arrived back at Hunter's Settlement early that afternoon, feeling poorly, but well enough to spend the remainder of the day reading.

13

Hope and Despair

During the final week of November and the opening days of December, 1744, Brainerd worked diligently with an unidentified group of individuals to erect a small cottage in which he could live by himself through the coming winter. The Hunter settlers may have helped in the construction of that sturdy little abode, which stood intact for the next fifty-plus years. It was located just a quarter of a mile from the native village of Clistonwackin and about two hundred yards from a large bend in the Delaware River at the site of present-day Martin's Creek.

His spirits sank the first Tuesday in December when most of the local natives went together to participate in an idolatrous feast and dance. Two days later, for the first time since arriving at the Forks, he devoted an entire day to fasting and prayer. This was a protracted season of intense personal introspection and rededication as well as of fervently seeking the Lord's blessing on his ministry efforts. The next day he sought to minister to the natives who had just returned from their idolatrous feast, but found it very difficult to do so under those deeply discouraging circumstances: 'Then visited the Indians and preached to 'em. But under inexpressible dejection: I had no heart to speak to them, and could not do it but as I forced myself: I knew they must hate to hear me, as having but just got home from their idolatrous feast and devil worship.'

Crossing the Delaware, he preached twice the following Sunday, December 9, at Greenwich, New Jersey, about ten miles from his new cottage. The events of the day reveal how seriously he approached the preaching task:

In the first discourse I had scarce any warmth or affectionate longing for souls. In the intermission season I got alone among the bushes and cried to God for pardon of my deadness; and was in anguish and bitterness that I could not address souls with more compassion and tender affection: Judged and condemned myself for want of this divine temper: Though I saw I could not get it as of myself any more than I could make a world. In the latter exercise, blessed be the Lord, I had some fervency, both in prayer and preaching; and especially in the application of my discourse was enabled to address precious souls with affection, concern, tenderness and importunity. The Spirit of God, I think, was there; as the effects were apparent, tears running down many cheeks.

As he visited and preached to the Indians on Wednesday of that same week, he was heartened to find his interpreter, Moses Tattamy, under marked concern for his own soul. That development was both a comfort and a new cause of concern for the earnest evangelist. He immediately went to prayer: 'I longed greatly for his conversion; lifted up my heart to God for it while I was talking to him: Came home and poured out my soul to God for him: Enjoyed some freedom in prayer, and was enabled, I think, to leave all with God.'

He dedicated the entire next day as well to praying about the matter. The season of supplication, however, turned into a discouraging struggle with wandering thoughts and a spirit of pride:

Thursday, December 13. Endeavored to spend the day in fasting and prayer, to implore the divine blessing, more especially on my poor people; and in particular, I sought for converting grace for my interpreter, and three or four more under some concern for their souls. ... Some freedom I had in pleading for these poor concerned souls, several times; and when interceding for them, I enjoyed greater freedom from wandering and distracting thoughts than in any part of my supplications: But in the general, was greatly exercised with wanderings; so that in the evening it seemed as if

I had need to pray for nothing so much as for the pardon of sins committed in the day past, and the vileness I then found in myself. The sins I had most sense of were pride and wandering thoughts, whereby I mocked God. The former of these cursed iniquities excited me to think of writing, or preaching, or converting heathen, or performing some other great work, that my name might live when I should be dead. My soul was in anguish and ready to drop into despair, to find so much of that cursed temper. With this and the other evil I labored under, viz., wandering thoughts, I was almost overwhelmed, and even ready to give over striving after a spirit of devotion; ...

Despite such struggles, God's timely encouragement awaited him when he ministered to the natives the following Tuesday. After discoursing for nearly an hour 'without any power to come close to their hearts' he at last began to feel and speak with fervency. In addition, Tattamy translated the address with obvious earnestness: 'My interpreter also was amazingly assisted; and I doubt not but "the Spirit of God was upon him" (1 Sam. 19:23) (though I had no reason to think he had any true and saving grace, but was only under conviction of his lost state).'

Their combined appeal, empowered by the Spirit of God, made a strong impression on the audience. Presently tears began to run down the cheeks of most of the adults. One elderly man wept openly and seemed convinced of the importance of what was being taught. 'I stayed with them a considerable time, exhorting and directing them,' he reported afterwards, 'and came away lifting up my heart to God in prayer and praise, and encouraged and exhorted my interpreter to "strive to enter in at the strait gate" (Luke 13:24).'

As has already been seen, Tattamy's interest toward spiritual matters had been somewhat awakened the previous summer. But that interest had rather quickly declined and for two or three months he had slipped back into a largely 'careless and secure' spiritual state. That fall, however, he became ill and languished for several weeks. During that time he came to have a deep and abiding concern for his soul. His spiritual burden weighed so heavily on his mind that he started having trouble sleeping at night. Day and night he had little rest. He seemed like a different man to his fellow natives, who could not help but notice and be amazed at the change in his outlook and behavior.

After he had sought to obtain God's mercy for quite some time, he came to picture in his mind's eye an impassable mountain before him. He thought he was pressing toward heaven, but found his way so hedged about with thorns that he couldn't progress an inch further. He supposed if he could just make his way through the thorns and briers and climb up the first steep pitch of the mountain, there might be some hope for him to scale it. But looking this way and that he could find no way through the thorns. Though he labored for a time to get through, all was in vain and he realized it was impossible. After that he gave up his striving as a futile effort that would never succeed under his own power.

Brainerd feared the Indian's spiritual conflicts might be no more than the result of an overactive imagination. But before he could question Tattamy, the native further revealed: 'I am in a miserable and perishing condition. I see plainly what I have been doing all my days, and I have never done one good thing. I have not been so bad as some other people in some things – I have not been used to steal, quarrel and murder. And I have done many things which folks call good – I have been kind to my neighbors. But all this does me no good now. I see that all was bad, and that I never have done one good thing.' Of the latter statement, Brainerd clarified: 'meaning that he had never done anything from a right principle and with a right view, though he had done many things that were materially good and right.' These additional remarks convinced Brainerd that Tattamy really did comprehend the true nature of his lost spiritual condition and that he was not in any way still trying to depend on his own good works to save himself.

Brainerd was not yet persuaded that his interpreter had become a born-again Christian. Nevertheless, he and others noted evident changes that took place in the native's life at that time:

But these exercises of soul were attended and followed with a very great change in the man, so that it might justly be said, he was become another man, if not a new man. His conversation and deportment were much altered, and even the careless world could not but admire what had befallen him to make so great a change in his temper, discourse, and behavior. And especially there was a surprising alteration in his public performances. He now addressed the Indians with admirable fervency, and scarce knew when to leave off; and sometimes when I had concluded my discourse, and was returning homeward, he would tarry behind to repeat and inculcate what had been spoken.[1]

As Brainerd returned to his cottage after ministering to the Indians that Tuesday, December 18, he sensed that God was beginning to do a significant stirring work among them. Reflexively he went to prayer: 'Came home and spent most of the evening in prayer and thanksgiving; and found myself much enlarged and quickened. Was greatly concerned that the Lord's work, which seemed to be begun, might be carried on with power to the conversion of poor souls and the glory of divine grace.' Throughout the remainder of the week he frequently poured out his heart in petition and praise along similar lines.

Unfortunately, beginning the very next week and continuing for the better part of two months, he experienced considerable physical indisposition and the spiritual and psychological struggles that often accompany poor bodily health. While he sought to soldier through his ministerial and devotional activities, it would prove to be one of the most difficult periods of his adult ministry. His low physical and psychological condition, combined with a weighty concern for the welfare of the Indians, nearly sabotaged his preaching efforts one Sunday:

1. Brainerd recorded an account of Tattamy's spiritual conviction and subsequent conversion in the July 21, 1745, entry of his Journal. See Dwight, *Memoirs of David Brainerd*, pp. 210-14, and *The Life and Diary of David Brainerd* (Grand Rapids: Baker, 1999), pp. 207-12.

Lord's Day, January 27. Had the greatest degree of inward anguish that almost ever I endured: I was perfectly overwhelmed, and so confused, that after I began to discourse to the Indians, before I could finish a sentence, sometimes I forgot entirely what I was aiming at; or if, with much difficulty, I had recollected what I had before designed, still it appeared strange and like something I had long forgotten and had now but an imperfect remembrance of. I know it was a degree of distraction occasioned by vapory disorders, melancholy, spiritual desertion, and some other things that particularly pressed upon me this morning with an uncommon weight, the principal of which respected my Indians.

Interestingly, both that evening and the following Saturday night, God used a season of family prayer, most likely in Alexander Hunter's home, to ease His faithful servant's despondency. Brainerd did not identify the family, but Edwards noted that the missionary continued to attend family prayer with the Hunters even after his cottage had been built and he no longer boarded with them. Of that Sunday Brainerd recorded:

In the evening this gloom continued still till family prayer, about nine o'clock, and almost through this until I came near the close, when I was praying (as I usually do) for the illumination and conversion of my poor people; and then the cloud was scattered so that I enjoyed sweetness and freedom, and conceived hopes that God designed mercy for some of them. ...

His depression reached a horrific depth on the first day of February, a Friday. Relief again came during family prayer with the Hunters the next evening. He approached his day of public ministry on Sunday with some trepidation, but the Lord again helped him:

Lord's Day, February 3. In the morning I was somewhat relieved of that gloom and confusion that my mind has of late been greatly exercised with: Was enabled to pray with some composure and comfort. But however, went to my Indians trembling; for my soul remembered 'the wormwood and the gall' (Lam. 3:19) (I might almost say the hell) of Friday last; and I was greatly afraid I should be obliged again to drink of that 'cup of trembling' (Isa. 51:17), which was inconceivably more bitter than death, and made me long for the grave more, unspeakably more, than for hid treasures; yea, inconceivably more than the men of this world long for such treasures. But God was pleased to hear my cries, and to afford me great assistance; so that I felt peace in my own soul; ...

He preached the following Sunday at Greenwich, New Jersey. That evening he rode eight miles to visit a dying man, whom he found unconscious and unresponsive upon his arrival. The ailing man died at dawn the next day, and Brainerd revealed, 'I was affected at the sight.' He spent the morning praying and conversing with the mourners. Returning to Greenwich, he preached there on the hopeful words of Psalm 89:15: 'Blessed is the people that know the joyful sound: they shall walk, O Lord, in the light of Thy countenance.' The results were encouraging: 'Several persons were much affected. And after meeting, I was enabled to discourse, with freedom and concern, to some persons that applied to me under spiritual trouble.'

Those events left him with 'a solemn sense of death' throughout the remainder of the week. His reflections of that Monday, February 11, might seem morbid to some, but are worthy of consideration:

In the evening, was in the most solemn frame that almost ever I remember to have experienced: I know not that ever death appeared more real to me ... Oh, how great and solemn it appeared to die! Oh, how it lays the greatest honor in the dust! And oh, how vain and trifling did the riches, honors, and pleasures of the world appear! I could not, I dare not, so much as think of any of them: for death, death, solemn (though not frightful) death appeared at the door. Oh, I could see myself dead, and laid out, and enclosed in my coffin, and put down into the cold grave, with greatest solemnity, but without terror!

His health appears to have turned a corner that week. After mentioning earlier in the week that he was 'exceeding weak' and 'much exercised with vapory disorders,' he recorded on Thursday, 'Enjoyed health and freedom in my work.' References to physical weakness or illness were absent from his diary in the following weeks.

The next Sunday proved to be a special day of ministry for him as he discoursed to a sizable congregation of settlers, some of whom had traveled a great distance to attend the day's services, on a sun-bathed hillside at Hunter's Settlement:

> Lord's Day, February 17. Preached to the white people (my interpreter being absent) in the wilderness upon the sunny side of a hill: Had a considerable assembly, consisting of people that lived (at least many of them) not less than thirty miles asunder; some of them came near twenty miles. I discoursed to 'em, all day, from John 7:37. 'Jesus stood and cried, saying, If any man thirst,' etc. In the afternoon it pleased God to grant me great freedom and fervency in my discourse; and I was enabled to imitate the example of Christ in the text, who 'stood and cried.' I think I was scarce ever enabled to offer the free grace of God to perishing sinners with more freedom and plainness in my life. And afterwards I was enabled earnestly to invite the children of God to come renewedly, and drink of this fountain of water of life, from whence they have heretofore derived unspeakable satisfaction. It was a very comfortable time to me: There were many tears in the assembly; and I doubt not but that the Spirit of God was there, convincing poor sinners of their need of Christ.

When Tattamy had still not returned a full week later, Brainerd was perplexed how to prosecute his ministry to the Indians. He engaged a Dutchman to interpret for him as he attempted to preach to the natives, but discovered the settler 'was but poorly qualified for the business.'

Afterwards he discoursed to a small group of settlers on John 6:67, 'Then said Jesus unto the twelve, Will ye also go away?'

The sermon spoke not only to his audience, but also to his own spiritual condition and need:

> I felt freedom to open the love of Christ to his own dear disciples: When the rest of the world forsakes Him, and are forsaken by Him, that He calls them no more, He then turns to His own and says, 'Will ye also go away?' I had a sense of the free grace of Christ to His own people, in such seasons of general apostasy, and when they themselves in some measure backslide with the world. Oh, the free grace of Christ, that He seasonably minds His people of their danger of backsliding, and invites them to persevere in their adherence to Himself! I saw that backsliding souls, who seemed to be about to 'go away' with the world, might return, and welcome, to Him immediately; without anything to recommend them; notwithstanding all their former backslidings.
>
> And thus my discourse was suited to my own soul's case: for, of late, I have found a great want of this sense and apprehension of divine grace; and have often been greatly distressed in my own soul, because I did not suitably apprehend this 'fountain opened to purge away sin' (Zech. 13:1); and so have been too much laboring for spiritual life, peace of conscience, and progressive holiness, in my own strength: But now God showed me, in some measure, 'the arm of all strength' (Isa. 62:8), and 'the fountain of all grace' (Rev. 21:6). In the evening I felt solemn, devout, and sweet, resting on free grace for assistance, acceptance, and peace of conscience.

His long, dark winter seems to have passed. In the days that immediately followed, he sometimes complained of spiritual dullness and expressed longings after greater spiritual life and holy fervency, but frequently experienced refreshing, invigorating influences of God's Spirit.

14

Seeking a Missionary Colleague

Brainerd's diary on Wednesday, March 6, 1745, reveals for the first time some significant thoughts about his future ministry plans that presumably he had been contemplating for some time. He spent most of that day preparing for a journey to New England. There he desired to explore the possibility of recruiting a colleague to share in his ministry and to determine the feasibility of raising financial support for that individual. Following that trip, he hoped to spend most of the summer ministering to the natives along the Susquehanna River.

As he prayed about the journey to New England, he brought one special concern before the Lord: 'Was afraid I should forsake the "fountain of living waters," and attempt to derive satisfaction from "broken cisterns" (Jer. 2:13), my dear friends and acquaintances, with whom I might meet in my journey. I looked to God to keep me from this vanity in special [especially], as well as others.'

His concern in that regard certainly did not indicate a lack of appreciation for human friendships. Rather, precisely because he cherished 'dear friends,' he feared he might seek deeper satisfaction from his interaction with them than from his personal fellowship with God. His obvious appreciation of friendships is clearly seen through perspectives he penned following a visit from some acquaintances on the eve of his journey:

> Towards night, and in the evening, was visited by some friends, some of whom, I trust, were real Christians; who

discovered [manifested] an affectionate regard to me, and seemed grieved that I was about to leave them; especially seeing I did not expect to make any considerable stay among them, if I should live to return from New England. Oh, how kind has God been to me! How has he raised up friends in every place where His Providence has called me! Friends are a great comfort; and 'tis God that gives them; 'tis He makes them friendly to me.

He set out on Thursday, March 7. Edwards devoted only one paragraph to summarizing the journey, which lasted nearly five weeks. He preserved Brainerd's diary entry of March 21, recorded after his visit with an unidentified minister in New England, as that notation stated the primary purpose of the trip:

Contrived with him how to raise some money among Christian friends, in order to support a colleague with me in the wilderness (I having now spent two years in a very solitary manner) that we might be together; as Christ sent out his disciples, two and two: And as this was the principal concern I had in view, in taking this journey, so I took pains in it, and hope God will succeed it, if for His glory.

For all his love of solitude in order to insure having adequate opportunity for private communion with the Lord, he had come to realize it was not good for him to carry out such a demanding and discouraging ministry on his own. While needing time alone with God, he also needed the company of a committed Christian with whom he could share mutual fellowship and encouragement as well as the burden of ministry.

He first visited several ministerial acquaintances in New Jersey, then went to New York. After that he ventured to various parts of Connecticut. Assuming he visited his home area, it may have been at that time he learned that his sister, Jerusha, had given birth to her eighth child two months earlier. She named the son David Brainerd Spencer in his honor.

While at Woodbury, Connecticut, on March 15, he penned a letter 'in greatest haste' to fellow missionary John Sergeant in Stockbridge, Massachusetts. The letter reveals his ongoing interest in Sergeant's ministry as well as his desire to support him and other of their ministerial acquaintances. Though his own finances were pinched at the present time, he was doing what he could to assist his fellow ministers materially:

> I long to hear of your affairs; and especially how things are like to turn out with respect to your plan of a free boarding school, which is an affair much upon my heart amidst all my heavy concerns, and I can learn nothing whether it is likely to succeed or not.
>
> I fully designed to have given something considerable for promoting that good design; but whether I shall be able to give anything, or whether it will be my duty to do so under present circumstances, I know not. I have met with sundry losses lately, to the value of sixty or seventy pounds, New England money. In particular, I broke my mare's leg last fall in my journey to Susquehanna, and was obliged to kill her on the road and prosecute my journey on foot, and I can't get her place supplied for fifty pounds. And I have lately moved [formally requested] to have a colleague or companion with me, for my spirits sink with my solitary circumstances. And I expect to contribute something to his maintenance, seeing his salary must be raised wholly in this country and can't be expected from Scotland.
>
> I sold my teakettle to Mr Jo. Woodbridge, and an iron kettle to Mr Timothy Woodbridge, both which amounted to something more than four pounds, which I ordered them to pay to you for the school. I hope you will use the money that way; if not, you are welcome to it for yourself. I desire my teapot and bed ticking may be improved to the same purpose.
>
> As to my blankets, I desired Mr Woodbridge to take the trouble of turning them into deerskins. If he has not done it, I wish he would, and send the skins to Mr Hopkins, or, if it might be, to Mr Bellamy.[1]

---

1.   Pettit, *Life of David Brainerd*, pp. 582-3.

Joseph and Timothy Woodbridge were sons of Rev. John Woodbridge, who graduated from Harvard in 1694 and pastored at West Springfield, Massachusetts, until he was accidentally killed, in 1718, by a falling tree. Joseph and Timothy's mother, Jemima Eliot Woodbridge, was a granddaughter of John Eliot, Massachusetts' famous 'Apostle to the Indians' in the previous century. Timothy moved to Stockbridge early in the settlement's history to assist Sergeant in his ministry to the Indians, and Joseph joined them there a short time later.[2]

During his return trip to the Forks of the Delaware, Brainerd met a number of ministers when they gathered in Woodbridge, New Jersey, several miles south of Elizabethtown, 'to consult about the affairs of Christ's kingdom, in some important articles.' Unfortunately, his 600-mile journey failed to produce a colleague who would be willing to join him in Indian work. But he had received encouragement from ministers and others who said they thought supporting funds would be forthcoming once a suitable candidate was identified.

He arrived back at the Forks on Saturday, April 13, full of thanksgiving to God for keeping him safe throughout the long journey. The next day, Easter Sunday, he felt fatigued, but was enabled to preach effectively to a sizable assembly of settlers who had gathered 'from all parts round about' for worship. Rather than employing a traditional Easter text, he discoursed freely from Ezekiel 33:11: 'Say unto them, As I live, saith the Lord God, I have no pleasure in the death of the wicked; but that the wicked turn from his way and live.'

He did not linger at the Forks, but traveled the very next week some fifty miles south to Philadelphia. There he sought the Governor's help in obtaining permission from the leaders of the Iroquois Confederacy for him to live at the Susquehanna and to instruct the natives of that region. No record of the precise content of his meeting with Deputy Governor George Thomas has been preserved. From what Brainerd reported to a group of Indians he visited at the Susquehanna the following month, the Governor was

---

2. Pettit, *Life of David Brainerd*, p. 560.

favorable to the prospect of his settling and teaching in that area for a period of two years, and had even 'given him orders to that effect.'

While traveling to and from Philadelphia, he lodged with Charles Beatty, pastor of the Presbyterian Church at Neshaminy, located about a dozen miles north of the City of Brotherly Love. Beatty, who was four years Brainerd's senior, was a 1742 graduate of a frontier school known as the Log College, which had operated in Neshaminy for years. The college was headed by William Tennent, Sr., the father of Gilbert Tennent, one of the prominent evangelists around whom considerable controversy had swirled during the recent Awakening. The senior Tennent had established the institution to help supply the need for trained clergymen on the rapidly expanding frontier. The same year Beatty graduated, the ailing Tennent retired and the college closed.

Beatty replaced Tennent as the pastor of Neshaminy's New Side congregation the following year. He would go on to have a fruitful and colorful career of nearly thirty years' duration there. He was spoken of in Benjamin Franklin's *Autobiography* as the army chaplain during the French and Indian War of 1756 who rationed the daily gill (four fluid ounces) of rum to his troops to insure their presence at prayer services. His extensive ministry travels took him to western Pennsylvania and Ohio, the Southern Colonies, England, Scotland, Holland and Barbados in the West Indies, where he died of yellow fever in 1772.[3]

On Saturday, April 20, 1745, Brainerd's twenty-seventh birthday, he joined Beatty in traveling a few miles south to Abington, located between Neshaminy and Philadelphia. The Abington congregation was pastored by Richard Treat, a 1735 Yale graduate who was one year older than Brainerd. Earlier in his ministry Treat had served as supply pastor for the churches of Lower Providence and Old Norriton, several miles west of Neshaminy. When the evangelist John 'Hell-fire' Rowland came to the region in 1741, the Norriton church split. Old Siders literally locked him out of their building, leading New Siders to form another congregation and erect a building at Charlestown, five

---

3.   Wynbeek, *Beloved Yankee*, pp. 129-30.

miles to the west. Treat served as pastor of that new congregation as well as of the church in Abington, where he died in 1778.[4]

The purpose of Brainerd and Beatty's brief trip to Abington was to assist Treat in administering the Lord's Supper 'according to the method of the Church of Scotland.' On the frontier, sizable multitudes sometimes traveled from miles around to receive communion, thus necessitating the assistance of visiting ministers. Preparation for the Lord's Supper usually began with a service of prayer and fasting on Thursday, at which time communion tokens in the form of small, distinctive metal discs were distributed to approved participants. Final preparatory services were held on Saturday, the actual communion service took place on Sunday, and the multi-day affair ended with a service of thanksgiving on Monday.

Another distinctive feature of the Church of Scotland's form of communion was that all communicants were served the elements while seated at tables. There they surrendered their tokens before being served the specially baked bread and the wine. When vast numbers of people received communion, they were served in relays at the tables. Psalms were sung as groups of participants filed to and from the linen-covered tables. The ministers in charge would take turns dispensing the elements. Sometimes those services lasted seven or eight hours or were even carried over to another day. At other times long rows of tables were set up in groves outside the church to facilitate the serving of large groups.[5]

When Brainerd and Beatty arrived that Saturday they found Treat preaching a preparatory sermon. Brainerd followed with a message from one of his favorite preaching texts, Matthew 5:3. He preached with 'great freedom and tenderness,' and his message made a noticeable impact on the auditors: 'The assembly was sweetly melted, and scores were all in tears.'

The next morning Treat preached in the church while Beatty addressed the throng of worshipers outside. That afternoon Brainerd preached to the entire assembly outdoors from Revelation 14:4:

4. Pettit, *Life of David Brainerd*, p. 291.
5. Wynbeek, *Beloved Yankee*, p. 131.

'These are they which follow the Lamb whithersoever He goeth. These were redeemed from among men, being the firstfruits unto God and to the Lamb.'

Both Beatty and Brainerd discoursed again the next day, bringing to a close the solemn observance. The missionary spoke from John 7:37, the same text he had used with great effectiveness at Hunter's Settlement two months earlier. The two ministers returned to Neshaminy that same day, and Brainerd continued on to his own home at the Forks on Tuesday.

After preaching at Craig's Settlement the following weekend, he returned to his cottage on Monday, April 29, thoroughly weakened. The next day he was confined to his bed, feeling too weak to read, meditate or pray constructively. That led him to comment on the necessity he had come to learn of disengaging himself from active ministry pursuits under such weakened circumstances so that he might be restored to engage in those pursuits once again. For a man who was so conscientious about using every moment of time in consecrated service of the Lord, that continued to be a difficult lesson to accept:

> Oh, how heavily does time pass away when I can do nothing to any good purpose; but seem obliged to trifle away precious time! But of late, I have seen it my duty to divert myself by all lawful means, that I may be fit, at least some small part of my time, to labor for God. And here is the difference between my present diversions and those I once pursued, when in a natural [unregenerate] state. Then I made a god of diversions, delighted in them with a neglect of God, and drew my highest satisfaction from them: Now I use them as means to help me in living to God: fixedly delighting in Him, and not in them, drawing my highest satisfaction from Him. ... And those things that are the greatest diversion, when pursued with this view, don't tend to hinder, but promote my spirituality; and I see now, more than ever, that they are absolutely necessary.

That Friday, May 3, he was able to ride out and spend some time with the nearby natives. It was the first time he had visited them since leaving on his journey to New England nearly two months earlier.

15

A DIFFICULT AND DISAPPOINTING ITINERATION

Despite his ongoing weakness, Brainerd was determined to carry out his plan of traveling to the Susquehanna region and ministering to the Indians there through the summer. On Wednesday, May 8, therefore, he set out on that journey with Moses Tattamy. After spending the first night in the open woods, they were overtaken on the second day by a cold northeasterly storm. Having no cover and no way of making a fire in the heavy downpour, they decided to press forward in hopes of stumbling across some source of shelter.

To make matters worse, their horses had eaten some poisonous vegetation at the place they had camped the night before and were too sick to be ridden. The men were forced to make their way on foot while driving their horses through the rain. Providential mercy led them to discover an abandoned bark hut shortly before darkness set in, and they were able to spend the night there.

Once they reached the Susquehanna, they traveled along it a distance of about 100 miles, visiting many Indians. They encountered members of seven or eight distinct tribes, to whom Brainerd was able to preach the Gospel by using different interpreters. He was encouraged by the openness of some natives to Christian instruction but discouraged by the opposition of others. In an unspecified location along the way, he was pleasantly surprised to meet some of the Indians he had formerly ministered to at Kaunaumeek. They had since moved to the Susquehanna and seemed delighted to see and hear him again.

The Susquehanna was the last important Indian river before the Pennsylvania tribes were forced further west to the Allegheny and Ohio Rivers. At that time the entire length of the Susquehanna was controlled by the Six Nations Confederacy, also known as the Iroquois Confederacy. Originally that federation was called the Five Nations Confederacy, being made up of five Iroquois tribes from New York – Cayugas, Mohawks, Oneidas, Onondagas and Senecas. In 1722 the Tuscaroras, an Iroquoian-speaking tribe that a decade earlier had been forced out of North Carolina, joined the Iroquois league. The region over which that powerful confederacy exercised its authority stretched some 500 miles from central New York to as far south as North Carolina.

The Susquehanna was also home to a number of other tribes – Delawares, Tutelos, Susquehannas, Canay, Nanticokes and Shawnees – that had migrated to the region from various locations both nearby and far away.[1] With so many tribal groups congregated along the Susquehanna, it is not hard to comprehend why Brainerd had such an abiding interest in ministering in that region.

The principal Indian town he visited during the present itineration was Shamokin, at the junction of the West and North Branches of the Susquehanna River (the site of modern Sunbury and not to be confused with present Shamokin, thirteen miles to the southeast). Ancient Shamokin was one of the four largest Indian settlements in Pennsylvania at the time, with nearly 300 natives living in upwards of fifty houses. It was actually comprised of three tribes – Delawares, Senecas and Tutelos – that lived in separate villages on each side of the river and on an island in the middle of the waterway. The tribes spoke separate languages that were wholly unintelligible to each other.

Moral conditions at Shamokin were abysmal, as Brainerd described: 'The Indians of this place are accounted the most drunken, mischievous, and ruffianly fellows of any in these parts: and Satan seems to have his seat in this town in an eminent manner.'

On the west bank at Shamokin resided an important Delaware chief named Sassoonan who had lived there with his people since

---

1. For further information concerning these tribes, see Wynbeek, *Beloved Yankee*, pp. 135-6.

1732. Though now very old, nearly blind and in extremely poor health, he was still loved and respected by his tribesmen and maintained his rule over them. He had also proven intelligent and loyal in his dealings with settlers through the years, having attended many of the important conferences involving natives and the Penn government.

Sassoonan's Achilles' heel was his weakness for liquor. In 1731, after killing one of his own nephews in a drunken brawl, he petitioned Penn officials to curtail the supply of liquor to the Indians. Unfortunately, he and his fellow natives didn't want to prohibit the whiskey trade altogether, but only desired that 'no Christian should carry any rum to Shamokin' where they lived. When they wanted liquor they would send for it themselves and in that way would not be wholly deprived of it. Such an expedient, however, proved unsuccessful. Two years after this visit of Brainerd at Shamokin, Pennsylvania's veteran Indian agent, Conrad Weiser, reported that Sassoonan 'has been drunk for these two or three years almost constantly.'

On the east side of the Susquehanna at Shamokin lived a prominent Iroquois chief, Shikellamy. Born of either Cayuga or French parents, he had been captured and adopted by the Oneidas when only two years old, then grew up to become one of their chieftains. He had resided at Shamokin since 1728 and in 1731 had supported Sassoonan in his liquor control petition. At that time Shikellamy, acting as overlord of all tributary tribes on the Susquehanna, delivered an ultimatum to the Penn government: If the liquor trade were not more carefully regulated, friendly relations with the Iroquois Confederacy would cease. Now, fourteen years later, he had just been promoted to executive deputy of the Grand Council of the Six Nations.

Unlike Sassoonan, Shikellamy maintained strict sobriety. He was highly respected by Indians and settlers alike as possessing marked intelligence, sagacity, dignity, refinement and kindness. He, too, had attended most of the important government conferences, and, in addition, had accompanied Conrad Weiser on a number of long, hazardous peace missions to the Iroquois in New York. In return for those services, Weiser hired eight young Germans to build a sizable, shingled house for Shikellamy at Shamokin.

In 1743 Weiser and Shikellamy had helped to negotiate the crucial treaty between the Six Nations and the English against the French. At the present time, in the spring of 1745, it was vitally important that that peace accord be maintained. That very month an expeditionary force from New England sailed and attacked France's Fort Louisbourg on Cape Breton (at the easternmost tip of present Nova Scotia, Canada). Should the Iroquois Confederacy capitulate and join the Canadian French, the English colonies would be greatly imperiled.[2]

Brainerd's primary goal in visiting Shamokin, of course, was not to promote such peace, but rather to seek to establish a Christian mission among the native tribes there. While there, he assembled the Delawares in Shikellamy's house and encouraged them to start gathering for worship and prayer on Sundays as the settlers did. He shared with them his desire to build a house there for that purpose and to stay with them for two years. He also related the Governor's approval of his plans and concluded by stating he would be glad if the Indians would hearken to him.

To those proposals Shikellamy solemnly responded: 'We are Indians, and don't wish to be transformed into white men. The English are our Brethren, but we never promised to become what they are. As little as we desire the preacher to become an Indian, so little ought he to desire the Indians to become preachers.' The chief concluded emphatically, 'He should *not* build a house here; they don't want one.'

If Brainerd wrote about this event in his diary, Jonathan Edwards preserved no record of it. An account of the meeting was shared by Shikellamy's people with Conrad Weiser and a trio of Moravians who arrived at Shamokin just a few days after Brainerd and Tattamy's departure.

Weiser had been born in Germany and raised in the Reformed Church, but now served with the Moravians. The delegation with which he traveled on this occasion was headed by Bishop Jacob

2. Wynbeek, *Beloved Yankee*, pp. 136-8.

Spangenberg. After arriving in Shamokin the bishop recorded in his journal, 'We were told that two ministers and an Indian had been lately here – probably it was the Presbyterian Brainerd and his interpreter Tatami.' Fortunately Spangenberg also preserved a summary of the report the Indians shared with him about their meeting with Brainerd at Shikellamy's house.[3]

The bishop's allusion to 'two ministers' is an intriguing one. In summarizing this itineration to the Susquehanna, Edwards made no mention of another minister traveling with Brainerd and Tattamy. Some have speculated that Eliab Byram accompanied them on this trip, as he had the previous fall when the missionary first ventured to the Susquehanna region.

After spending a week at Shamokin, from Tuesday, May 21, to Monday, May 27, Weiser and the Moravians, accompanied by Shikellamy and one of his three sons, left on a ten-day trip to Onondaga, New York. There they obtained permission from the Iroquois to establish a mission at Wyoming Valley, northeast of Shamokin.

Spangenberg also related that after Shikellamy effectively vetoed Brainerd's proposal, he and his companions 'departed for Philadelphia the next day.' Whether he actually intended to go to Philadelphia, or whether the Shamokin Indians merely presumed that was his destination when he continued downriver in that general direction, is not known.

It was likely at this juncture that the rigors Brainerd had been undergoing during the first two weeks of the trip proved too much for his fragile health, and he suddenly became gravely ill. According to Edwards:

> He spent a fortnight among the Indians on this river; and passed through considerable labors and hardships, frequently lodging on the ground, and sometimes in the open air; and at length he fell extremely ill, as he was riding in the wilderness, being seized with an ague followed with a burning fever and extreme pains in his head and bowels,

---

3. Wynbeek, *Beloved Yankee*, pp. 138-9.

attended with a great evacuation of blood; so that he thought he must have perished in the wilderness: But at last coming to an Indian trader's hut, he got leave [permission] to stay there; and though without physic [purging medicine] or food proper for him, it pleased God, after about a week's distress, to relieve him so far that he was able to ride.

He made his way to Juniata, an island thirty-five miles south of Shamokin, where the Juniata River flowed into the Susquehanna. Some Shawanese lived there whom Shikellamy had found the most difficult of all the Susquehanna tribes to control against the persistent and increasing enticements of the French to gain their loyalty. A group of the feared Nanticokes, with their reputation for great skill at witchcraft, also resided there. Having formerly lived among or near settlers in Maryland, many Nanticokes had considerable understanding of the English language. Brainerd described them as 'very vicious, drunken, and profane, although not so savage as those who have less acquaintance with the English.'

The Nanticokes also had unique burial customs that other Indian tribes did not share. They placed deceased bodies in close-slatted cribs above ground. After a corpse had thoroughly decomposed for a year or longer, the remaining bones were removed from the crib, washed and scraped, then buried underground with a degree of ceremony. The bones were exhumed and carried with the Nanticokes from place to place during their migrations.

Somewhat surprisingly, Brainerd received quite a positive reception from the Indians at Juniata. Edwards reported that 'a considerable number' of natives there 'appeared more free from prejudices against Christianity than most of the other Indians' the missionary had visited elsewhere during the trip. The itinerant himself commented, 'They appeared friendly, and gave me encouragement to come and see them again.'

On this occasion Brainerd also met a 'devout and zealous' native reformer whom he described as a 'restorer of what he supposed was the ancient religion of the Indians.'[4] This man performed a ceremonial

---

4. Brainerd's account of his interaction with the native reformer is recorded in his *Journal* entry for September 21, 1745 (Pettit, *Life of David Brainerd*, pp. 329-30).

dance in his presence, dressed in attire that was quite frightening in appearance. A great coat of shaggy bear skins covered every part of his body and reached to his toes. He wore bear skin stockings and a bear-skin hood over his head. A wooden mask, painted half black and half tawny, and bearing 'an extravagant mouth, cut very much awry,' hid his face. As he danced, he vigorously shook a tortoise shell rattle containing dried corn.

When the reformer approached him, dancing furiously, Brainerd reflexively shrank back, although it was the middle of the day and he knew who the man was. He later elaborated on the native's unnerving appearance and gestures: 'But of all the sights I ever saw among them, or indeed anywhere else, none appeared so frightful or so near akin to what is usually imagined of infernal powers; none ever excited such images of terror in my mind.'

The reformer bemoaned the fact that the Indians had become 'very degenerate and corrupt.' He shared that until four or five years earlier he had been just like his fellow natives. Then his heart became so greatly distressed over the general degradation of the Indians that he could no longer live among them. Instead, he went out to dwell alone in the woods for several months. In time, he claimed, God comforted his heart and showed him what he should do. Since then, he professedly had known God and tried to serve Him.

He also claimed that now he loved all people, whoever they happened to be, in a way he never before had. Other Indians verified the concern he manifested for them. They related that he vehemently opposed strong liquor and that he would 'go crying into the woods' when he could not dissuade them from consuming it. As to the reformer's influence on his fellow natives, Brainerd remarked, 'I perceived that he was looked upon and derided amongst most of the Indians as a precise zealot, that made a needless noise about religious matters.'

He treated Brainerd with uncommon courtesy. He seemed to appreciate some aspects of Christian teaching, but strongly disliked other facets of it. When he agreed with something Brainerd was teaching, he stated, 'Now that I like: so God has taught me.' He flatly rejected the existence of the Devil and declared that no such creature was known to the Indians of earlier times. He believed that departed souls all went southward where the good souls were admitted into a beautiful town with spiritual walls. Evil souls, however, were doomed to hover forever around the walls, vainly attempting to enter.

From Juniata, Brainerd and Tattamy ventured back to the Forks of the Delaware, arriving there on Thursday, May 30. They had traveled 340 miles in twenty-three days. As quite often happened, Brainerd returned from the journey very weak in body and under considerable mental dejection. The following Sunday, however, he was able to preach with some success to both Indians and settlers.

Again, he did not tarry at the Forks. On Friday, June 7, he rode the nearly forty miles back to Neshaminy, where he had been invited by Charles Beatty to assist in a communion observance. Though thoroughly fatigued from the long ride in the heat, he preached effectively to a considerable audience that Saturday afternoon from Isaiah 40:1, 'Comfort ye, comfort ye my people, saith your God.'

At least three thousand people were on hand for Sunday's communion service. Beatty preached in the morning, and Brainerd assisted in the administration of the Lord's Supper that followed. Toward the end of the sacred observance he extemporized to the vast throng on the same passage he had used as his sermon text at the Forks the previous Sunday – Isaiah 53:10, 'Yet it pleased the Lord to bruise him ...' He reported: 'Here God gave me great assistance in addressing sinners: And the Word was attended with amazing power; many scores, if not hundreds, in that great assembly, consisting of three or four thousand, were much affected; so that there was a very "great mourning," like "the mourning of Hadadrimmon" (Zech. 12:11).'

The next morning, as the protracted communion observance was concluded, he again sensed the Lord's special blessing and enablement as he preached on a text he had been meditating on in his personal devotions the previous week – Psalm 17:15, 'I shall be satisfied, when I awake, with Thy likeness.' He relished a further day of meaningful Christian fellowship at Neshaminy:

> Tuesday, June 11. Spent the day mainly in conversation with dear Christian friends; and enjoyed some sweet sense

of divine things. Oh, how desirable it is to keep company with God's dear children! These are the 'excellent ones of the earth, in whom,' I can truly say, 'is all my delight' (Ps. 16:3). Oh, what delight will it afford to meet them all in a state of perfection! Lord, prepare me for that state!

Those days of ministry and fellowship at Neshaminy likely brought a measure of encouragement at a time when he sorely needed it. He had recently returned from the Susquehanna physically exhausted and 'exceedingly depressed with a view of the unsuccessfulness of my labors.' With the exception of Moses Tattamy and his wife, who by that time had become believers, he was not aware of any Indians who had been brought to saving faith in Christ as a result of his more than two years of ministry as a missionary among them.

He had come to view himself as being a burden to the Scottish Society and had started thinking seriously of resigning his mission. He 'almost resolved' that he would do so at the end of the present year if by that time he had no improved prospect of special success in his ministry. Later he would write of his inner contemplations during that discouraged season:

I cannot say I entertained these thoughts because I was weary of the labors and fatigues that necessarily attended my present business, or because I had light and freedom in my own mind to turn any other way; but purely through dejection of spirit, pressing discouragement, and an apprehension of its being unjust to spend money, consecrated to religious uses, only to civilize the Indians, and bring them to an external profession of Christianity. This was all that I could then see any prospect of having effected, while God seemed, as I thought, evidently to frown upon the design of their saving conversion by withholding the convincing and renewing influences of His blessed Spirit from attending the means I had hitherto used with them for that end.[5]

5. Dwight, *Memoirs of David Brainerd*, p. 246; *Life and Diary of David Brainerd* (Baker edition), p. 244.

Carrying such weighty musings in his heart, he crossed the Delaware into New Jersey after leaving Charles Beatty's home on Wednesday, June 12. There he spent seven days visiting several ministers in Maidenhead (now Lawrenceville, southwest of Princeton), New Brunswick and other towns in the vicinity. Unknown to him, God was about to lead him into a dramatic new phase of Indian ministry.

16

THE SPIRIT'S STIRRING

On Tuesday, June 18, 1745, Brainerd set out from New Brunswick, New Jersey, traveling south. His destination was an Indian village he had heard of named Crossweeksung, eight miles southeast of Trenton. Along the way that afternoon he came to Cranberry (modern Cranbury), fifteen miles south of New Brunswick, and stopped to spend the night at the home of Rev. Charles McKnight. After emigrating from Ireland in 1740 and attending the Log College, McKnight had preached at the Forks of the Delaware for a time before being installed as the pastor of both Cranberry and Allentown the previous year.[1] Brainerd frequently lodged in McKnight's home while carrying out his ministry in Crossweeksung in the weeks and months that followed.

Continuing on the next day, he traveled another thirteen miles to Crossweeksung (present Crosswicks). The town had been settled by Quakers in 1681, the same year Philadelphia was established. The site of an iron ore bog that was extensively worked, Crossweeksung township in Brainerd's day boasted four mills and a tannery, all of which had been in operation for many years.[2]

After nearly a century of European settlement in New Jersey, few Indians remained in the region. Remnant Delawares lived on the outskirts of towns, eking out their livelihood by making baskets, brooms and wooden utensils to sell to the settlers.

---

1. Pettit, *Life of David Brainerd*, p. 297.
2. Wynbeek, *Beloved Yankee*, p. 148.

They maintained some contact with Indians at the Forks of the Delaware and further west.

Brainerd's outlook as he began that new ministry venture was not at all optimistic, as he later revealed:

> In this [discouraged] frame of mind I first visited these Indians at Crossweeksung, apprehending it was my indispensable duty, seeing I had heard there was a number in these parts, to make some attempts for their conversion to God, though I cannot say I had any hope of success, my spirits being now so extremely sunk. I do not know that my hopes respecting the conversion of the Indians were ever reduced to so low an ebb since I had any special concern for them, as at this time.[3]

When he first arrived at Crossweeksung he discovered that only a few Indians – all women and children – were there. He further learned that the natives of that region were widely scattered, living in small groups of just two or three families, with those tiny settlements being between six and thirty or more miles from Crossweeksung.

He preached to the four women he found there that day. They listened attentively and appeared well disposed to what he had to say. After finishing his discourse, he informed them he would willingly visit them again the following day. That evening he was so exhausted he was 'scarce able to walk or sit up' and complained to his diary, 'Oh, how tiresome is earth! How dull the body!'

When he returned to preach the next evening he found that the four women who had made up his audience the day before had traveled ten and fifteen miles to gather their friends to come and hear him. 'These also appeared as attentive, orderly, and well disposed as the others,' he reported. 'And none made any objection, as Indians in other places have usually done.'

That Friday he rode more than twenty miles northeast to Freehold, where William Tennent, Jr., pastored the largest

---

3. Dwight, *Memoirs of David Brainerd*, p. 246; *Life and Diary of David Brainerd* (Baker edition), p. 244.

Presbyterian congregation in the area. William, Jr., was the younger brother of Gilbert and the second son of their father, founder of the Log College. After attending the college, William, Jr., succeeded his younger brother, John, who had died in 1732 at age twenty-five, as pastor of Freehold's Presbyterian Church. Though quieter than his more prominent older brother (Gilbert), William was also a noted revivalist who, under God, had carried the Awakening to Freehold. He faithfully served there from 1733 until his death at age seventy-two in 1777.[4] Brainerd's 'sinking spirits' received a boost and he felt holy longings for God rekindled in his soul through the Christian conversation he was able to enjoy at Tennent's home.

The following day he returned to Crossweeksung, where he preached to a gathering of nearly thirty natives. Various auditors, some of them shedding many tears, had obviously begun 'to feel their misery and perishing state, and appeared concerned for a deliverance from it.' He spent considerable time talking to them about both their spiritual misery and its remedy through faith in Christ.

'My soul was much refreshed and quickened in my work,' he wrote afterwards. 'This was indeed a sweet afternoon to me.' He was so encouraged, in fact, that he further reflected: 'I was then willing to live, for the dear kingdom of Christ; and yet death appeared pleasant: so that I was in some measure in a strait between two, having a desire to depart. I am often weary of this world, and want to leave it on that account: But 'tis desirable to be drawn, rather than driven out of it.'

After preaching to an even larger group of natives the next day, Sunday, June 23, he made these interesting revelations: 'Not a word of opposition was heard from any of them against Christianity, although in times past they had been as opposite to anything of that nature, as any Indians whatsoever. And some of them not many months before were enraged with my interpreter, because he attempted to teach them something of Christianity.' Exactly when and where Tattamy had interacted with these New Jersey Delawares is not known.

4. Pettit, *Life of David Brainerd*, p. 299.

Though his physical and emotional strength were depleted, the eagerness of the natives to receive further spiritual instruction motivated him to minister to them again the following day. Because of his exhaustion, he may have had to rest from preaching for a couple of days. The next recorded occasion he spoke to the natives was on Thursday, when about forty attentive people gathered to hear him. Full of joyous gratitude, he then wrote: 'My soul rejoiced to find that God enabled me to be faithful, and that He was pleased to awaken these poor Indians by my means. Oh, how heart-reviving and soul-refreshing is it to me to see the fruit of my labors!'

A day later the Indians requested that he begin preaching to them twice daily, a request he happily granted. In addition to preaching to between forty and fifty individuals on Sunday and Monday, he spent considerable time visiting with the natives more privately to determine what they were remembering of the truths he had been communicating. He was pleased and even amazed at the measure of knowledge some had acquired in just a few days.

He had not forgotten about the Indians back at the Forks. Rather, he considered it his duty to visit them, as soon as his health allowed. When he informed the Crossweeksung natives on Tuesday, July 2, of his intention to do so, they earnestly inquired when he planned to return and expressed a great desire to receive further spiritual instruction.

'I wish God would change my heart,' one female native told him that day through her many tears.

'I want to find Christ,' another woman stated.

An old man who had once been one of their chiefs wept bitterly with concern for his soul. Brainerd promised to return to them as quickly as his health and business elsewhere would permit.

He was more than a little concerned that the strong spiritual impressions being made upon a number of the Crossweeksung Indians might decline and wear off once the ministry of God's Word ceased among them. He could not but hope that God would maintain and further promote the spiritual work He had begun among the natives, and he realized the Lord was perfectly capable of doing so, even without the means of preaching. Still, due to his many past disappointments, he struggled with doubts and fears:

> At the same time, I must confess that I had often seen encouraging appearances among the Indians elsewhere prove wholly abortive; and it appeared the favor would be so great, if God should now, after I had passed through so considerable a series of almost fruitless labors and fatigues, and after my rising hopes had been so often frustrated among these poor pagans, give me any special success in my labors with them. I could not believe, and scarce dared to hope that the event would be so happy, and scarce ever found myself more suspended between hope and fear, in any affair, or at any time, than this.

He also revealed that the current openness of the Crossweeksung natives to spiritual instruction seemed to stem from his earlier ministry at the Forks of the Delaware. While visiting at the Forks some time earlier, one or two of the Crossweeksung Indians had heard him preach and had come under conviction. Returning to their home in New Jersey, they sought to point out to their acquaintances the evils of idolatry.

'And although the other Indians seemed but little to regard, but rather to deride them,' Brainerd explained, 'yet this, perhaps, has put them into a thinking posture of mind, or at least, given them some thoughts about Christianity, and excited in some of them a curiosity to hear, and so made way for the present encouraging attention.' That, in turn, heartened him that God might yet use his earlier efforts in other places to bear significant spiritual fruit among the Indians of those locations.

That same Tuesday, July 2, he rode the nearly thirty miles north to New Brunswick. Edwards reports that Brainerd was so 'beat out by constant preaching' that he 'found it necessary to give himself some relaxation.' He spent a week in New Jersey, therefore, visiting several ministers and carrying out some necessary business, before proceeding to the Forks of the Delaware. When he arrived there on Friday, July 12, he was still very weak in body, but strong in spirit.

The convicting work of God's Spirit that he had witnessed at Crossweeksung appears to have accompanied him back to the Forks, at least to a degree:

> Lord's Day, July 14. Discoursed to the Indians twice, several of whom appeared concerned, and were, I have reason to think, in some measure convinced by the Divine Spirit of their sin and misery; so that they wept much the whole time of divine service.

> Thursday, July 18. Preached to my people, who attended diligently, beyond what had been common among these Indians: and some of them appeared concerned for their souls.

The following Sunday he had the great joy of baptizing his first Indian converts, Moses Tattamy and his wife. Of them he testified:

> They are both persons of some experimental knowledge in religion; have both been awakened to a solemn concern for their souls; have to appearance been brought to a sense of their misery and undoneness in themselves; have both appeared to be comforted with divine consolations; and it is apparent both have passed a great, and I cannot but hope a saving, change.

He elaborated further on the spiritual transformation he had observed in Tattamy's life during the past half year:

> His change is abiding, and his life, so far as I know, unblemished to this day, though it is now more than six months since he experienced this change; in which space of time he has been as much exposed to strong drink, as possible, in divers places where it has been moving free as water; and yet has never, that I know of, discovered any hankering desire after it. He seems to have a very considerable experience of a spiritual exercise, and discourses feelingly of the conflicts and consolations of a real Christian. His heart echoes to the

soul-humbling doctrines of grace, and he never appears better pleased than when he hears of the absolute sovereignty of God, and the salvation of sinners in a way of mere free grace. He has likewise of late had more satisfaction respecting his own state, has been much enlivened and assisted in his work, so that he has been a great comfort to me.

And upon a view and strict observation of his serious and savory conversation, his Christian temper, and unblemished behavior for so considerable a time, as well as his experience I have given an account of, I think that I have reason to hope that he is 'created anew in Christ Jesus to good works' (2 Cor. 5:17; Eph. 2:10).

Five days later Brainerd baptized Tattamy's children after holding a preaching service with the Indians. Tattamy is known to have had at least five children, but it is not clear how many of them were baptized on that occasion. Some of the other natives stated that witnessing the baptism of Tattamy and his family members had done more to awaken their personal spiritual concern than anything they had seen or heard before.

On the last day of July he set out again for Crossweeksung. After completing the seventy-mile journey in just two days, he sent word around to the Indians, informing them of his return and inviting them to attend a preaching service that Saturday, August 3. He spoke from Revelation 22:17 – 'And whosoever will, let him take the water of life freely' – and felt like the Lord helped him in something of an exceptional manner to portray Jesus Christ to them as a kind and compassionate Savior who was inviting distressed and perishing sinners to accept everlasting mercy. Of the twenty adults who listened to his discourse, all but two were in tears as he spoke.

Charles McKnight had invited Brainerd to assist him in administering the Lord's Supper at his church in Cranberry the following day, August 4. The missionary complied with that request, and took with him a group of nearly fifty Indians, adults and children, who by that time had arrived at Crossweeksung to receive his instruction. They attended the several discourses that were delivered that day, and their spiritual concern was heightened through what they heard and saw.

He preached the second of two messages that concluded the communion observance on Monday. Taking John 7:37 as his text, he addressed his remarks especially to the Indians who sat in a group by themselves at the meeting. That evening he again discoursed to the natives, the majority of them being at the house where he lodged while in Cranberry. He found them all engaged in conversation about spiritual matters and expressing concern about the condition of their souls. Tattamy, who had been ministering among them day and night, was of much assistance to many in those discussions.

That day one native woman appeared to gain comfort and assurance that she had been brought into a saving relationship with Jesus Christ. She had been greatly concerned for her soul ever since first hearing Brainerd preach the previous June, but that day came to be at peace spiritually.

That young woman, Brainerd's first convert from Crossweeksung, was the sole surviving child of Weequehela, the last great sachem among the Delawares in New Jersey in the early 1700s. He once owned much land, many horses and cattle, as well as black slaves. He frequently entertained governors and other important white men in his home, which was fully furnished with English furniture, silverware, calico curtains and featherbeds.

In 1727 a land dispute developed between Weequehela and his English neighbor, Captain John Leonard. On more than one occasion, Leonard reportedly extorted large tracts of land from Weequehela after getting him drunk. Following a particularly grievous instance of such extortion, Weequehela, after becoming sober and realizing what had happened, shot Leonard dead, then surrendered peacefully to white authorities.

When his people offered to break him out of jail he refused, stating that it would not be right for a king to run away. He also exhorted them to live in peace with their pale-faced brethren. He was hanged at Perth Amboy, west across the bay from Staten Island. A reprieve from the Governor arrived too late, after he was already dead.

Following the chief's death, his widow and four or five children, one of them being only a few days old, were badly mistreated and deprived of all their property and possessions. Within a short time all of them except a three-year-old daughter of Weequehela died. During her difficult childhood she saw her aunt killed by a settler.

When Brainerd came to Crossweeksung, this daughter of Weequehela would have been about twenty years old and may have already been married to her husband, Stephen Calvin. Her husband, a man of high intelligence and goodwill, was one of the Indians who assisted Brainerd as an interpreter.

She would later tell her children and grandchildren that Brainerd was the first white man she could ever love, having suffered so much at their hands and always having feared them. One of her grandchildren testified of her: 'She loved David Brainerd very much because he loved his heavenly Father so much that he was willing to endure hardships, traveling over mountains, suffering hunger, and lying on the ground that he might do her people good. And she did everything she could for his comfort.'[5]

---

5   Thomas Brainerd, *Life of John Brainerd*, pp. 460-1; Wynbeek, *Beloved Yankee*, pp. 155-8.

17

Days of God's Power

The next morning Brainerd discoursed to the Indians at the house where they had been lodging while at Cranberry. By that time many of the natives' hearts had become exceedingly tender, so much so that after he had spoken just 'a few words' about their spiritual concerns they began to weep freely. Many sobbed or groaned.

After their delegation returned to Crossweeksung that same day, he preached to them again in the afternoon. Some fifty-five individuals were present, about forty of whom he judged as being 'capable of attending divine service with understanding.' They listened intently as he expounded from 1 John 4:10, 'Herein is love, not that we loved God, but that he loved us, and sent his Son to be the propitiation for our sins.' By the close of his message all but three of the forty who understood were weeping and crying out bitterly under heavy conviction.

> They all, as one, seemed in an agony of soul to obtain an interest in Christ; and the more I discoursed of the love and compassion of God in sending His Son to suffer for the sins of men; and the more I invited them to come and partake of His love, the more their distress was aggravated, because they felt themselves unable to come. It was surprizing to see how their hearts seemed to be pierced with the tender and melting invitations of the Gospel, when there was not a word of terror spoken to them.

That day two Indians received relief from their spiritual distress. After questioning them individually and concluding that their newfound comfort was based on a solid scriptural understanding, he asked them, 'What would you like God to do further for you?'

'We want Christ to wipe our hearts completely clean,' they responded.

He preached the following day from Isaiah 53:3-10, of the Suffering Servant who bore the sins of God's people. Many continued to be greatly distressed over the condition of their souls and several lay flat on the ground crying incessantly for mercy. He found it remarkable that as soon as newcomers arrived from outlying areas, the Spirit of God seemed to seize them with concern for their souls. Two more individuals found definite spiritual relief that day while a third person seemed to have gained a degree of such comfort.

The next day – Thursday, August 8, 1745 – stands as the single most outstanding day in Brainerd's ministry career. He preached to a gathering of about sixty-five Indians that afternoon, relating 'with uncommon freedom' the parable of the invitation to the heavenly banquet from Luke 14:16-23. Then, suddenly, came the gracious, overwhelming moving of God's Spirit for which he had so long hoped and prayed:

> There was much visible concern among them while I was discoursing publicly; but afterwards when I spoke to one and another more particularly, whom I perceived under much concern, the power of God seemed to descend upon the assembly like 'a rushing mighty wind' (Acts 2:2), and with an astonishing energy bore down all before it.
>
> I stood amazed at the influence that seized the audience almost universally, and could compare it to nothing more aptly than the irresistable force of a mighty torrent, or swelling deluge, that with its insupportable weight and pressure bears down and sweeps before it whatever is in its way! Almost all persons of all ages were bowed down with concern together, and scarce one was able to withstand the shock of this surprizing operation! Old men and women who had been

drunken wretches for many years, and some little children not more than six or seven years of age, appeared in distress for their souls, as well as persons of middle age. And 'twas apparent these children (some of them at least) were not merely frightened with seeing the general concern; but were made sensible of their danger, the badness of their hearts, and their misery without Christ, as some of them expressed it. The most stubborn heart was now obliged to bow. ...

They were almost universally praying and crying for mercy in every part of the house, and many out of doors, and numbers could neither go nor stand: Their concern was so great, each one for himself, that none seemed to take any notice of those about them, but each prayed as freely for themselves; ... I believe rather, that they thought nothing about any but themselves and their own states, and so were every one praying apart, although all together. ...

This concern in general was most rational and just; those who had been awakened any considerable time complained more especially of the badness of their hearts; and those newly awakened [complained more especially] of the badness of their lives and actions past; and all were afraid of the anger of God and of everlasting misery as the desert of their sins.

Those who had lately obtained relief were filled with comfort at this season; they appeared calm and composed, and seemed to rejoice in Christ Jesus: And some of them took their distressed friends by the hand, telling them of the goodness of Christ and the comfort that is to be enjoyed in Him, and thence invited them to come and give up their hearts to Him. And I could observe some of them in the most honest and unaffected manner (without any design of being taken notice of) lifting up their eyes to heaven as if crying for mercy, while they saw the distress of the poor souls around them.

Among those overwhelmed with conviction that day was one of the native leaders who up to that point had been self-righteous. He felt secure about his own spiritual standing because he knew more about Christian matters than most of his fellow Indians. Just the day before he had told Brainerd with a great degree of confidence that he had been a Christian for more than ten years. Now, however, he was brought under solemn concern about his own spiritual welfare and wept bitterly.

Another individual who fell under pressing conviction was an old powwow who was known to be a murderer and a notorious drunkard.[1] This man was from the Forks of the Delaware and had sometimes attended Brainerd's meetings throughout the year he ministered there. But late in 1744 or early in 1745 the conjurer murdered a promising young Indian. That wrongdoing, according to Brainerd, 'threw him into some kind of horror and desperation,' so that for several months afterwards he stayed away from the missionary and refused to hear him preach. Eventually the evangelist had an opportunity to visit with the troubled native and to encourage him that even his sin of murder might be forgiven for Christ's sake.

After that he again attended many of Brainerd's sermons. At the same time, however, he continued his conjuring practices. The other natives were convinced he possessed great supernatural power and readily paid heed to him. Their high opinion of him and his superstitious practices seemed to be an insurmountable obstruction that kept many of the Indians from receiving the Christian Gospel. So great was that hindrance, in fact, that Brainerd often thought it would be a great favor to his efforts if God would bring the man's life to an end. But the Lord, in His infinite grace and wisdom, had other plans for the old powwow.

The first indication of his having genuine concern for the welfare of his soul had come after he witnessed the baptism of Moses Tattamy and his wife the previous month. When that concern continued, he accepted the invitation of one of his fellow Indians to join him in following Brainerd to Crossweeksung to hear more of his preaching. Now, on this day of God's Spirit bringing mighty conviction upon the natives gathered there,

1. Brainerd related the story of this man's protracted period of conviction and eventual conversion in his *Journal* on May 9, 1746 (Pettit, *Life of David Brainerd*, pp. 391-5).

the conjurer wept profusely and cried for mercy. He upbraided himself for not being even more concerned than he was, now that he saw his danger was so very great.

Another 'remarkable instance of awakening' that took place that same day involved a young Indian woman from a distance away who had heard something strange was happening among the natives and came to see what was the matter. On her way to Crossweeksung, she stopped to visit the white preacher, about whom she had heard so much, at his lodgings. In conversing with her, he concluded she had never realized or considered before that day that she had a soul. When he informed her of his intention to preach again presently to her people, she laughed and seemed to mock. But continuing on to where the Indians were gathered, she was in the audience when he spoke that day.

He had not proceeded far in his discourse before she became convinced that she had a soul. Before he had finished the message she was so convicted of her sin and misery and so distressed with concern for her soul's salvation that she cried out incessantly. She was unable to stand and could not even sit on her seat without being held up. After the public service ended, she lay flat on the ground praying earnestly. She didn't seem to notice and gave no response to those who spoke to her.

Brainerd listened closely to hear what she was praying. Repeatedly she kept verbalizing the burden of her heart, '*Guttummaukalummeh wechaumeh kmeleh Ndah*' – 'Have mercy on me, and help me to give You my heart.' So great was her burden that she continued to pray incessantly for hours.

Natives were not the only ones brought under conviction. A number of settlers were among Brainerd's auditors on that occasion. They were curious about what a missionary would have to say to 'savages' but not necessarily concerned about their own spiritual condition. He noted, however, that some of the settlers were 'much awakened' and 'appeared to be wounded with a view of their perishing state.'

The awakening continued in power the next day. That Friday afternoon he preached to a gathering of about seventy people, explaining and applying the parable of the sower from

Matthew 13. Many were in tears and some cried out in anguish of soul. This response was elicited, he was careful to clarify, 'although I spoke not a word of terror, but on the contrary, set before them the fullness and all-sufficiency of Christ's merits, and His willingness to save all that came to Him; and thereupon pressed them to come without delay.'

This commotion caused some who were scattered about, paying little heed to his discourse, to gather around to see what was happening. He continued his Gospel invitation in the same vein till all but two or three of his hearers were 'melted into tears and cries' and seemed 'in the greatest distress to find and secure an interest in the great Redeemer.' Some who had exhibited only a slight emotional response the previous day now seemed to be cut to the heart. Throughout the assembly the level of anxious concern appeared to be nearly as prevalent as it had been the day before. Again, nearly everyone seemed to be mourning and crying for themselves with little apparent awareness of others around them. 'Guttummaukalummeh, guttummaukalummeh – Have mercy upon me, have mercy upon me!' was the common cry.

On Saturday he spoke from Luke 19:10, 'For the Son of man is come to seek and to save that which was lost.' He had not preached long before the house where they met was filled with cries and groans. One man, who up to that point had given no indication of having experienced awakening, was brought under piercing conviction: 'He said all the wickedness of his past life was brought fresh to his remembrance, and he saw all the vile actions he had done formerly as if done but yesterday.' But another individual who had been under pressing distress day after day suddenly received spiritual peace. 'Could not but rejoice and admire at divine goodness in what appeared this day,' Brainerd related. 'There seems to be some good done by every discourse: some newly awakened every day and some comforted.'

A number of 'careless spectators of the white people, some Quakers and others' were among his audience when he preached on the parable of the prodigal son Sunday morning. As a result of the influence of those spiritually careless settlers: 'Observed no such remarkable effect of the Word upon the assembly as in days past.' Things changed that afternoon, however, when he spoke on part of the Apostle Peter's Pentecost sermon:

> And at the close of my discourse to the Indians, made an address to the white people, and divine truths seemed then to be attended with power both to English and Indians. Several of the white heathen were awakened and could not longer be idle spectators, but found they had souls to save or lose as well as the Indians; and a great concern spread through the whole assembly, so that this also appeared to be a day of God's power, especially towards the conclusion of it, as well as several of the former [days], although the influence attending the Word seemed scarce so powerful now as in some days past.

He reported that the natives who had received spiritual relief and comfort now appeared humble and devout, and conducted themselves in an agreeable and Christian manner. The tenderness of conscience they manifested was refreshing to him. Noting one morning that an Indian woman was very sad, he inquired as to the cause of her sorrow. She confessed to becoming angry with her child the evening before, and was now fearful lest her ire had been inordinate and sinful. She was so grieved over the possible offense that, since awaking before dawn that morning, she had been weeping for several hours.

On Wednesday, August 14, less than one week after the sudden spiritual stirring began, a native came to him under deep conviction about a perplexing issue. Some time earlier the man had put away his wife and taken another woman, a common practice among the Indians. Now he seemed fully convinced of his sin in the affair and eager to know what God would have him to do to rectify the situation. Brainerd addressed the issue with forthrightness, wisdom and maturity. The results were nothing short of astounding, given the short period of time the Indians had been exposed to Christian teaching:

> When the law of God respecting marriage had been opened to them, and the cause of leaving his wife inquired into; and

when it appeared she had given him no just occasion by unchastity to desert her, and that she was willing to forgive his past misconduct and to live peaceably with him for the future, and that she moreover insisted on it as her right to enjoy him; he was then told that it was his indispensible duty to renounce the woman he had last taken and receive the other who was his proper wife and live peaceably with her during life, with which he readily and cheerfully complied, and thereupon publicly renounced the woman he had last taken and publicly promised to live with and be kind to his wife during life, she also promising the same to him. And here appeared a clear demonstration of the power of God's Word upon their hearts. I suppose a few weeks before the whole world could not have persuaded this man to a compliance with Christian rules in this affair.

Brainerd feared this incident might prejudice some of the natives against the moral teachings of Christianity as being overly strict. But he was happily able to report: 'it seemed to have a good, rather than an ill, effect among the Indians, who generally owned that the laws of Christ were good and right respecting the affairs of marriage.'

Two days later he presented part of Jesus' bread of life discourse from John 6:26-34. Afterward he spoke individually with various people who were under distressing conviction:

There was a great concern for their souls spread pretty generally among them: But especially there were two persons newly awakened to a sense of their sin and misery, one of whom was lately come, and the other had all along been very attentive, and desirous of being awakened, but could never before have any lively view of her perishing state. But now her concern and spiritual distress was such, that I thought I had never seen *any* more pressing. Sundry old men were also in distress for their souls; so that they could not refrain from weeping and crying out aloud, and their bitter groans were the most convincing as well as affecting evidence of the reality and depth of their inward anguish. God is powerfully at work among them!

He was astute enough to realize that not everyone was being genuinely converted, even in the midst of this mighty spiritual stirring: 'some few, who felt a commotion in their passions in days past, seem now to discover that their hearts were never duly affected.'

Another feature of the awakening arrested his attention, causing him to give full credit for the stirring to God alone:

> I never saw the work of God appear so independent of means as at this time. I discoursed to the people, and spoke what (I suppose) had a proper tendency to promote convictions, and God's manner of working upon them appeared so entirely supernatural, and above means, that I could scarce believe He used me as an instrument, or what I spake as means of carrying on His work: for it seemed, as I thought, to have no connection with, nor dependence upon means in any respect. ... God seemed (as I apprehended) to work entirely without them: so that I seemed to do nothing and indeed to have nothing to do but 'stand still and see the salvation of God' (Exod. 14:13), and found myself obliged and delighted to say, 'Not unto us,' not unto instruments and means, 'but to Thy name be glory' (Ps. 115:1).

On Tuesday, August 20, he rode the more than twenty miles to William Tennent's church at Freehold where he was to preach. Besides being the largest Presbyterian congregation in the region, that prominent church had an additional distinction: Founded in 1682 by former New England settlers and Scottish immigrants, it had been the first regularly constituted Presbyterian church in America.[2]

Doubtless the Freehold congregants had heard about the dramatic awakening taking place among the Indians through Brainerd's ministry and were eager to hear one of his powerful sermons. Naturally, he would have preferred to represent himself well in such a prestigious setting. But perhaps as a reminder to all that spiritual awakening is the work of God rather than of man,

2. Wynbeek, *Beloved Yankee*, p. 164.

the Lord saw fit to allow him to struggle that day, even though he employed one of his favorite preaching texts. His resigned response to that embarrassing disappointment was exemplary:

> Near noon I rode to Freehold and preached to a considerable assembly, from Matt. 5:3. It pleased God to leave me to be very dry and barren; so that I don't remember to have been so straightened for a whole twelve month [year] past. God is just, and He has made my soul acquiesce in His will in this regard. 'Tis contrary to 'flesh and blood' (Heb. 2:14) to be cut off from all freedom in a large auditory, where their expectations are much raised; but so it was with me: And God helped me to say 'Amen' to it; good is the will of the Lord. In the evening I felt quiet and composed, and had freedom and comfort in secret prayer.

Back at Crossweeksung that Saturday, he met privately with the natives who had professed faith in Christ to prepare them for baptism the next day. On Sunday morning he preached from Luke 15 on the parable of the lost sheep. 'A multitude' of spiritually careless settlers were present that day, and he tried to address them in particular at the close of his message. Their discourteous, uninterested response proved deeply discouraging to him: 'could not so much as keep them orderly; for scores of them kept walking and gazing about, and behaved more indecently than any Indians I ever addressed; and a view of their abusive conduct so sunk my spirits that I could scarce go on with my work.'

Despite that discouragement, he proceeded with the baptismal service that was planned for the afternoon. Great indeed must have been his joy and thanksgiving as he baptized twenty-five Indians, including fifteen adults and ten children. After the crowd of white spectators had departed, he called together the newly baptized believers:

> ... [I re]minded them of the solemn obligations they were now under to live to God, warned them of the evil and dreadful consequences of careless living, especially after this public profession of Christianity; gave them directions for

their future conduct, and encouraged them to watchfulness and devotion by setting before them the comfort and happy conclusion of a religious life. This was a desirable and sweet season indeed! Their hearts were engaged and cheerful in duty, and they rejoiced that they had in a public and solemn manner dedicated themselves to God. Love seemed to reign among them!

As he instructed the believers, they tenderly and affectionately joined hands with one another 'as if their hearts were knit together.' All this made a strong impression on some of the other Indians. They wept bitterly, wishing that they shared in the joy and spiritual comfort some of their fellow natives now obviously possessed.

The next day he preached to nearly 100 Indians from John 6:51-55. Two more natives gained relief and rest for their distressed and weary souls. In addition, an old man who throughout his life had been an 'obstinate idolater' willingly surrendered his rattles to his fellow Indians. The rattles, which had commonly been used in conjunction with idolatrous feasts and dances, were quickly destroyed. Commented Brainerd: 'And this [was done] without any attempt of mine in the affair, I having said nothing to him about it; so that it seemed 'twas nothing but just the power of God's Word, without any particular application to this sin, that produced this effect.'

He had become 'fully convinced' it was now his duty to make another itineration to the Indians along the Susquehanna River. He knew this was the time of year to find them generally at home. 'Would you be willing,' he asked the new Christians at Crossweeksung, 'to spend the remainder of the day in prayer for me, that God will go with me and succeed my endeavors for the conversion of those poor souls?'

They happily complied. He left them about an hour and a half before sunset, and they commenced their prayer meeting shortly after his departure. They continued earnestly in prayer until they thought it was about the time when they normally went to bed for the night. Exiting the house where they had been meeting, they discovered that the morning star was at a considerable height. Only then did they realize they had prayed through most of the night and it would soon be dawn!

18

Ministering Where Satan Reigns

Upon leaving Crossweeksung, Brainerd took a roundabout journey of five days traveling to the Forks of the Delaware. Along the way he again paid a visit to the Governor of Pennsylvania in Philadelphia in order to obtain a letter of recommendation that could be shared with the Indian chiefs of the Susquehanna region.

After arriving at the Forks the last day of August, he preached to the Indians there on Sunday, September 1, 1745. He returned to one of his favorite Gospel preaching texts, the parable of the great banquet, in Luke 14:16-23. 'The Word appeared to be attended with some power,' he reported, 'and caused some tears in the assembly.' Afterward he discoursed to a number of settlers who were present, and observed that many of them, too, wept. That included some who had formerly been as careless and unconcerned about spiritual matters as the Indians.

Two days later he discoursed to the natives from Isaiah 53:3-6. As he did, 'the divine presence seemed to be in the midst of the assembly, and a considerable concern spread amongst them.' Various people seemed to be awakened to their spiritual need, including two exceedingly dull individuals who previously would hardly ever stay awake while he was preaching.

On Wednesday he rode the fifteen miles to Craig's Settlement where he preached a Gospel message from Luke 14:23. Again, many in the audience were in tears and unbelievers seemed to be 'in some measure' awakened to their spiritual needs. He remarked afterward, 'Blessed be the Lord that lets me see His work going on in one place and another.'

Back at the Forks the next day, he spoke to the Indians on the parable of the sower and afterwards conversed with various individuals. Some wept and even cried out in spiritual distress. Others seemed to be seized with surprise at this sudden spiritual stirring and with concern about their own spiritual welfare. Various of these natives had gone with him to Crossweeksung, had witnessed the mighty convicting power of God's Word there and, in some cases, had themselves been brought to faith.

He asked one of the men, who had come to be at peace spiritually and who had been manifesting promising evidences of genuine conversion, why he now wept. The man responded, 'When I think how Christ was slain like a lamb and spilt His blood for sinners, I cannot help crying when I am all alone.' Having said that, he again burst into tears.

Turning to the man's wife, who had also gained abundant comfort for her soul, Brainerd asked her why she was weeping. 'I am grieved that the Indians here will not come to Christ as well as those at Crossweeksung,' she answered.

Only a few natives were present to hear his morning and afternoon messages on Sunday, September 8, but the Word of God seemed to fall with convicting power. Most of those present were in tears, and various ones cried out in concern for their souls.

Not all the Indians at the Forks were receptive toward the missionary and his message. Some of them were very upset with their fellow natives for listening to his preaching, and lately had resorted to biting ridicule of those who were under spiritual conviction:

> There are sundry Indians in these parts who have always refused to hear me preach, and have been enraged against those that have attended my preaching. But of late they are more bitter than ever, scoffing at Christianity, and sometimes asking my hearers how often they have cried, and whether they han't [have not] now cried enough to do the turn, etc.; so that they have already 'trial of cruel mockings' (Heb. 11:36).

On Monday he set out for the Susquehanna. He traversed the 120 miles from the Forks to Shamokin in five days. Jonathan Edwards revealed: 'He performed the journey under a considerable degree of melancholy, occasioned at first by his hearing that the Moravians were gone before him to the Susquehanna Indians.'

Only in very recent years had the missions-motivated Moravians of Germany succeeded in gaining a foothold in America, and that primarily in Pennsylvania. Due to their pietism and pacifism, they were initially viewed with suspicion and opposed by many Protestant denominations. For Moravians, coming to salvation did not involve, as it did for Puritans, a protracted process of spiritual distress which was only gradually relieved as one gained a certainty that God had drawn him to saving faith in Christ. Whereas the Puritans insisted on seeing lifestyle fruit to verify one's Christian profession, Moravian missionaries were content with a simple profession of faith on the part of their converts. Moravians rejected the Puritans' strict system of catechizing new believers in biblical doctrine. They, instead, placed their emphasis on the believer's personal spiritual experiences. At that time the Moravians also had an unhealthy fixation on the blood and wounds of Christ on the cross that was repugnant to most American Protestants. (That unfortunate, unbalanced fascination was later corrected.)

Because of these several significant differences in theological and practical emphasis, it is not surprising that Brainerd was discouraged when he learned that Moravian missionaries had been carrying out their work among the Susquehanna Indians whom he hoped to reach. He would have viewed various aspects of the Moravians' work as misguided and spiritually unhealthy.

Upon arriving at Shamokin on Friday, September 13, he was kindly received and entertained by the Indians. But he was distressed by the 'heathenish dance and revel' they held in the house where he was obliged to stay that night. He repeatedly entreated them to desist for the sake of one of their own friends there in the house who was very ill and whose disorder was greatly aggravated by all the noise and commotion. All his appeals, however, were to no avail.

The next day he visited the Delaware chief, Sassoonan. The chief had been deathly ill when Brainerd was at Shamokin four months earlier but now was recovered. The evangelist spent the afternoon visiting with Sassoonan and others about Christianity. The results were more encouraging than he had anticipated: 'The king appeared kindly disposed and willing to be instructed. This gave me some encouragement that God would open an effectual door for my preaching the Gospel here, and set up His kingdom in this place.'

He again visited and was kindly received by Sassoonan on Sunday. He discoursed to some Indians that afternoon, but unfortunately many of the natives in that locale were so inebriated throughout the few days he was there that he was unable to speak to them. Monday morning was spent visiting the Indians from house to house and encouraging them 'to be friendly to Christianity.'

That evening he went to another part of town where the Indians were sober. Almost certainly that was the portion of Shamokin where the Iroquois chief Shikellamy and his people resided. 'Having first obtained the king's cheerful consent,' Brainerd gathered nearly fifty people and preached to them. They were surprisingly attentive and showed considerable desire to receive further instruction.

He was very encouraged by that apparent interest. As he returned to his 'poor hard lodgings' with Moses Tattamy, his faithful interpreter and his only companion on this itineration, he was 'rejoicing in hopes that God designed to set up His kingdom here, where Satan now reigns in the most eminent manner.'

Most of the Shamokin Indians left town the next day to go on a hunting expedition. Brainerd and Tattamy set out downriver for Juniata and arrived there on Thursday, September 19. The missionary likely went to Juniata with a hopeful outlook because the natives there had given him a friendly reception the previous spring and had encouraged him to return to visit them again. Now, however, he was deeply disappointed and discouraged to find them determined to 'retain their pagan notions and persist in their idolatrous practices.'

Nearly all the Indians were busily engaged in preparing for a great idolatrous sacrifice and dance that were to be held the next night. Because of those preparations, he had no opportunity to gather them for a preaching service. To make matters worse, Tattamy, who did not speak or understand the language of the Juniata natives, had to leave to attend to some pressing business elsewhere. So Brainerd's only available interpreter was an idolatrous pagan. He attempted to dialogue privately about spiritual matters with some of the Indians but with no apparent success.

Nearly 100 natives gathered Friday evening to dance around a large fire. The fat of ten deer that had been sacrificed for the occasion was burned in the fire, sometimes raising the flames 'to a prodigious height.' The dancers yelled and shouted so loudly that Brainerd estimated they could have easily been heard at a distance of two miles or more. After dancing throughout nearly the entire night, the Indians ate the sacrificial meat, then retired to their separate lodgings.

He felt entirely alone that night without even a single Christian companion, as well as troubled and dejected at the 'idolatrous revel.' He walked to and fro till both his body and mind were 'pained and much oppressed.' At length he slipped into a small corncrib where he slept on the poles.

On Sunday he again attempted to share a Christian message with the local natives. 'As soon as they were well up in the morning,' he tried to gather them together, but quickly discovered they had other intentions that day. About noon they brought together all their powwows in an effort to determine the cause of a widespread sickness on the island at that time. Many individuals had been suffering from a fever and bloody flux. About half a dozen conjurers set to work 'playing their juggling tricks' and carrying out a variety of unusual and fantastic actions that were apparently intended to have some influence on the unseen world of spirits:

> In this exercise they were engaged for several hours, making all the wild, ridiculous, and distracted motions imaginable; sometimes singing, sometimes howling, sometimes extending their hands to the utmost stretch, spreading all their fingers;

and seemed to push with them as if they designed to fright something away, or at least keep it off at arms end; sometimes stroking their faces with their hands, then spurting water as fine as mist; sometimes setting flat on the earth, then bowing down their faces to the ground; wringing their sides, as if in pain and anguish; twisting their faces, turning up their eyes, grunting, puffing, etc. ... Some of them, I could observe, were much more fervent and devout in the business than others, and seemed to chant, peep, and mutter with a great degree of warmth and vigor, as if determined to awaken and engage the powers below.

While all this was going on he had crept near and sat down, undetected, not more than thirty feet from the powwows. Holding his Bible in his hand and praying fervently, he was determined if possible to 'spoil their sport and prevent their receiving any answers from the infernal world.' After the conjurers had carried out their 'hideous charms and incantations' for more than three hours, they exhausted themselves and eventually gave up the effort.

As they broke up the powwow he attempted to discourse with them about Christianity. But they refused to listen to him and soon dispersed to their homes. Their refusal to even consider the teachings of Christianity and their steadfast commitment to pagan beliefs and practices was totally deflating to him:

A view of these things, while I was entirely alone in the wilderness, destitute of the society of anyone that so much as 'named the name of Christ' (2 Tim. 2:19), greatly sunk my spirits, gave me the most gloomy turn of mind imaginable, almost stripped me of all resolution and hope respecting further attempts for propagating the Gospel and converting the pagans, and rendered this the most burdensome and disagreeable Sabbath that ever I saw. But nothing, I can truly say, sunk and distressed me like the loss of my hope respecting their conversion. This concern appeared so great, and seemed to be so much my own, that I seemed to have nothing to do on earth if this failed: And a prospect of the greatest success in the saving conversion of souls under

Gospel light [i.e., in places where the Gospel was already being preached] would have done little or nothing towards compensating for the loss of my hope in this respect; and my spirits now were so damped and depressed that I had no heart nor power to make any further attempts among them for that purpose, and could not possibly recover my hope, resolution, and courage, by the utmost of my endeavors.

The next morning he left Juniata and set out on the return trip to the Forks of the Delaware. Feeling very weak, he traveled slowly. Throughout the journey he was also dogged by deep discouragement. Thankfully, however, while at Craig's Settlement that weekend, God brought refreshment and encouragement to his heart through seasons of private prayer and profitable interaction with fellow believers.

He returned to his own house at the Forks on Monday. The next day, October 1, he preached to the Indians there and visited privately with a number of them about their spiritual concerns. He also invited them to accompany him (or to follow him at their earliest convenience) in returning to Crossweeksung, a suggestion that several natives readily accepted.

Two days later he left the Forks. Shortly after his arrival at Crossweeksung that Saturday, he preached to the Indians on John 14:1-6. As before, the divine presence was immediately sensed in that assembly. He was struck by the difference in spiritual responsiveness between these natives and those he had recently attempted to evangelize. He was careful to credit the difference to the working of God's sovereign grace:

Oh, what a difference is there between these and the Indians I had lately treated with upon Susquehanna! To be with those seemed like being banished from God and all His people; to be with these like being admitted into His family, and to the enjoyment of His divine presence! How great is the change lately made upon numbers of these Indians, who not many months ago were many of them as thoughtless and averse to Christianity as those upon Susquehanna! And how astonishing is that grace that has made this change!

19

Progress of a Remarkable Work of Grace

Brainerd preached to the spiritually hungry Crossweeksung Indians morning, afternoon and evening on Sunday, October 6, 1745. His limited strength being depleted from his recent itineration and the exertions of the day, he returned to his lodgings shortly after the evening service concluded. The natives, however, continued praying together for an additional two hours.

Likely he pushed himself to instruct the eager natives three times that day because on the morrow he again needed to leave them for a time. Along with other ministers from New Jersey, he had been asked to serve on a council to assist and advise the congregation of East Hampton, Long Island, in working through 'affairs of difficulty in that church.'

When the ministerial delegates arrived at East Hampton they found the congregation deeply divided over whom to call as the pastoral replacement for the ailing Nathaniel Huntting. (A year and a half had passed since Brainerd declined the invitation of that church to become its settled pastor.) A majority of the congregation had agreed upon a suitable candidate and went so far as to convene the present council for the purpose of ordaining him as their pastor. But when the council members discovered that a formidable minority in the congregation opposed the candidate they declined to proceed with the ordination.

Less than a year later, the situation was happily resolved when Samuel Buell, Brainerd's ardent friend at Yale, was installed as pastor of the East Hampton parish. Following his graduation from Yale, Buell had experienced considerable success as an evangelist, first as Edwards' apprentice in Northampton, then at other places. The East Hampton congregation accepted Buell unanimously. He served as pastor there for fifty-two years, preaching some 10,000 sermons in his lifetime before dying at age eighty-two in 1798.[1]

The importance of the council's business and Brainerd's concern for the spiritual welfare of the East Hampton church lay so heavily on his mind that he slept but little for several successive nights. He did experience soul-refreshing seasons of personal devotions and of conversation with fellow ministers. As had often happened before, so during this journey he experienced special divine assistance in the public ministry opportunities that were afforded him, while at the same time sensing his 'extreme vileness and unprofitableness.'

He arrived back at Crossweeksung on Wednesday, October 23. The following weekend he assisted in a communion observance that was held at 'a neighboring congregation,' perhaps again Charles McKnight's in Cranberry. A number of the Crossweeksung Indians readily accepted his invitation to accompany him on that occasion. Most of them now understood some English, so they attentively attended the several preaching services that were held during the three-day affair.

As Brainerd addressed a large crowd outdoors that Sunday, a native woman who had never before considered religious teaching and who had only reluctantly accepted her friends' invitation to attend the meeting, was instantly seized with pressing concern for her own spiritual welfare. She expressed a great desire to return home, more than forty miles' distance, to call her husband to come hear the preaching so that his spiritual concern might be similarly awakened.

After Brainerd preached to another sizable gathering on Monday morning, the Indians, eager to receive further instruction from God's Word, asked if there would be another sermon that day, either before the solemnity concluded or back at Crossweeksung. After they returned home later in the day, he obliged them by discoursing from Matthew 22:1-13 on the parable of the wedding banquet.

1. Wynbeek, *Beloved Yankee*, pp. 174-5, 228-9.

The Word of God at this time seemed to fall upon the assembly with a divine power and influence, especially toward the close of my discourse: There was both a sweet melting and bitter mourning in the audience. The dear Christians were refreshed and comforted. Convictions revived in others, and sundry persons newly awakened who had never been with us before, and so much of the divine presence appeared in the assembly that it seemed 'this was no other than the house of God, and the gate of heaven' (Gen. 28:17). ...

Not altogether surprisingly, given the significant emotional letdown that pastors quite commonly experience after a blessed but taxing period of ministry, his spirits plummeted the very next day: 'Was much dejected and greatly perplexed in mind: Knew not how to see anybody again, my soul was so sunk within me.' But this time he battled the despondency with corrective perspectives: 'Oh, that these trials might make me more humble and holy! Oh, that God would keep me from giving way to sinful dejection, which may hinder my usefulness!'

About noon that same day he rode out and viewed 'the Indian lands at Cranberry.' Presumably those were properties the natives owned in that vicinity. Eventually he hoped to see a native settlement established on some of that property.

When he preached from Luke 16:17 the following Sunday, November 3, he noted: 'There was some apparent concern and affection in the assembly, though far less than has been usual of late.' After the preaching service he baptized fourteen more Indians – six adults and eight children. One of the adults was a woman nearly eighty years old while two others, both men about fifty years of age, had formerly been 'singular and remarkable, even among the Indians, for their wickedness.' Both those men had been notorious drunkards as well as excessively quarrelsome, and one of them was a past murderer. Brainerd had delayed the baptism of those two individuals for 'many weeks' after they first began to show evidence of having undergone a spiritual transformation. He wanted to make sure the fruit of their conversion would be abiding.

John 11 was the subject of his sermon the next day. He especially emphasized the Lord's 'power and ability to raise dead souls (such as many of them then felt themselves to be) to a spiritual life.' Various individuals who had just recently come to Crossweeksung from distant locations were brought under pressing concern about their spiritual condition that day. This was especially true of one woman who not long before had arrived at a meeting drunk, railed against the Christians and did all she could to disrupt their worship. Now she was so distressed that she could find no spiritual relief apart from the prospect of gaining 'an interest in Christ' (i.e., a share in His work of saving sinners).

That same day Brainerd baptized another child, bringing to forty-seven the total number of Indians to have received the ordinance. That number was made up of twenty-three adults and twenty-four children; thirty-five from the vicinity of Crossweeksung and twelve from the Forks of the Delaware. 'And through rich grace,' he was delighted to report, 'they have none of them as yet been left to disgrace their profession of Christianity by any scandalous or unbecoming behavior.'

He spent the remainder of that week traveling to various parts of New Jersey in order to solicit funds 'for the use of the Indians' and to recruit a schoolmaster to come and instruct the natives. Such funds were later used not only to support a native school, but also to help the Indians regain mortgaged properties and establish a community of their own.

The following Monday, November 11, he crossed over to Newtown (modern Queens Borough), Long Island, to attend a presbytery meeting. Unfortunately, his horse was stolen while there on Wednesday night. On Friday he was prevented by a violent wind from taking the ferry back to New Jersey and apparently needed to spend the night at the ferry house. Though the company there left something to be desired, he was able to pass the time comfortably and profitably enough:

And although some were drinking and talking profanely, which was indeed a grief to me, yet my mind was calm and composed. And I could not but bless God, that I was not like to spend an eternity in such company. In the evening I sat down and wrote with composure and freedom; and can say (through pure grace) it was a comfortable evening to my soul, an evening I was enabled to spend in the service of God.

He spent the next few days in Elizabethtown, finalizing preparations of an account of his ministry activities among the Indians of New Jersey and Pennsylvania during the past five months, since June 19, when he first arrived at Crossweeksung. That report was provided at the request of the Scottish Society. Early the following year – 1746 – the society commissioners published the account under the title: *Mirabilia Dei inter Indicos; Or the Rise and Progress of a remarkable Work of Grace, Among a number of the Indians, In the Provinces of New Jersey and Pennsylvania.* That publication eventually became part one of what is now commonly referred to as 'Brainerd's Journal.' (As will be seen in a later chapter, part two of the Journal was published late that same year and covered the period from November 24, 1745, to June 19, 1746.)

To the narrative of part one of the Journal, Brainerd appended a series of reflections on some of the remarkable aspects of the awakening at Crossweeksung. Of the many positive spiritual fruits that had issued from the awakening, he elaborated:

I doubt not that many of these people have gained more doctrinal knowledge of divine truths, since I first visited them in June last, than could have been instilled into their minds by the most diligent use of proper and instructive means for whole years together, without such a divine influence. Their pagan notions and idolatrous practices seem to be entirely abandoned in these parts. They are regulated and appear regularly disposed in the affairs of marriage. They seem generally divorced from drunkenness, their darling vice, the 'sin that easily besets them' (Heb. 12:1); so that I do not know of more than two or three who have been my steady hearers, that have drunk to excess since I first visited them, although before it was common for some or other of them to be drunk almost every day. Some of them seem now to fear this sin in particular more than death itself.

A principle of honesty and justice appears in many of them, and they seem concerned to discharge their old debts, which they have neglected, and perhaps, scarce thought of for years past. Their manner of living is much more decent and comfortable than formerly, having now the benefit of that money which they used to consume upon strong drink. Love seems to reign among them, especially those who have given evidences of having passed a saving change. ...

He also summarized the efforts he had put forth on behalf of the Indians at Crossweeksung and elsewhere. Since the beginning of March, he revealed, he had ridden over 3,000 miles in seeking to propagate Christian knowledge among them. He informed the Scottish Society of his lengthy journey to New England the previous spring in an effort to find a missionary colleague as well as his recent appeal to the ministers of New Jersey for funds to support a native school. In concluding his report, he spoke of the fatiguing labors involved in his ministry and reiterated his urgent desire to have a colleague join him in the work. Those appended remarks were dated November 20, 1745, his final day at Elizabethtown on that occasion.[2]

After returning to Crossweeksung, Brainerd immediately resumed his practice of preaching to the natives several times per week. On Saturday, November 30, he spent several hours visiting privately with some of the Indians about their personal spiritual concerns. When, late in the day, he preached from Luke 16:19-26 on the story of the rich man and Lazarus, the response of the natives followed the pattern he had observed earlier:

The Word made powerful impressions upon many in the assembly, especially while I discoursed of the blessedness of Lazarus 'in Abraham's bosom' (Luke 16:22). This, I could perceive, affected them much more than what I spoke of

---

2. The appendix to part one of the Journal is found in: Dwight, *Memoirs of David Brainerd*, pp. 245-53; *The Life and Diary of David Brainerd* (Baker edition), pp. 243-53.

the rich man's misery and torments. And thus it has been usually with them. They have almost always appeared much more affected with the comfortable than the dreadful truths of God's Word. And that which has distressed many of them under convictions, is that they found they wanted, and could not obtain, the happiness of the godly. At least they have often appeared to be more affected with this than with the terrors of hell. But whatever be the means of their awakening, 'tis plain, numbers are made deeply sensible of their sin and misery, the wickedness and stubbornness of their own hearts, their utter inability to help themselves, or to come to Christ for help, without divine assistance; and so are brought to see their perishing need of Christ to do all for them, and to lie at the foot of sovereign mercy.

He spent the first week of December attending a presbytery meeting at Connecticut Farms (modern Union), a suburb of Elizabethtown and part of Jonathan Dickinson's parish. On Sunday, December 8, he was back at Crossweeksung and preached on the story of the blind man in John 9. Of the noticeably lessened outward response to the message that day, he commented:

There appeared no remarkable effect of the Word upon the assembly at this time. The persons who have lately been much concerned for their souls seemed now not so affected nor solicitous to obtain an interest in Christ as has been usual; although they attended divine service with seriousness and diligence.

Such have been the 'doings of the Lord' (Ps. 77:11-12) here in awakening sinners and affecting the hearts of those who are brought to solid comfort, with a fresh sense of divine things from time to time, that 'tis now strange to see the assembly sit with dry eyes, and without sobs and groans!

By no means, however, had he and the Indians seen the last of the dramatic responses to the preaching of God's Word that would occur at Crossweeksung. While there would be periods of ebbing, the work of God's Spirit would continue to flow quite freely and strongly among the natives there.

20

THE CONTINUED STIRRING

The Indians had built a small hut for Brainerd to live in that was located among their growing number of residences at Crossweeksung. He spent most of Monday, December 9, procuring supplies with which to set up his private residence, but did not appreciate needing to be distracted with those temporal concerns: 'Enjoyed little satisfaction through the day, being very much out of my element.' He was able to move into the tiny dwelling late Tuesday afternoon.

When he spoke to the natives Thursday evening from the parable of the ten virgins in Matthew 25: 'There appeared in many persons an affectionate concern for their souls; although the concern in general seemed not so deep and pressing as it had formerly done. Yet it was refreshing to see many melted into tears and unaffected sobs; some with a sense of divine love, and some for want of it!'

Monday night, December 16, he shared the parable of the importunate neighbor in Luke 11. Pointing out Christ's command and encouragement to ask for divine favors, he urged the Indians to request a new heart 'with utmost importunity.' As a result, much spiritual concern was manifested in the assembly and one woman in particular became greatly distressed. Of her he related: 'She was brought to such an agony in seeking after Christ that the sweat ran off her face for a considerable time together, although the evening was very cold; and the bitter cries were the most affecting indication of the *inward* anguish of her heart.'

The following Saturday evening, he instituted a new form of instruction among the natives, involving the use of the

Westminster Shorter Catechism. After posing a question to the Indians from the catechism, he received their answers, then expanded on and clarified points as needed. He also sought to point out some practical application of the doctrinal issue under consideration.

The story of the rich and self-righteous young ruler in Matthew 19 was the focus of his sermon the next morning. A number of Indians who had just recently arrived at Crossweeksung were in the audience that day. They had formerly lived among Quakers and, according to Brainerd: 'had imbibed some of [their] errors; especially this fundamental one, viz., that if men will but live soberly and honestly, according to the dictates of their own consciences (or the light within) there is then no danger or doubt of their salvation.'

He had generally found those types of individuals, with their self-righteous foundation to stand upon, much harder to deal with concerning spiritual matters than were total pagans who made no pretenses of possessing any Christian knowledge. But on this occasion the Spirit and Word of God broke through to the newcomers: 'However, they all, except one, appeared now convinced that this sober honest life, of itself, was not sufficient to salvation; since Christ Himself had declared it so in the case of the young man; and seemed in some measure concerned to obtain that change of heart which I had been laboring to show them the necessity of.'

The following Wednesday was Christmas Day. Neither the New England Puritans nor the Quakers of that era observed Christmas as a holiday. Some other settlers did, often in a thoroughly worldly fashion. Just two years earlier, a Quaker named John Woolman recorded in his journal what he had witnessed at Mount Holly, fifteen miles south of Crossweeksung: 'About the time called Christmas, I observed that many people from the country, and dwellers in town, resorting to public houses [taverns], spent their time in drinking and vain sports, tending to corrupt one another; on which account I was much troubled.'[1]

---

1. Wynbeek, *Beloved Yankee*, p. 182.

To avoid any such ill influence on the natives under his care, Brainerd was careful to gather them for Christian instruction that Christmas Day: 'The Indians having been used upon Christmas days to drink and revel among some of the white people in these parts, I thought it proper this day to call them together and discourse to them upon divine things: which I accordingly did from the parable of the barren fig tree, Luke 13:6-9.'

Several individuals who in the past had scarcely ever been moved with any spiritual concern, that day suddenly seemed shocked and roused in their hearts. 'The power attending divine truths seemed to have the influence of the earthquake rather than the whirlwind upon them,' he commented, apparently signifying that the truths of Scripture jolted rather than overwhelmed them.

He also reminded the natives that day of the duty of husbands and wives from Ephesians 5:22-33. In his journal he noted that he had reason to think this marital instruction was a 'word in season' (Prov. 15:23; Isa. 50:4).

The following evening, December 26, an elderly woman was led by the hand into his cottage.[2] She appeared to be 'very childish through age' and incapable of being taught spiritual or doctrinal truths. As she appeared to be in 'extreme anguish,' he asked her what was troubling her.

'My heart is distressed, and I fear I shall never find Christ,' she responded.

'When did you begin to be concerned?' he probed.

'I have heard you preach many times. But I never knew anything about it. I never felt it in my heart till the last Sabbath. And then it came all at once as if a needle had been thrust into my heart. Since that time I've had no rest day or night.'

She went on to relate that on Christmas Eve a number of Indians were gathered in the house where she lived and were discoursing about Christ. Suddenly their conversation so pricked her heart that she could not even sit up, but fell down on her bed.

---

2. This incident and Brainerd's responses to it is recorded in: Dwight, *Memoirs of David Brainerd*, pp. 262-4; *Life and Diary of David Brainerd* (Baker edition), pp. 261-4.

At that time she appears to have had some sort of a vision. She was afterward certain she had not merely fallen asleep and had a dream.

In her vision she saw two paths, one very broad and crooked turning to the left and the other straight and very narrow leading up a hill to the right. After following the latter path for some time she came to a dark place where a bar seemed to obstruct her way. At that point she remembered what she had heard Brainerd say about striving to enter in at the strait gate. Just as she was thinking of climbing over the bar, she came back to consciousness of her surroundings in the house. Whereupon she became very distressed because she concluded she had turned back and forsaken Christ. She feared there was now no hope of mercy for her.

Brainerd's first response to her vision was one of wariness and skepticism. He thought it 'might be a design of Satan to bring a blemish upon the work of God here by introducing visionary scenes, imaginary terrors, and all manner of mental disorders and delusions, in the room [place] of genuine convictions of sin, and the enlightening influences of the blessed Spirit.'

He considered declaring the vision to be one of Satan's devices and to caution the Indians against it and similar experiences. But he determined first to question the woman further to see if she possessed a level of spiritual understanding that was adequate to account for her present distressing concern. As he queried her about man's fallen state and about the condition of her own heart, she surprised him by answering rationally. 'I thought it was next to impossible, if not altogether so,' he observed, 'that a pagan who was become a child through age should in that state gain so much knowledge by any mere human instruction, without being remarkably enlightened by a divine influence.'

He then reminded her of the provision made in the Gospel for the salvation of sinners. He also emphasized Christ's ability and willingness to save to the uttermost all, old as well as young, who come to Him for salvation. 'Ay, but I cannot come,' she instantly replied. 'My wicked heart will not come to Christ; I do not know how to come.' As she spoke those words, tears were in her eyes and she struck her breast in obvious anguish of spirit.

'She seems to be really convinced of her sin and misery and her need of a change of heart, and her concern is abiding and constant,' he commented further. 'So that nothing appears but that this exercise may have a saving issue. Indeed it seems hopeful, seeing she is so solicitous to obtain an interest in Christ that her heart (as she expresses it) prays day and night.'

Two days later – Saturday, December 28 – he catechized the Indians in the miseries of man in his fallen state and urged the unregenerate to strive to obtain a saving interest in Christ. Many natives were 'melted into tears and sobs' and two or three 'appeared to be brought to the last exercises of a preparatory work and reduced almost to extremity.'

Late the next morning he spoke on the new birth from John 3:1-5 to a mixed audience of natives and settlers. After announcing his intention to preach again in the early afternoon, he retired to his cottage for a brief rest. But in less than half an hour the Indians, with tears in their eyes, began to enter his house one by one to inquire what they should do to be saved. The small dwelling was soon filled with cries and groans.

> They all flocked together upon this occasion, and those whom I had reason to think in a Christless state were almost universally seized with concern for their souls. ... So astonishingly prevalent was the operation upon old as well as young, that it seemed as if none would be left in a secure and natural state, but that God was now about to convert all the world. And I was ready to think then that I should never again despair of the conversion of any man or woman living, be they who or what they would.
>
> ... A number might now be seen rejoicing that God had not taken away the powerful influence of His blessed Spirit from this place, refreshed to see so many 'striving to enter in at the strait gate' (Matt. 7:13), and animated with such concern for them that they wanted 'to push them forward,' as some of them expressed it. At the same time numbers both of men and women, old and young, might be seen in tears, and some in anguish of spirit, appearing in their very

> countenances like condemned malefactors bound towards
> the place of execution, with a heavy solicitude sitting in
> their faces: So that there seemed here (as I thought) a lively
> emblem of the solemn day of accounts, a mixture of heaven
> and hell, of joy unspeakable, and anguish inexpressible!

So strong was the pressing concern and fervent emotions of the
natives at that time that he concluded he could not possibly
interrupt it by having another formal worship service as he had
earlier proposed. Instead, he spent the entire afternoon and on
into the early evening visiting with one Indian after another and
sometimes addressing all of them together.

The next day he penned a letter to Eleazer Wheelock, pastor of
the North Parish at Lebanon, Connecticut. Along with the letter,
he sent a transcribed copy of the Journal account he had prepared
for the Scottish Society six weeks earlier. The correspondence
reveals he had learned that Wheelock was attempting to raise
funds for a missionary colleague to join Brainerd in his work.
He hoped that as Wheelock and others in that region read the
Journal they would be encouraged in their efforts on behalf of the
Indian mission.

Brainerd spent several hours on Tuesday visiting the natives
from house to house and conversing with them about their
spiritual concerns. 'The Indians are now gathered together from
all quarters to this place,' he reported, 'and have built them little
cottages, so that more than twenty families live within a quarter
of a mile of me. A very convenient situation in regard both of
public and private instruction.'

The following day, January 1, 1746, he gratefully acknowledged
the Lord's support in the past and consecrated himself to serve
even more to God's glory in the future:

> I am this day beginning a new year; and God has carried
> me through numerous trials and labors in the past. He has
> amazingly supported my feeble frame; for 'having obtained
> help of God, I continue to this day' (Acts 26:22). Oh, that
> I might live nearer to God this year than I did the last. The

business I have been called to, and enabled to go through, I know has been as great as nature could bear up under, and what would have sunk and overcome me quite without special support. But alas, alas! Though I have done the labors and endured the trials, with what spirit have I done the one and borne the other? How cold has been the frame of my heart oftentimes! And how little have I sensibly eyed the glory of God in all my doings and sufferings! I have found that I could have no peace without filling up all my time with labors; and thus 'necessity has been laid upon me' (1 Cor. 9:16); yea, in that respect I have loved to labor: But the misery is, I could not sensibly labor for God as I would have done. May I for the future be enabled more sensibly to make the glory of God my all!

21

CONVICTION, CONVERSIONS AND OPPOSITION

As 1746 dawned, Brainerd met with fresh opportunities to evangelize individuals who had virtually no prior knowledge of Christianity:

> January 2. Visited some persons newly come among us, who had scarce ever heard anything of Christianity (except the empty name) before. Endeavored to instruct them particularly in the first principles of religion, in the most easy and familiar manner I could. There are strangers from remote parts almost continually dropping in among us, so that I have occasion repeatedly to open and inculcate the first principles of Christianity.

When he preached the following Sunday morning, January 5, on the miracle of Jesus healing the man with the withered hand, there was no outward response from his hearers. But when they met again late that same afternoon, there was such a stirring among the natives he thought it best to change his original teaching plan:

> Near night I proposed to have proceeded in my usual method of catechizing. But while we were engaged in the first prayer, the power of God seemed to descend upon the assembly in such a remarkable manner, and so many appeared under pressing concern for their souls, that I thought it much more expedient to insist upon the plentiful provision made by divine grace for the redemption of perishing sinners, and

to press them to a speedy acceptance of the great salvation, than to ask them questions about doctrinal points. What was most practical seemed most seasonable to be insisted upon, while numbers appeared so extraordinarily solicitous to obtain an interest in the great Redeemer.

He also baptized two Indians – a woman and a child – that day. Two Sundays earlier that same woman, having submitted entirely to the concept of God being absolutely sovereign over whether or not she would come to salvation, had declared she would be glad for God to send her to hell if that was His will for her! Rather than experiencing divine judgment, however, she had received deep and abiding comfort that her soul had been saved through faith in Christ Jesus.

That same woman had asked the missionary, 'Were you not sent to preach to the Indians by some good people who live a great way off?'

'Yes, by the good people of Scotland,' he replied.

'My heart loved those good people so last evening,' she revealed, 'that I couldn't help praying for them nearly all night. My heart will go to God for them.'

Despite experiencing marked physical weakness in the days to follow, Brainerd's spirits remained strong. Wednesday evening, during a refreshing time of private prayer: 'I had great hopes of the ingathering of precious souls to Christ; not only among my own people, but others also. I was sweetly resigned and composed under my bodily weakness; and was willing to live or die, and desirous to labor for God to the utmost of my strength.' Similarly, on Thursday: 'Was still very weak and much exercised with vapory disorders. In the evening, enjoyed some enlargement and spirituality in prayer. Oh, that I could always spend my time profitably, both in health and weakness!'

A number of Indians were under obvious conviction as he preached from Isaiah 55:6 on Sunday morning and as he catechized that evening. 'The Spirit of God seems from time to time to be striving with numbers of souls here,' he observed. 'They are so frequently and repeatedly roused that they seem unable at present to lull themselves asleep.'

The following day, January 13, he was visited by various individuals who were deeply concerned about the welfare of their souls. In his Journal he spoke candidly of the physical and emotional strain that such constant evangelistic work was for him:

> 'Tis a most agreeable work to treat with souls who are solicitously inquiring 'what they shall do to be saved' (Acts 2:37; 16:30). And as we are never to be 'weary in well doing' (Gal. 6:9; 2 Thess. 3:13), so the obligation seems to be peculiarly strong when the work is so very desirable. And yet I must say, my health is so much impaired, and my spirits so wasted with my labors and solitary manner of living (there being no human creature in the house with me), that their repeated and almost incessant applications to me for help and direction are sometimes exceeding burdensome, and so exhaust my spirits that I become fit for nothing at all, entirely unable to prosecute any business sometimes for days together. ...

As he visited with the Indians again the next day a new concern surfaced. It seemed to him that some of the natives were becoming overly eager to conclude they had been savingly converted:

> Spent some time in private conferences with my people, and found some disposed to take comfort, as I thought, upon slight grounds. They are now generally awakened, and 'tis become so disgraceful, as well as terrifying to the conscience, to be destitute of religion, that they are in imminent danger of taking up with any appearances of grace, rather than to live under the fear and disgrace of an unregenerate state.

After catechizing the Indians on Saturday evening, January 18, he remarked, 'This method of instructing I find very profitable.' He further revealed that at first he feared that type of teaching might tend 'only to enlighten the head, but not to affect the heart.' But it had become apparent that those exercises were being 'remarkably blessed' in both those respects.

Brainerd spent the following week in Elizabethtown conferring with the Scottish Society commissioners about various aspects of the ministry to the Indians. One urgent matter discussed was the imminent danger the Crossweeksung natives were in of losing much of their land. In times past they had accrued debt through excessive drinking. Some settlers were seeking to take advantage of the Indians by having various ones of them arrested and by confiscating their land. Brainerd knew if the natives lost their hunting lands they would not be able to remain together as a congregation.

The commissioners approved the use of a portion of the funds they had been collecting from a number of churches to eliminate the debt. Upon returning to Crossweeksung, Brainerd was able to pay off debts on behalf of the Indians amounting to over eighty pounds, thus enabling them to retain their lands.

Another red-letter day in the Crossweeksung ministry occurred later that same week. Friday, January 31, brought the arrival of the individual whom Brainerd had chosen and hired to be a schoolmaster for the Indians. Though Brainerd never revealed the schoolmaster's name, he may have been Ebenezer Hayward. Four and a half years later, in the July 30, 1750, issue of *The New York Gazette Revived*, John Brainerd, David's successor in the Crossweeksung Indian work, listed Hayward's estate. Acting as executor of the estate, John described Hayward as 'Indian Schoolmaster at Bethel, in New Jersey, deceased.'[1] (Bethel was the name John gave the Crossweeksung Indian settlement shortly after beginning his ministry there in 1747.)

The schoolmaster received a hearty welcome from all the Indians. Brainerd promptly distributed a few dozen primers to the children and young people. The very next day – Saturday, February 1 – the teacher held his first school session. Normally about thirty young children and teens attended the school during the daytime and around fifteen married people participated in night classes.

A marked discouragement followed close behind the series of blessings Brainerd had experienced in his Crossweeksung ministry that week:

1. Pettit, *The Life of David Brainerd*, p. 359.

Lord's Day, February 2. Preached from John 5:24-25. There appeared (as usual) some concern and affection in the assembly ... After public worship, my bodily strength being much spent, my spirits sank amazingly; and especially on hearing that I was so generally taken to be a Roman Catholic, sent by the Papists to draw the Indians into an insurrection against the English, that some were in fear of me, and others were for having me taken up by authority and punished. Alas, what will not the devil do to bring a slur and disgrace on the work of God! Oh, how holy and circumspect had I need to be! Through divine goodness I have been enabled to mind my own business in these parts, as well as elsewhere; and to let all men and all denominations of men alone, as to their party notions; and only preached the plain and necessary truths of Christianity, neither inviting to nor excluding from my meeting any of any sort of persuasion whatsoever. Towards night, the Lord gave me freedom at the throne of grace in my first prayer before my catechetical lecture: And in opening the 46th Psalm to my people, my soul confided in God, although the wicked world should slander and persecute me, or even condemn and execute me as a traitor to my king and country. Truly God is 'a present help in time of trouble' (Ps. 46:1).

'My spirits were still much sunk,' he wrote on Monday, 'with what I heard the day before of my being suspected to be engaged in the Pretender's interest.' The historical backdrop of the fallacious accusations against him was this: In the Bloodless or Glorious Revolution of 1688, William III (a Protestant) replaced the deposed James II (a Catholic) as Britain's monarch. James II's son was James Edward Stuart, dubbed by his political opponents as the Old Pretender, and his grandson was Charles Edward, the Young Pretender. In September of 1745 Charles gathered a Highland army to aid his exiled father in regaining the throne.[2]

News that a rebellion against the Crown had broken out in Scotland had reached the American colonies less than a month

2.   Wynbeek, *Beloved Yankee*, pp. 189-90.

earlier, on January 8. Some used the occasion to cast aspersions on Brainerd's ministry by claiming that he was a Catholic and a supporter of James Edward Stuart. His comment on the situation makes it clear his opponents were knowingly being deceitful in spreading the report: 'What they pretended gave them reason for this opinion,' he explained, 'was that they understood I had a commission from Scotland. Whereupon they could with great assurance say, "All Scotland is turned to the *Pretender*, and this is but a popish plot to make a party for him here." '

The further faulty accusation – that Brainerd intended to draw the Indians into an insurrection against the English – had another set of recent events at its root. Many New Jersey land titles were in a state of confusion. Numerous early homesteaders purchased land directly from the Indians without securing proper titles. Later, when wealthy persons secured legal title to large tracts of land, ignoring prior claims, feelings ran high as one settler after another lost his land.

An ugly riot resulted from one such case involving a home-steader named Samuel Baldwin. He had been jailed in Newark for refusing to pay bail, pending his trial for cutting trees on land he claimed was his own. On September 19, 1745, 150 men armed with clubs, axes and crowbars broke into the Newark jail to free him. A number of the rioters boasted that they would return with twice their number as well as 100 Indians.

The only sizable group of Indians in New Jersey was the growing community of natives gathered around Brainerd at Crossweeksung. But any fair-minded, clear-thinking individual should have readily realized that they posed no threat. Indeed, when twice the number of September rioters had returned to assail Newark again in January, less than a month before, not a single Indian accompanied them from anywhere.[3]

Brainerd further related his various distresses concerning the entire affair:

> It grieved me that after there had been so much evidence of
> a glorious work of grace among these poor Indians, as that
> the most carnal men could not but take notice of the great

3. Ibid., pp. 188-9.

change made among them, so many poor souls should still suspect the whole to be only a Popish Plot, and so cast an awful reproach on this blessed work of the divine Spirit; and at the same time wholly exclude themselves from receiving any benefit by this divine influence. This put me upon searching whether I had ever dropped anything inadvertently that might give occasion to any to suspect that I was stirring up the Indians against the English: and could think of nothing, unless it was my attempting sometimes to vindicate the rights of the Indians, and complaining of the horrid practice of making the Indians drunk, and then cheating them out of their lands and other properties: And once, I remembered, I had done this with too much warmth of spirit. And this much distressed me; thinking that this might possibly prejudice them against this work of grace, to their everlasting destruction. ...

By repeatedly bringing those concerns to the Lord in prayer that first Sunday in February and in the week that followed, he was able to gain a large measure of relief from his anxiety over them.

A significant conversion process was taking place in yet another native's life just at that same time. When Brainerd conducted a catechism session that first Saturday evening in February, the old powwow who the previous August had followed him from the Forks of the Delaware to Crossweeksung fell under extreme spiritual distress.[4] He trembled for hours that night, perceiving that he was just about to drop into hell and had no power to rescue himself or to relieve his anxiety.

But when Brainerd saw him the next night, he appeared remarkably composed. When the missionary asked how he was doing, a fascinating conversation unfolded.

'Tis done, 'tis done, 'tis all done now,' responded the Indian.

'What do you mean?'

'I can never do any more to save myself. 'Tis all done forever. I can do no more.'

---

4. The first part of this man's story was related in chapter 17. The remainder of his testimony as recorded here is found in Pettit, *Life of David Brainerd*, pp. 393-5.

'Can you not do a little more rather than to go to hell?'

'My heart is dead. I can never help myself.'

'What do you think will become of you then?'

'I must go to hell.'

'Do you think 'tis right that God should send you to hell?'

'Oh, 'tis right. The devil has been in me ever since I was born.'

'Did you feel this when you were in such great distress last evening?'

'No, I did not then think it was right. I thought God would send me to hell, and that I was then dropping into it. But my heart quarreled with God and would not say 'twas right He should send me there. But now I know 'tis right, for I've always served the devil, and my heart has no goodness in it now, but is as bad as ever it was.'

For several days the man remained in that same frame of mind. 'And yet,' added Brainerd, "twas plain he had a secret hope of mercy, though imperceptible to himself, which kept him not only from despair but from any pressing distress. So that instead of being sad and dejected, his very countenance appeared pleasant and agreeable.'

At various times the native asked him when he would preach again, and seemed desirous to hear the Word of God daily. Up to that point Brainerd had 'labored in the best manner I could' to represent to him Christ's ability and willingness to save lost sinners in his exact condition. But since that approach had brought no special comfort to the Indian, he now decided to take a different tack by using the man's own words in an effort to lead him to the place of spiritual conversion and assurance:

'Why do you want to hear me preach, seeing your heart is dead and all is done, since you can never help yourself and you expect that you must go to hell?'

'I love to hear you speak about Christ for all.'

'But what good will that do you if you must go to hell at last?'

'I would have others come to Christ, if I must go to hell myself.'

"Twas remarkable in this season,' Brainerd commented, 'that he seemed to have a great love to the people of God, and nothing affected him so much as the thoughts of being separated from them. This seemed to be a very dreadful part of the hell he thought himself doomed to.'

During those days the native was extremely diligent and attentive not only in hearing the Word of God but also in praying privately and attending daily family prayer. Finally, at the end of the week, while Brainerd was discoursing publicly: 'he seemed to have a lively, soul-refreshing view of the excellency of Christ, and the way of salvation by Him, which melted him into tears and filled him with admiration, comfort, satisfaction and praise to God; since which he has appeared to be a humble, devout, and affectionate Christian.'

Throughout much of that same week Brainerd had been so weak physically that he needed 'to consume considerable time in diversions' rather than devoting all his time to ministry and spiritual exercises. But by that Saturday, February 8, he was able to spend a significant part of the day visiting the Indians from house to house and conversing with them about their spiritual concerns.

God's Spirit continued to bless his diligent efforts the next day. As he preached from Mark 10 that morning on the story of the blind man: 'Divers in particular, who have generally been remarkably stupid and careless under the means of grace, were now awakened and wept affectionately.' That same day he baptized two adults and a child.

When he catechized the natives that evening another man who had been a 'vile drunkard' was 'remarkably awakened' to his spiritual need. As had been the case with the conjurer eight days earlier, this individual appeared to be in great anguish of soul and wept and trembled till nearly midnight.

22

MINISTERING TO EXHAUSTION

Though still quite weak, Brainerd set out again for the Forks of the Delaware on Monday, February 10. On this occasion he took with him six of the most serious and spiritually knowledgeable Christians from Crossweeksung. Among that number was the newly converted conjurer whose influence had formerly discouraged many natives at the Forks from embracing Christianity. Brainerd recollected that some of the Forks Indians were obstinately opposed to Christianity, so much so that some of them had refused to listen to him preach in times past. He hoped that as the Crossweeksung natives conversed with them about spiritual matters it might help to convince them of the truth and importance of Christianity.

The response of the Forks Indians was mixed when he and the Crossweeksung Christians met with them for the first time on Sunday, February 16. He thought it likely that various of the Forks Indians could not have been prevailed upon to attend the meeting in the first place if it had not been for his Crossweeksung companions. As he preached: 'Some of them who had, in times past, been extremely averse to Christianity, now behaved soberly, and some others laughed and mocked. However, the Word of God fell with such weight and power that sundry seemed to be stunned, and expressing a willingness to hear me again of these matters.'

Following the public service, he spent some time trying to convince those who had mocked what he taught. For his efforts he received at least some encouragement: 'And had reason to think, from what I observed then and afterwards, that my endeavors took considerable effect upon one of the worst of them.' He also was heartened by the friendly, though somewhat guarded, reception he received from his former acquaintances at the Forks: 'Those few Indians then present, who used to be my hearers in these parts ... seemed somewhat kindly disposed toward, and glad to see me again, although they had been so much attacked by some of the opposing pagans that they were almost ashamed or afraid to manifest their friendship.'

Another old powwow who still resided at the Forks threatened to bewitch him and the Crossweeksung Christians. The recently converted former conjurer zealously withstood him. After challenging the man to do his worst to them, the new Christian stated: 'I myself used to be just as great a conjurer as you are. Yet despite that, as soon as I felt in my heart that Word which these [Christian] people loved, my power of conjuring immediately left me. So it would you, if you did but once feel it in your heart. And you have no power to hurt them, nor so much as to touch one of them.'

After spending considerable time the next day visiting the Indians at their respective homes, Brainerd gathered them together for a public service. As he shared from Acts 8 of Philip evangelizing the city of Samaria, the Indians listened attentively, some with tears and sobs.

The Christians from Crossweeksung continued to visit with their fellow natives throughout the day and evening. They repeated the truths he had shared in his messages and sometimes prayed and sang psalms. They also talked with each other in the hearing of their hosts about the great things God had done for them and others at Crossweeksung.

On Tuesday Brainerd made the thirty-mile round trip to preach to the Irish people at Craig's Settlement. The following day he again ministered to the Forks natives, both individually and collectively. As a result: 'Divers of the Indians here seemed to have their prejudices and aversion to Christianity removed, and appeared well disposed and inclined to hear the Word of God.'

A small group of 'High Dutch people' traveled eight and ten miles from their homes to hear him speak on Thursday. These were immigrants, originally from the upper provinces of Germany, who in recent years had settled in the Forks region. They had seldom heard the Gospel preached, but various ones of them had lately been on a thoughtful search for salvation. After listening attentively to his message, they declared that never in their entire lives had they received such enlightening instruction concerning the way of salvation.

The next day he preached not only to some of those same High Dutch, but also to a number of 'Low Dutch,' recent German immigrants from the Palatinate and the Lower Rhine. Various Indians also attended the service, including two who the previous Sunday had ridiculed Christianity. Now they 'behaved soberly.'

On Sunday, February 23, he preached once more to the Forks Indians, sharing from John 6 Christ's teachings about Himself as the bread of life. After the service he visited various individual natives and invited them to come and stay for a time at Crossweeksung. There they could hear divine truth taught regularly and would not be subject to the scoffing and temptations of opposing unbelievers. Some of them promised to do so soon.

When he left the next day, the Crossweeksung Christians stayed behind with one of their number who had fallen gravely ill. While making his way back to Crossweeksung by the following Saturday, Brainerd preached along the way each day but one.

That Sunday, March 2, some of the native evangelists who had lingered at the Forks returned to Crossweeksung, though without their still-ailing comrade. They were accompanied by two of the Indians from the Forks who had promised to visit Crossweeksung. 'May the Lord meet with them here,' Brainerd recorded his heartfelt desire. 'They can scarce go into a house now but they will meet with Christian conversation, whereby, 'tis hopeful, they may be both instructed and awakened.'

He was obviously glad to be back with his Christian congregation. That night he spoke with pleasure of that group of believers and again reflected on the amazing spiritual transformation that had taken place among them just in the past several months:

I know of no assembly of Christians where there seems to be so much of the presence of God, where brotherly love so much prevails, and where I should take so much delight in the public worship of God, in general, as in my own congregation; although not more than nine months ago they were worshipping devils and dumb idols under the power of pagan darkness and superstition! Amazing change this! Effected by nothing less than divine power and grace! ...

After meeting with the natives for prayer, singing and instruction from the Word on Wednesday evening, he revealed: 'Their present situation is so compact and commodious that they are easily and quickly called together with only the sound of a conch shell, so that they have frequent opportunities of attending religious exercises publicly; which seems to be a great means, under God, of keeping alive the impressions of divine things in their minds.'

The following Sunday, March 9, he preached in the morning on the story from Luke 10 of Mary and Martha hosting Christ and His disciples in their home. Many in the audience seemed concerned to obtain the 'one thing needful' of verse 42. The Christian natives applied that principle to their need of 'growing in grace' (2 Pet. 3:18).

He had intended to catechize the Indians that afternoon, but as had happened before, he found it necessary to adjust those plans in response to the moving of God's Spirit. As he offered the opening prayer 'in the Indian language (as usual),' there was such a divine stirring among the natives that he thought it best to return to his text and theme of the morning. A number of the believers were deeply affected with a sense of their own spiritual barrenness and some 'poor awakened sinners' appeared to be in anguish over their need for a Savior. There were 'many heavy groans, sobs and tears' in the assembly.

After the public service, numbers of natives followed him to his cottage where they sang and talked about spiritual matters. The presence of God was strongly sensed among them there also. As they sang, one woman in particular seemed to Brainerd to be filled 'with joy unspeakable and full of glory' (1 Pet. 1:8), as much or more than any other person he had ever seen.

Exactly one month earlier, on February 9, this woman had gained relief from her overwhelming spiritual distress by submitting herself completely to God's sovereign will in choosing either to save or condemn her. While realizing there was nothing she could do to save herself, she also knew that Christ might yet choose to save her, and in that she seemed to rest. Before that time Brainerd had scarcely ever seen anyone appear 'more bowed and broken under convictions of sin and misery' than she. Since then she had appeared to him and others to have undergone a saving transformation, although she herself seemed unaware of it until this very night, one month later:

> Since which time [February 9] she has seemed constantly to breathe the spirit and temper of the new creature: crying after Christ, not through fear of hell as before, but with strong desires after Him as her only satisfying portion. And has many times wept and sobbed bitterly, because (as she apprehended) she did not and could not love Him. When I have sometimes asked her why she appeared so sorrowful, and whether it was because she was afraid of hell, she would answer, 'No, I ben't distressed about that; but my heart is so wicked I can't love Christ'; and thereupon burst out into tears. But although this has been the habitual frame of her mind for several weeks together, so that the exercise of [saving] grace appeared evident to others, yet she seemed wholly insensible of it herself, and never had any remarkable comfort and sensible satisfaction till this evening.

Now, as he and the Indians sang songs at his house, she could not help but burst out in prayer and praises to God before them all. Weeping profusely, she cried out sometimes in English and sometimes in her native tongue: 'Oh, blessed Lord, do come, do come! Oh, do take me away, do let me die and go to Jesus Christ! I am afraid if I live I shall sin again! Oh, do let me die now! Oh, dear Jesus, do come! I can't stay, I can't stay! Oh, how can I live in this world? Do take my soul away from this sinful place! Oh, let me never sin any more! Oh, what shall I do, what shall I do? Dear Jesus, oh, dear Jesus.' In something of an ecstatic state, she continued incessantly to express those and similar sentiments for quite some time.

When she had regained her composure somewhat, Brainerd asked her, 'Is not Christ now sweet to your soul?'

Turning to him with tears in her eyes, she uttered with deepest sincerity and humility: 'I've many times heard you speak of the goodness and the sweetness of Christ, that He was better than all the world. But oh! I knew nothing what you meant. I never believed you! I never believed you! But now I know it is true!'

'And do you see enough in Christ for the greatest of sinners?' he queried further.

'Oh! Enough, enough! For all the sinners in the world if they would but come.'

'And could you not tell them of the goodness of Christ?'

In answer to that question, she turned to some unconverted individuals who were observing the conversation and obviously being affected by it. Fervently she appealed to them: 'Oh! There's enough in Christ for you, if you would but come! Oh, strive, strive to give up your hearts to Him.'

When Brainerd then mentioned the glory of heaven and that there is no sin in that world, the woman 'again fell into the same ecstasy of joy and desire of Christ's coming.' She began repeating her former expressions: 'Oh, dear Lord, do let me go! Oh, what shall I do, what shall I do? I want to go to Christ! I can't live! Oh, do let me die.' Quite overwhelmed by this 'sweet frame,' she continued in it for more than two hours before being able to make her way back to her own home.

On their own the Indians gathered again late the next afternoon to sing, pray and discuss spiritual matters. Seeing their earnestness in these exercises, Brainerd joined them, praying with them and giving 'a word of exhortation.'

Very much by contrast, he was dissatisfied with the social interaction he experienced three days later. Where and with whom it took place was not divulged. Of the occurrence he wrote obliquely: 'On Thursday, spent considerable time in company, on a special occasion; but in perplexity, because without savory religious conversation.'

The warning from Hebrews 2:1-3 not to neglect 'so great salvation' was the subject of his sermons the following Sunday morning and afternoon. That same day he baptized the woman whose joyous conversion had become so apparent the previous Sunday. At night his cottage was again crowded with spiritually thirsty Indians, and he ministered to them to the extent of his limited physical and emotional capacities: 'My house being thronged with my people in the evening, I spent the time in religious exercises with them, till my nature was almost spent. They are so unwearied in religious exercises, and insatiable in their thirsting after Christian knowledge, that I can sometimes scarce avoid laboring so, as greatly to exhaust my strength and spirits.'

The exertion, in fact, proved too much for him. In the early part of the week that followed he became very ill and dejected. As is not uncommon with people in a weakened and discouraged condition, his situation appeared worse to him than it actually was. He feared his illness would render him permanently unserviceable in the work of the Lord and, therefore, desired to die.

Rather than give in to such a bleak outlook, however, he left Crossweeksung in search of assistance from a physician. Happily, he succeeded, though unfortunately the identity of the doctor was not preserved. In condensing this portion of Brainerd's diary, Jonathan Edwards summarized simply: 'In the latter part of the week he was in some measure relieved of his illness, in the use of means prescribed by a physician.'

While he was away that week, the remainder of the native evangelists who had remained at the Forks of the Delaware with their gravely ill companion returned to Crossweeksung. When they arrived on Wednesday, March 19, most of the Indians, of their own accord, gathered together to thank God for raising back to health the one who had been sick and for bringing safely home all those who had been absent for several weeks. Without their beloved missionary to guide them, the Indians asked the schoolmaster to assist in the special thanksgiving observance, which consisted of much fervent prayer and singing.

23

Preparing a New Settlement

Brainerd was back at Crossweeksung by that Saturday, March 22, 1746. In the previous week about fifteen adult Indians had arrived who were strangers to the natives already residing there. Since some of the newcomers had not had any previous exposure to Christian teaching, Brainerd attempted to tailor his sermons Sunday morning and afternoon to their spiritual condition and limited understanding. That morning he spoke on God's existence and perfections as well as man's creation in a sinless state followed by his fall into sin. In the afternoon he delineated God's glorious provision to redeem apostate creatures by providing His own Son to suffer for them, thus satisfying divine justice on their behalf.

While the Indians, including the newcomers, were attentive, there was no special stirring among them that day. As a result: 'Near sunset I felt an uncommon concern upon my mind, especially for the poor strangers, that God had so much withheld His presence and the powerful influence of His Spirit from the assembly in the exercises of the day; and thereby denied them of that matter of conviction which I hoped they might have had.'

In that frame of mind he visited several houses and, in a spirit of earnest concern, dialogued privately with various individuals. His efforts seemed to have little success until he came to a house where some of the new arrivals were staying. There the solemn truths he shared 'appeared to take effect, first upon some children, then upon divers adult persons that had been somewhat awakened before, and afterwards upon several of the pagan strangers.' He continued his discourse with some fervor till nearly everyone in the house was weeping, many of them aloud, and 'appeared earnestly concerned to obtain an interest in Christ.'

Natives from the neighboring houses quickly began to gather to witness what was happening. As a result, that home became so overcrowded they needed to dismiss to a larger house where they normally met for public worship. The full congregation gathered immediately, and Brainerd preached on an obvious Gospel text, Luke 19:10: 'For the Son of man is come to seek and to save that which was lost.'

Five or six of the newcomers, both men and women, seemed to be considerably awakened to their spiritual need. One 'very rugged' young man, who at first seemed as if nothing would move him, began to 'tremble like the jailer' (Acts 16:29) and wept for a long time. Brainerd further disclosed:

> The pagans that were awakened seemed at once to put off their savage roughness and pagan manners and became sociable, orderly, and humane in their carriage. When they first came, I exhorted my religious people to take pains with them (as they had done with other strangers from time to time) to instruct them in Christianity. But when some of them attempted something of that nature, the strangers would soon rise up and walk to other houses, in order to avoid the hearing of such discourses. Whereupon some of the serious persons agreed to disperse themselves into the several parts of the settlement. So that wherever the strangers went, they met with some instructive discourse and warm addresses respecting their souls' concern. But now there was no need of using policy in order to get an opportunity of conversing with some of them about their spiritual concerns; for they were so far touched with a sense of their perishing state, as made them tamely yield to the closest addresses that were made them respecting their sin and misery, their need of an acquaintance with, and interest in the great Redeemer.

The next day – Monday, March 24 – he conducted a census and discovered that there were then about 130 Indians gathered at

Crossweeksung. Another fifteen or twenty natives who were his 'stated hearers' were away from the settlement at that time.

That same day a number of the Indians were intending to set out for some of their lands in the vicinity of Cranberry, fifteen miles northeast of Crossweeksung. They desired to clear their lands for the purpose of establishing a permanent settlement there. They would build homes there as well as a school for their children and a church building for corporate worship. They also planned to plant and cultivate fields there, the soil at Cranberry being much more suitable for that purpose than was the ground at Crossweeksung.

Before they left, Brainerd called them together and sought to impress upon them the importance of being 'laborious, diligent and vigorous in the prosecution of their business.' He reminded them that planting season would soon be upon them and gave them specific, practical instructions on how to carry out their work. His own farming background doubtless qualified him to give those instructions, and he revealed in his journal that the Indians 'very much wanted' them. He also sought to provide the natives with a scriptural perspective on their undertaking by explaining and singing to them Isaac Watts' adaptation of Psalm 127:1-2:

> If God to build the house deny
> The builders work in vain;
> And towns, without His wakeful eye,
> An useless watch maintain.
>
> Before the morning beams arise,
> Your painful work renew,
> And 'till the stars ascend the skies
> Your tiresome toil pursue;
>
> Short be your sleep, and coarse your fare,
> In vain, till God has blessed;
> But if His smiles attend your care,
> You shall have food and rest.[1]

1. Wynbeek, *Beloved Yankee*, pp. 200-1.

He then closed the meeting with prayer, commending them and their undertaking to God. After the members of the work party departed for Cranberry: 'I got alone and poured out my soul to God, that He would smile upon these feeble beginnings, and that He would settle an Indian town that might be a "mountain of holiness" (Jer. 31:23).'

That evening he met with those who had stayed behind at Crossweeksung, including the newcomers who had just arrived the week before. As he preached from Acts 3 there was a visible response in the audience, especially when he expounded on verse 19: 'Repent ye therefore, and be converted, that your sins may be blotted out, when the times of refreshing shall come from the presence of the Lord.' Afterwards he put a straightforward question to the recent arrivals: 'Do you not now feel that your hearts are wicked, as I have taught you?'

One woman replied: 'Yes, I feel it now.' Her admission was seen to be even more significant when she divulged that even before coming to Crossweeksung she had heard that the white missionary taught the Indians that their hearts were entirely bad by nature and needed to be changed and made good by the power of God. Upon initially hearing that, she had insisted that her heart was not wicked and that she had never done anything bad in her life.

Brainerd noted that such seemed to be the outlook among the Indians universally before they came under the teaching of Scripture. 'They seem to have no consciousness of sin and guilt,' he revealed, 'unless they can charge themselves with some gross acts of sin contrary to the commands of the second table [of the ten commandments].'

The next day the schoolmaster became seriously ill with pleurisy, and Brainerd spent the remainder of the week closely attending him. At night he slept on the floor, presumably so the ailing teacher would have a bed. His own limited strength quickly declined under those heavy demands, and his spirits fell to a considerable degree.

He was able that Thursday to visit a number of Indians in one of their homes. Various individuals seemed to be much affected as he inquired about their spiritual state and urged on them the infinite importance of being born again. 'I find particular and close dealing with souls in private is often very successful,' he observed.

The following week found him still heavily occupied with caring for the schoolmaster. As a result, his strength and spirits continued to flag.

Following the usual Saturday catechism session on April 5, a number of Christian natives followed him to his home, eager to receive further spiritual instruction. As he spoke to them of their need to show a distinctive love for one other, he found his own heart overflowing with earnest love for them. In turn, the Indians' love for each other also became readily apparent:

> After public worship, a number of my dear Christian Indians came to my house; with whom I felt a sweet union of soul: My heart was knit to them; and I can't say I have felt such a sweet and fervent 'love to the brethren' (Eph. 6:23; 1 Pet. 1:22) for some time past: And I saw in them appearances of the same love. This gave me something of a view of the heavenly state; and particularly that part of the happiness of heaven which consists in the communion of saints: and this was affecting to me.

The natives were sobered by his sermon on Matthew 7:21-23 the next morning. Some of them, troubled by the fact that they had done so little of the Heavenly Father's will, expressed concern lest they had deceived themselves in taking up a false hope that they had truly been saved. One man was brought under 'very great and pressing concern' for his spiritual welfare. He divulged that his uneasiness and distress were not caused by any particular sin. Rather, they sprang from the fact that he had never done the will of God at all, but had sinned continually, so had no claim to the kingdom of heaven.

That afternoon Brainerd shared Christ's directives in Matthew 18 concerning church discipline. The Christians were deeply affected, especially when they heard that an offender who continued obstinately in sin was, in the end, to be treated as a pagan who has no part among God's people. He commented on their reaction: 'This they seemed to have the most awful apprehensions of: a state of heathenism, out of which they were so lately brought, appearing very dreadful to them.'

He again perceived that God blessed his house-to-house visitation efforts later that same day: 'After public worship I visited sundry houses to see how they spent the remainder of the Sabbath, and to treat with them solemnly on the great concerns of their souls: And the Lord seemed to smile upon my private endeavors, and to make these particular and personal addresses more effectual upon some than my public discourses.'

With a view to beginning to prepare some of the Christian natives to receive communion at some time in the future, that Monday evening he instructed the Indians from 1 Corinthians 11:23-26. He discoursed on 'the institution, nature, and ends of the Lord's Supper' as well as the qualifications and necessary preparations in order to rightly participate in the ordinance. Various individuals seemed deeply touched by the great love that Christ manifested in instituting this provision for the comfort of His people, especially since He did so the night before His crucifixion, just at the time when He was entering upon His sharpest sufferings.

The next day, April 8, Brainerd rode to Elizabethtown for a presbytery meeting. Throughout much of that week he labored under 'an awful gloom.' His dejection began to ease on Saturday evening, and the following day he preached to a Dutch and English audience at Staten Island. Back in Elizabethtown on Monday, April 14, his spirits were 'raised and refreshed.' That Thursday night he preached a love-filled Gospel message to Jonathan Dickinson's congregation: 'My heart was melted for the dear assembly, and I loved everybody in it; and scarce ever felt more love to immortal souls in my life; my soul cried, "Oh, that the dear creatures might be saved! Oh, that God would have mercy on them!" '

The following Sunday, April 20, was his twenty-eighth birthday. Both his morning and afternoon expositions at Crossweeksung that day were devoted to Luke 24's account of Christ's resurrection appearances. 'Our meeting was very full,' he noted, 'there being sundry strangers present who had never been with us before.'

After the evening catechism meeting, at which time the Christians again seemed to have their 'hearts knit together in love' (Col. 2:2), he further remarked of God's continued blessings at Crossweeksung: 'This was a sweet and blessed season, like many others that my poor people have been favored with in months past! God has caused "this little fleece" to be repeatedly wet with the blessed "dews" (Judg. 6:37) of His divine grace, while all the earth around has been comparatively dry.'

During his recent visit to Elizabethtown he had sought advice from the Scottish Society commissioners concerning the possibility of some of his congregants receiving communion. Having determined to hold that observance the following Sunday, April 27, he consecrated that Friday as a solemn time of fasting, prayer and instruction to prepare his people.

In his Journal he listed additional reasons for their observing the day of prayer and fasting: to humble themselves before God on account of the apparent withdrawal, at least in measure, of the Spirit's influence that had been so prevalent among natives of all ages; because of the rising appearance of carelessness, vanity and vice among some who previously had seemed to be affected by divine truths and sensible of their perishing state; to seek divine blessing on their efforts in establishing a peaceable settlement and 'commodious' Christian congregation at Cranberry; to ask God to 'blast and defeat all the attempts that were or might be made against that pious design.' Of the latter concern, he noted further:

> There being at this time a terrible clamor raised against the Indians in various places in the country [region], and insinuations as though I was training them up to cut peoples' throats. Numbers wishing to have them banished out of these parts, and some giving out great words in order to fright and deter them from settling upon the best and most convenient tract of their own lands, threatening to molest and trouble them in the law, pretending a claim to these lands themselves, although never purchased of the Indians.

The entire congregation, rather than just those who intended to receive communion the following Lord's Day, participated in Friday's services. The whole day was devoted to worship, prayer and teaching from the Word. At day's end Brainerd briefly summarized 'the substance of the doctrine of the Christian faith' and the believing Indians cheerfully reaffirmed their assent to it. He also led them in renewing the commitment they had previously made at the time of their baptism. In it they publicly surrendered themselves to God the Father, Son and Holy Spirit, affirming Him to be their God. At the same time they renounced their past idolatrous and superstitious practices and pledged to follow Scripture as the rule of their lives. They also promised to walk together in love, to watch over themselves and one another and to lead serious, devoted lives. 'This solemn transaction was attended with much gravity and seriousness,' he reported, 'and at the same time with utmost readiness, freedom, and cheerfulness.'

The following afternoon he discoursed publicly on Christ's instituting of communion in Matthew 26, and emphasized the concept of receiving the ordinance in a worthy manner. He also baptized two adults, one of them being the man who on Sunday, April 6, became greatly distressed because he realized he had never done God's will. Since then, according to the watchful missionary, the native had 'obtained spiritual comfort upon good grounds.'

In the evening he took one more opportunity to prepare the communicants by catechizing on the nature and purpose of the ordinance. Upon hearing the Indians' responses to his queries, he testified he had 'abundant satisfaction' respecting their doctrinal understanding of the ordinance and their fitness to receive it. Commenting on a couple of specific aspects of their understanding, he wrote:

> They were likewise thoroughly sensible that 'twas no more than a seal or sign, and not the real body and blood of Christ; that 'twas designed for the refreshment and edification of the soul, and not for the feasting of the body. They were also acquainted with the end of the ordinance, that they were therein called to commemorate the dying love of Christ.

On Sunday morning he preached on the purpose of Christ's death as revealed in Titus 2:14. Afterward he administered the Lord's

Supper to twenty-three natives, the number of men and women being nearly equal. Five or six others who would have qualified to receive the ordinance were away at the Forks of the Delaware at the time.

'The ordinance was attended with great solemnity, and with a most desirable tenderness and affection,' he related. 'And 'twas remarkable that in the season of the performance of the sacramental actions, especially in the distribution of the bread, they seemed to be affected in a most lively manner, as if Christ had been really crucified before them.'

The demands of the morning's ministry left him considerably worn out, forcing him to rest for some time that afternoon. After recouping a degree of strength, he walked from house to house and visited privately with most of the communicants. Nearly all of them reported having been spiritually refreshed at the Lord's Table.

He spoke again on Titus 2:14 that evening. Some of the Christians afterward told him they had never before felt such strong desires to be completely redeemed from all iniquity. He was also delighted that various individuals whom he had 'never observed under any religious impressions before' seemed to be awakened to their spiritual need on that occasion.

A message on Christ's words from John 14:15 – 'If ye love me, keep my commandments' – concluded the solemnity the next day. Of the spirit of affectionate devotion to the Lord that the communicants exhibited at that service, he remarked, 'They seemed willing to have their "ears bored to the door posts of God's house" (Exod. 21:6), and to be His servants forever.'

Sensing that God's Spirit was stirring in the congregation in a special way, he 'thought it proper to improve this advantageous season, as Hezekiah did the desirable season of his great Passover (2 Chron. 31), in order to promote the blessed reformation begun among them.' Consequently he proposed they should enter again into a covenant before God, pledging to watch over themselves and one another lest they should dishonor the name of Christ by falling into sinful practices. He challenged them especially to guard against the sin of drunkenness and the temptations leading to it, as well as any 'appearance of evil' (1 Thess. 5:22) in that regard.

The Christian natives readily entered into the proposed covenant. Brainerd, 'in the most solemn manner I was capable of,' called God to witness their agreement and reminded the natives of the guilt they would bring upon themselves if they were to violate it. 'It was a season of amazing solemnity! And a divine awe appeared upon the face of the whole assembly in this transaction! Affectionate sobs, sighs, and tears were now frequent in the audience.'

Almost as an afterthought, he concluded his journal entry for that Monday with a terse notation: 'Baptized six children this day.'

He left the next day to attend another set of presbytery meetings in Elizabethtown. He did not linger there, but hastened back to rejoin the Indians, knowing they were relocating that same week to their new settlement near Cranberry.

24

'ONE CONTINUED FLAME FOR GOD'

The Indians' new settlement was located one and a half miles northeast of Cranberry, at the head of Wigwam Brook. Brainerd joined them there on Saturday, May 3, 1746. Because he had no house of his own at the new location, he was obliged to board with an English family that lived 'some distance' from the natives. The less-than-ideal arrangement left him feeling 'somewhat uneasy and dejected' that Saturday evening.

The next morning he preached to the Indians from Mark 4:5 on the seed sown on stony ground. Through the message he sought to remind them that there was reason 'to fear lest many promising appearances and hopeful beginnings in religion might prove abortive.' After discoursing on Romans 8:9 that afternoon, he spent several hours conversing privately with various Christians, laboring 'to regulate some things I apprehended amiss among some of them.'

On Monday he gave the natives further instruction concerning their farming endeavors. He was increasingly convinced that, for the sake of their spiritual welfare, they needed to become more industrious and more fully acquainted with husbandry techniques and practices. Only in that way would they be able to provide for themselves the necessities and comforts of life and to avoid the many temptations to which their present dependence upon settlers exposed them.

That Friday, May 9, he sought to woo those who had not yet embraced the Gospel by preaching on John 5:40, 'And ye will not come to me, that ye might have life.' That message was delivered 'in the open wilderness,' since the Indians at that time had 'no house for public worship ... nor scarce any shelters for themselves.' That same day he had the joy of baptizing the former conjurer who had come to saving faith during the first week of February.

The next morning he rode to nearby Allentown, where he had been invited to assist Charles McKnight in a communion observance being held there that weekend. He preached on Titus 2:14 in the afternoon but was afterward grieved, believing he had inadequately expounded such an important text and theme:

> God was pleased to carry me through with some competency of freedom; and yet to deny me that enlargement and power I longed for. In the evening my soul mourned, and could not but mourn, that I had treated so excellent a subject in so defective a manner, that I had borne so broken a testimony for so worthy and glorious a Redeemer. And if my discourse had met with the utmost applause from all the world (as I accidentally heard it applauded by some persons of judgment), it would not have given me any satisfaction: Oh, it grieved me to think that I had had no more holy warmth and fervency, that I had been no more melted in discoursing of Christ's death, and the end and design of it!

After assisting in the administration of the Lord's Supper on Sunday morning, he again preached at the afternoon service, this time with greater satisfaction from Luke 9:30-31:

> Enjoyed special freedom, from the beginning to the end of my discourse, without interruption. Things pertinent to the subject were abundantly presented to my view, and such a fullness of matter that I scarce knew how to dismiss the various heads and particulars I had occasion to touch upon. And, blessed be the Lord, I was favored with some fervency and power, as well as freedom; so that the Word of God seemed to awaken the attention of a stupid [spiritually ignorant] audience, to a considerable degree.

Part of his diary entry on the following Friday, May 16, reveals that he was having uncertainty over God's will for his future ministry endeavors:

> When I attempted to look to God respecting my worldly circumstances and His providential dealings with me in regard of my settling down in my congregation, which seems to be necessary and yet very difficult and contrary to my fixed intention for years past, as well as my disposition, which has been and still is, at times especially, to go forth and spend my life in preaching the Gospel from place to place, and gathering souls 'afar off' (Eph. 2:17) to Jesus the great Redeemer; when I attempted to look to God with regard to these things, and His designs concerning me, I could only say 'The Will of the Lord be done' (Acts 21:14): "Tis no matter for me' (Gal. 2:6). The same frame of mind I felt with respect to another important affair I have lately had some serious thoughts of: I could say, with utmost calmness and composure, 'Lord, if it be most for Thy glory, let me proceed in it; but if Thou seest that it will in any wise hinder my usefulness in Thy cause, oh, prevent my proceeding: for all I want, respecting this world, is such circumstances as may best capacitate me to do service for God in the world.'

What was the other 'important affair' he had recently been contemplating? Some have interpreted it as a guarded allusion to his consideration of the possibility of seeking a wife. More likely he was referring to a prospect he would write of again less than a week later: 'my great desire of enjoying conveniences and opportunities for profitable studies.'

His patience was tested when he preached at the Cranberry settlement the next Sunday morning. In the early part of his sermon on Revelation 3:20, a group of ill-mannered settlers crowded between him and the Indians. Their obvious inconsiderateness and disdain toward the natives caused him to feel 'peevish and provoked' and proved to be 'a great temptation' to him. 'But blessed be God,' he was able to report afterwards, 'I got these shackles off before the middle of my discourse, and was favored with a sweet frame of spirit in the latter part of the exercise; was full of love, warmth, and tenderness in addressing my people.'

In the intermission between worship services he took the opportunity to visit more privately with a number of people about the kindness and patience of Christ in standing and knocking, thus continuing His gracious calls to sinners who had long rejected His grace. That line of appeal seemed to have some effect on various individuals. Despite the fact that some tears were present in the congregation as he expounded further on the same text that afternoon: 'The appearance of the audience under divine truths was comparatively discouraging; and I was ready to fear that God was about to withdraw the blessed influence of His Spirit from us.'

Of his outlook at the end of that somewhat discouraging day he wrote: 'In the evening I was grieved that I had done so little for God. Oh, that I could be "a flame of fire" in the service of my God!' His expressed desire – to serve God as well and as tirelessly as did the angels – was an allusion to Hebrews 1:7 (citing Ps. 104:4): 'And of the angels He saith, Who maketh His angels spirits, and His ministers a flame of fire.'

He continued to ponder whether the Lord would have him to serve in a settled or itinerate ministry. For several days he thought he perceived it was 'the design of Providence' he should settle at Cranberry with the congregation God had enabled him to gather. He found his heart somewhat engaged by the prospect and started making plans in his own mind how he could hasten such a permanent settlement. On Thursday, May 22, he wrote of that possibility:

> And this, considering the late frequent sinking and failure of my spirits, and the need I stood in of some agreeable society, and my great desire of enjoying conveniences and opportunities for profitable studies, was not altogether disagreeable to me: Although I still wanted to go about far and wide in order to spread the blessed Gospel among benighted souls far remote; yet I never had been so willing to settle in any one place, for more than five years past, as I was in the foregoing part of this week.

'And yet,' he further divulged, '[I] was never fully determined, never quite pleased with the thoughts of being settled and confined to one place. ... For I never, since I began to preach, could feel any freedom to "enter into other men's labors" (John 4:38; 2 Cor. 10:15), and settle down in the ministry where the "Gospel was preached before" (Rom. 15:20); I never could make that appear to be my province.'

As he further contemplated these matters that same evening, he appears to have reached a conclusive decision in his heart. Of the possibility of entering a settled ministry with its attendant advantages he wrote at length:

> But now these thoughts seemed to be wholly dashed to pieces; not by necessity, but of choice: for it appeared to me that God's dealings towards me had fitted me for a life of solitariness and hardship; it appeared to me I had nothing to lose, nothing to do with earth, and consequently nothing to lose by a total renunciation of it: And it appeared just right that I should be destitute of house and home, and many comforts of life which I rejoiced to see others of God's people enjoy.
>
> And at the same time, I saw so much of the excellency of Christ's kingdom, and the infinite desirableness of its advancement in the world, that it swallowed up all my other thoughts; and made me willing, yea, even rejoice, to be made a pilgrim or hermit in the wilderness, to my dying moment, if I might thereby promote the blessed interest of the great Redeemer. And if ever my soul presented itself to God for His service, without any reserve of any kind, it did so now. The language of my thoughts and disposition (although I spake no words) now were, 'Here I am, Lord, send me; send me to the ends of the earth; send me to the rough, the savage pagans of the wilderness; send me from all that is called comfort in earth, or earthly comfort; send me even to death itself, if it be but in Thy service and to promote Thy kingdom.'
>
> And at the same time I had as quick and lively a sense of the value of worldly comforts as ever I had; but only saw them

infinitely overmatched by the worth of Christ's kingdom and the propagation of His blessed Gospel. The quiet settlement, the certain place of abode, the tender friendship which I thought I might be likely to enjoy in consequence of such circumstances, appeared as valuable to me, considered absolutely and in themselves, as ever before; but considered comparatively, they appeared nothing: Compared with the value and preciousness of an enlargement of Christ's kingdom, they vanished like the stars before the rising sun.

And sure I am, that although the comfortable accommodations of life appeared valuable and dear to me, yet I did surrender and resign myself, soul and body, to the service of God and promotion of Christ's kingdom; though it should be in the loss of them all. And I could not do any other, because I could not will or choose any other. I was constrained, and yet chose to say, 'Farewell, friends and earthly comforts, the dearest of them all, the very dearest, if the Lord calls for it; Adieu, Adieu; I'll spend my life, to my latest moments, "in caves and dens of the earth" (Heb. 11:38), if the kingdom of Christ may thereby be advanced.'[1]

After reaching the conclusions he did that evening, Brainerd entered into an intense season of private prayer for the ongoing expansion of God's kingdom. He was loath to bring that time of intercession to an end, but finally did so in order not to prevent the family he was boarding with from getting to sleep:

I found extraordinary freedom at this time in pouring out my soul to God for His cause; and especially that His kingdom might be extended among the Indians far remote; and I had

---

1. Some who postulate that Brainerd had a romantic interest in Jerusha Edwards have speculated that in bidding adieu to friends – including 'the dearest of them all, the very dearest' – he was speaking specifically of her. It has even been suggested, without a shred of corroborating evidence, that he originally penned those words in a letter to her, and that Jonathan Edwards manipulated them into the form of a diary entry. Such totally unfounded speculation is unacceptable because it presents fiction as fact and casts a completely unjustified shadow of suspicion over Edwards' use of source material in composing his account of Brainerd's life.

a great and strong hope that God would do it. I continued wrestling with God in prayer for my dear little flock here; and more especially for the Indians elsewhere; as well as for dear friends in one place and another; till it was bedtime and I feared I should hinder the family, etc. But oh, with what reluctancy did I find myself obliged to consume time in sleep! I longed to be as 'a flame of fire' (Heb. 1:7; Ps. 104:4), continually glowing in the divine service, preaching and building up Christ's kingdom to my latest, my dying moment.

He remained in the same frame of mind the next day and again expressed his desire to 'burn out in one continued flame for God.' In a rare statement of satisfaction with the devoted service he had rendered to the Lord, he stated, 'If ever I filled up a day with studies and devotion, I was enabled so to fill up this day.'

That same evening he was visited by his brother, John, who was then twenty-six years old and in his final year at Yale. Brainerd's only comment on the visit was that it was the first he had received from any of his close relatives since he had undertaken missionary service. In the outworkings of Providence, John would come to have a central role in the ongoing ministry to the Indians at Cranberry, though neither brother would have had any way of knowing that at the time of this visit.

Brainerd was very weak physically during the first half of the week to follow, but his spirits remained positive. He baptized five adults and five children following the afternoon preaching service on Sunday, June 1. Of the Lord's ongoing, but altered, work among the Indians he noted:

I have reason to hope that God has lately (at and since our celebration of the Lord's Supper) brought home to Himself sundry souls who had long been under spiritual trouble and concern: although there have been few instances of persons lately awakened out of a state of security. And those comforted of late seem to be brought in in a more silent way, neither their concern nor consolation being so powerful and remarkable as appeared among those more suddenly wrought upon in the beginning of this work of grace.

William Tennent asked him to assist in a communion observance that was held in Freehold the following weekend. The Cranberry Indians were also invited to attend the solemnity. Most of the natives who had previously received communion were communicants on this occasion as well. Modestly they sat by themselves at the last of several tables where the elements were served. Brainerd related the varied responses of both Indians and settlers to this shared observance:

> Those of my people who communicated seemed in general agreeably affected at the Lord's table, and some of them considerably melted with the love of Christ; although they were not so remarkably refreshed and feasted at this time, as when I administered this ordinance to them in our own congregation only.
>
> Some of the bystanders were affected with seeing these, who had been 'aliens from the commonwealth of Israel, and strangers to the covenant of promise,' who of all men had lived 'without God and without hope in the world,' now brought 'near to God' (Eph. 2:12-13) as His professing people, and sealing covenant with Him, by a solemn and devout attendance upon this sacred ordinance. And as numbers of God's people were refreshed with this sight, and thereby excited to bless God for the enlargement of His kingdom in the world, so some others (I was told) were awakened by it, apprehending the danger they were in of being themselves finally 'cast out,' while they saw others 'from the East and West,' preparing, and hopefully prepared in some good measure, to 'sit down in the kingdom of God' (Matt. 8:11-12).

That afternoon he was able to preach 'with uncommon freedom' from 2 Corinthians 5:20, 'Now then we are ambassadors for Christ, as though God did beseech you by us: we pray you in Christ's stead, be ye reconciled to God.' A considerable number of Indians met together early on Monday morning in a retired place in the woods to pray, sing and converse about spiritual matters. Some of the Freehold congregants were touched to see the natives engaged, a number of them with tears, in those religious exercises.

Brainerd's sermon that same morning from Genesis 5:24, 'And Enoch walked with God,' brought the sacred assembly to a close. Afterward he praised God for blessings experienced in that message and throughout the observance:

> God gave me enlargement and fervency in my discourse; so that I was enabled to speak with plainness and power; and God's presence seemed to be in the assembly. I found my strength renewed and lengthened out, even to a wonder; so that I felt much stronger at the conclusion than in the beginning of this sacramental solemnity. I have great reason to bless God for this solemnity, wherein I have found assistance in addressing others and sweetness in my own soul.

The following Friday, June 13, he preached to the Indians at Cranberry from 2 Corinthians 5:17 on being new creatures in Christ. After the message he baptized three adults and two children. One of those adults was the elderly woman whose spiritual distress and apparent vision he had reported in his diary nearly half a year earlier, on December 26.

He was invited to assist in yet another communion observance that same weekend, this one led by Eleazer Wales in Kingston, seven miles northwest of Cranberry. Wales, a 1727 graduate of Yale, had been the first pastor to serve at the Forks of the Delaware. In 1735 he accepted the call to Millstone (not quite ten miles north of Kingston), where he served till his death in 1750.[2]

Despite the fact that he was quite weak, Brainerd pushed himself to carry out his ministerial duties and experienced God's strengthening. On Saturday afternoon he preached, but nearly fainted in the pulpit. 'Yet God strengthened me when I was just gone [starting to fail],' he reported, 'and enabled me to speak His Word with freedom, fervency, and application to the conscience. And praised be the Lord; "out of weakness I was made strong" (Heb. 11:34).'

He preached to 'a vast multitude' Sunday afternoon, extending the invitations of Revelation 22:17. Afterward he wrote: 'God

2. Pettit, *Life of David Brainerd*, p. 408.

helped me to offer a testimony for Himself and to leave sinners inexcusable in neglecting His grace. I was enabled to speak with such freedom, fluency, and clearness as commanded the attention of the great.' Who exactly he meant by 'the great' is not known. Some have suggested the reference may have been to ecclesiastical dignitaries who were in the area for a ministerial gathering that was to take place the middle of the following week.

After delivering the final message of the solemnity on Monday he wrote with gratitude: 'Preached again; and God helped me amazingly, so that this was a sweet refreshing season to my soul and others. Oh, forever blessed be God for help afforded at this time, when my body was so weak, and while there was so large an assembly to hear.'

On Wednesday he attended the ministerial meeting that convened at Hopewell, about eight miles west of Kingston. When he returned to Cranberry the following day, June 19, he was accompanied by 'two of the Reverend Correspondents' of the Scottish Society, most likely Jonathan Dickinson and Aaron Burr. Through their brief visit, the commissioners doubtless desired not only to gain first-hand acquaintance with the current status of the ministry, but also to encourage Brainerd in his vital work.

That day was significant in that it marked the one-year anniversary of his ministry among the natives of New Jersey. In what would be the final diary entry included in his public Journal, he was careful to glorify God for the remarkable spiritual developments he had witnessed during that period:

> This day makes up a complete year from the first time of my preaching to these Indians in New Jersey. What amazing things has God wrought in this space of time for these poor people! ... How are morose and savage pagans in this short space of time transformed into agreeable, affectionate, and humble Christians! And their drunken and pagan howlings turned into devout and fervent prayers and praises to God! ... And 'now to Him that is of power to stablish them according to the Gospel and the preaching of Christ' (Rom. 16:25), 'to God only wise, be glory through Jesus Christ for ever and ever. Amen' (Rom. 16:27).

Before 1746 came to an end, the Scottish Society commissioners published what would later become known as the second part of Brainerd's Journal. Covering the period from November 24, 1745, to June 19, 1746, that portion of the Journal was initially published as an independent work entitled *Divine Grace Displayed; Or the Continuance and Progress of a remarkable Work of Grace Among some of the Indians Belonging to the Provinces of New Jersey and Pennsylvania.*

25

INVALUABLE INSIGHTS CONCERNING INDIAN MINISTRY

To the second portion of his Journal, Brainerd appended extensive observations on various aspects of his work among the Indians. Though voluminous, originally running to some 20,000 words in length, the addendum is well worth considering because it supplies a wealth of additional information about the natives, their beliefs, and Brainerd's methods and challenges in seeking to minister to them. While space limitations prohibit an extensive summary of the appendix here, some highlights will be shared in this chapter.[1]

Concerning the moral reformation that had taken place among the natives, he pointed out that there had hardly been an instance of drunkennesss – the Indians' 'darling vice' – among his hearers for the past several months. Three or four married couples who had previously separated and started living with someone other than their own spouse had now voluntarily dismissed those whom they had wrongfully taken and were once again living with their original mate in love and peace. Family prayers had become common, so that 'scarce a prayerless person was to be found among near an hundred of them.' The Lord's Day was seriously and faithfully observed, with care being taken by parents 'to keep their children orderly upon that sacred day.'

By that time he had baptized a total of thirty-eight adults and thirty-nine children. 'Many others' were under solemn concern

---

1. The appendix to the second part of Brainerd's Journal is preserved in full as Chapters IX and X in Dwight, *Memoirs of David Brainerd*, pp. 321-66.

for their souls but had not been baptized due to the absence of evidence of a saving change having taken place in their lives.

There had been only a 'very few instances' of sinful or inappropriate behavior among the natives who had made a profession of faith or even among those who were giving spiritual matters serious consideration: 'I do not know of more than three or four such persons who have been guilty of any open misconduct, since their first acquaintance with Christianity; and not one who persists in any thing of that nature.'

The Indians' answers to the questions he proposed in the catechism sessions showed they were gaining a good understanding of various Christian doctrines. Like the Lord's disciples in Luke 11, they had taken the initiative in asking him to instruct them in the proper method and matter of prayer. Having put forth considerable effort and manifested remarkable aptitude in learning to sing 'Psalm-tunes,' they were 'now able to sing with a good degree of decency in the worship of God.'

They were very desirous to learn the English language. Frequently the natives spoke English among themselves, and most of them had gained enough acquaintance with it to understand a considerable part of his discourses, even without an interpreter. He encouraged their learning of English so they could profit from good books (which could only be translated into their language with great difficulty and expense) and from hearing other ministers occasionally, either at neighboring churches or in their home setting.

Thirty to thirty-five children continued to attend the school during the daytime and fifteen to twenty married and single adults attended evening classes. 'The children learn with surprising readiness,' he related, 'so that their master tells me he never had an English school which learned, in general, comparably so fast.' Just four and a half months had elapsed since the school was established, but already several of the students were able to read effectively out of a Psalter or Testament. Each Wednesday and Saturday the pupils were instructed in the Westminster Shorter Catechism. Some of them could recite from memory well over half of it.

Brainerd provided a precise accounting of the monies (in pounds, shillings and even drams) that had been received and dispersed in his missionary efforts since October of 1745. Congregations in nearly twenty locations in three different colonies were listed as having contributed a total of 100 pounds in offerings to the Indian work. In addition to the eighty-two pounds, five shillings paid in January, 1746, to eliminate the Indians' debts and secure their lands, other funds had been used for: building the schoolhouse (three pounds, five shillings); paying the schoolmaster's wages (seventeen pounds, ten shillings); providing books for the school (three pounds). Brainerd had covered out of his own resources six pounds of expenses that exceeded the donations from the churches.

As he was nearing completion of the preceding portion of the addendum, he received from Ebenezer Pemberton a copy of a letter from the Scottish Society directors in Edinburgh, dated March 21, 1745. In those days it not uncommonly took a year or longer for a letter to cross the Atlantic between Europe and America. That was partly due to France's success in disrupting British shipping efforts to and from the Colonies.

Among other things, the letter instructed Brainerd to share the difficulties he had encountered in his ministry and the strategies employed for surmounting those hardships. He divulged that he had intentionally avoided saying too much about the difficulties of his ministry lest: his Journal be rendered 'very tedious'; it seem he was complaining unduly; people wrongly suppose he had exceptional capacity to persevere through trials. One can be glad he complied with the mission organization's directive to share along this line. Otherwise a significant amount of information not only about those challenges but also relating to the general beliefs of the Indians would have gone unrecorded. His observations in this portion of the addendum reflected his experiences in both Pennsylvania and New Jersey.

The initial difficulty he elaborated on was the rooted aversion to Christianity that generally prevailed among the natives. The first reason for that antipathy was the blatant moral abuses the Indians witnessed in the lives of settlers who claimed to be

Christians. Not being able to distinguish between actual and mere professing Christians, the natives tended to view and condemn all white people as being alike.

A second prejudicing factor was their constant fear that settlers were forming some design to enslave them. Some of them suspected that Brainerd had been sent among them to draw them together, under a pretense of kindness, so they could more easily be taken as slaves as blacks had been. They also feared they might be taken on the white men's ships and made to fight against their enemies.

The Indians also opposed Christianity because of their strong attachment to their own religious notions and forms of worship. So far as Brainerd had been able to ascertain upon careful inquiry, the natives believed in a plurality of invisible deities. Furthermore, they had a superstitious reverence for different kinds of animals, birds, fish and reptiles because they believed that the invisible divine powers communicated good to them through various of those living creatures. Describing a form of totem worship, he explained it this way:

> ... such a creature becomes sacred to the persons to whom he is supposed to be the immediate author of good, and through him they must worship the invisible powers, though to others he is no more than another creature. Perhaps another animal is looked upon to be the immediate author of good to another; and consequently he must worship the invisible powers by that animal. I have known a pagan [to] burn fine tobacco for incense, in order to appease the anger of that invisible power, which he supposed presided over rattlesnakes, because one of these animals was killed by another Indian near his house.

Before the arrival of settlers, some Indians had supposed there were four invisible powers who presided over the four corners of the earth. Others thought the sun was the only deity and that all things had been made by him. But after the coming of the settlers, the natives had generally concluded there were three, and only three, deities. They surmised that each of those deities had made one of the different types of people they were familiar with – blacks, whites and Indians.

The natives viewed their manner of living, which they held their god had expressly prescribed for them, as being vastly preferable to that followed by the whites. 'Hence they will frequently sit and laugh at the whites,' Brainerd revealed, 'as being good for nothing else but to plow and fatigue themselves with hard labor; while they enjoy the satisfaction of stretching themselves on the ground, and sleeping as much as they please; and have no other trouble but now and then to chase the deer, which is often attended with pleasure rather than pain.'

Many natives believed that at death the part of them to survive the body – referred to as the *chichung* ('the shadow') – would go southward to an unknown place of unending happy activities such as hunting, feasting, dancing and the like. Brainerd supposed they associated a more southerly location with increased comfort climate-wise and thus the logical place of perfect felicity.

Some Indians held to the notion of people in the afterlife experiencing either happiness or misery. Most, they thought, would be happy, while those who were not would be punished only with privation from felicity. The latter would have to remain outside the walls of that good world where happy souls dwelled. Their happiness or misery in the future life depended entirely upon their treatment of their fellow men in the present life.

The Indians frequently offered sacrifices to the invisible powers, but as one of Brainerd's interpreters explained to him: 'They sacrifice that they may have success in hunting and other affairs, and that sickness and other calamities may not befall them, which they fear in the present world, in case of neglect; but they do not suppose God will ever punish them in the coming world for neglecting to sacrifice.'

A final significant reason for the natives' aversion to Christianity was the influence of their powwows over them. These conjurers, it was commonly thought, possessed special power that enabled them not only to foretell future events and heal the sick but also to enchant or even fatally poison people through their magic divinations.

The conjurer whose conviction of sin and eventual Christian conversion were related in chapters 17 and 21 once shared with Brainerd a fantastic account of how he believed he had received his supernatural powers. The Indian claimed that even before he was born his spirit was admitted into the presence of a 'great man' who informed him that he loved and pitied him and desired to do good for him. Their meeting took place in a world above and at a vast distance from the earth. The great man was clothed with the day, which, according to the native relating the event, was the brightest day he ever saw and a day of many years, even of everlasting continuance. Everything of beauty in the earth – rocks, mountains, seas – were drawn on the great man and could be clearly seen in him.

The supernatural being revealed to the native that he would come down to earth, the specific woman who would be his mother, and some of the things that would happen to him in his life, including the fact that he would once be guilty of murder. When the Indian protested and asserted that he would never murder, the spirit replied, 'I have said it, and it shall be so.'

The great man asked the native what he would choose to do in life, and he responded that he wished to be first a hunter and afterwards a diviner. He was told he would have what he desired and that the great man's shadow (spirit) would accompany him to the earth and remain with him there. Their entire conference was reportedly carried on without any words being spoken between them. Even without the use of human language, they understood each other's thoughts, dispositions and proposals.

Throughout the Indian's life on earth, the great man's spirit accompanied him and continued to appear to him in dreams and in other ways, providing him with guidance concerning his hunting and other matters. As was seen in chapter 22, that spirit's influence continued in the native's life until he felt the power of God's Word upon his heart, at which time it entirely left him.

The second 'great difficulty' Brainerd shared concerning his ministry was the twin challenge of conveying divine truths in a way that the Indians could understand and of gaining their assent to those truths. There were no words in their language that corresponded directly to the English terms 'Lord, Savior, salvation, sinner, justice, condemnation, faith, repentance, justification, adoption, sanctification, grace, glory, heaven' and scores of other spiritually weighted concepts. Furthermore, there were no spiritual truths that he could take for granted the natives understood and possessed as he attempted to teach them other truths.

He was careful to clarify with the Indians that what he had to share with them had to do with 'the *conscious* part of the man' (the soul), especially with relation to its state after the death of the body. He sought to make it clear that he had not come to deal with them about mere temporal affairs of the present world. He found it necessary to emphasize that point because any time the Indians had been called together by white people in the past it had always been to discuss the sale of lands or some other secular business.

Sometimes he found it difficult even to gain a hearing for his opening discourses. At times, after distinguishing between the present and future state and telling them that it was his intent to teach concerning the life to come, the natives showed little concern or interest in such matters. Now and again they simply walked away before he had finished even half his message.

It was also 'next to impossible' to convince the Indians that they were sinners by nature and that their hearts were corrupt and sinful. Unless they could be charged with some gross act of immorality, they would not admit that they were sinful. And even when they were confronted with obvious abuses of their neighbor – behavior contrary to the second table of the Ten Commandments – they admitted only that the actions were wrong, but still denied that their hearts were sinful.

A third set of factors that had been 'an unspeakable difficulty and discouragement' to him in his work was the natives' 'inconvenient situations, savage manners, and unhappy method of living.' After briefly rehearsing the extremely difficult travel conditions he had endured in his itinerations in wilderness areas, he divulged:

> I have been often obliged to preach in their houses in cold
> and windy weather, when they have been full of smoke and

cinders, as well as unspeakably filthy; which has many times thrown me into violent sick headaches.

While I have been preaching, their children have frequently cried to such a degree, that I could scarcely be heard, and their pagan mothers would take no manner of care to quiet them. At the same time, perhaps, some have been laughing and mocking at divine truths; others playing with their dogs, whittling sticks, and the like; and this, in many of them, not from spite and prejudice, but for want of better manners.

To the full extent of his ability he had sought to impress upon the Indians the several benefits to be gained by diligently working to establish their own community: the cause of Christianity would be promoted among them; their own worldly comfort would increase; other natives would be more inclined to live among them, thus coming under the hearing of the Gospel; religious whites would be more encouraged to help them; the mouths of their detractors would be stopped; they could earn a living to meet their financial obligations, thus avoiding the trouble that would come upon them if they failed to do so.

The Indians, according to Brainerd, gave ready assent that such benefits would result, but changed little in their lifestyle. 'Though it must be acknowledged,' he was able to add, 'that those who appear to have a sense of divine things, are considerably amended in this respect, and it is to be hoped that time will make a yet greater alteration upon them for the better.'

He also spoke of the temptations the natives were exposed to through their 'wandering to and fro in order to procure the necessaries of life.' When they had gone to hunt among Indians in remote locations, they had been laughed at for hearkening to the white man's religion. Or among settlers, whom he said were 'more horribly wicked' than the natives, they fell prey to drunkenness and theft. The whites had often gotten them drunk, then stole the commodities – animal skins, baskets, brooms, shovels and the like – which they intended to trade for corn and other necessities of life for themselves and their families. 'For the labor, perhaps, of several weeks,' he lamented, 'they have thus got nothing but the satisfaction of being drunk once; and have not only lost their labor, but, which is infinitely worse, the impressions of some divine subjects that were made upon their minds before.'

The fourth and final primary difficulty that had attended his endeavors was 'the attempts, which some ill-minded persons have designedly made, to hinder the propagation of the Gospel, and a work of divine grace among the Indians.' When the spiritual awakening came to the New Jersey natives, some whites attempted to prejudice the Indians against Brainerd and the truths he taught them 'by the most base, unmanly, and false suggestions of things which had no foundation but in their own brains.' He was apparently accused of some sort of rank immorality. Of that slander he remarked that he 'might have added more ... had not delicacy forbidden me to mention what was too obscene.' Happily, he was able to add: 'But, through the mercy of God, they were never able, by all their abominable insinuations, flouting jeers, and downright lies, to create in the Indians those jealousies with which they desired to possess them; and so were never suffered to hinder the work of grace among them.'

He reiterated the problem of a number of the New Jersey Indians having been sued for debt and threatened with imprisonment. The natives informed him that they had faced those threats more since he started ministering among them than they had in the previous seven years. He speculated the reason for this was because the Indians had stopped frequenting the 'tippling houses' where they used to consume most of their material resources on strong liquor. Seeing that their hope of gaining further profit from the natives in that way was lost, the malicious settlers then resolved to collect on the Indians' pre-existing debts by having them thrown into prison and seizing their lands.

To overcome such a threat he pressed the Indians to pay off their debts as quickly as possible. He exhorted those who were largely free from debt, and who had pelts or money, to help their fellow natives who were heavily oppressed. 'Frequently upon such occasions,' he revealed, 'I have paid money out of my own pocket, which I have not as yet received again.'

26

FINAL SUSQUEHANNA JOURNEY

Brainerd was still 'very much amiss' when he returned to Cranberry on June 19, 1746, with two correspondents of the Scottish Society. Despite his poor physical condition, he preached to his congregation once on Saturday and twice on Sunday, June 22. Throughout the week that followed he remained feeble and despondent.

Both his morning and afternoon messages the next Sunday centered on Jesus' words from John 14:19, 'Yet a little while, and the world seeth me no more; but ye see me: because I live, ye shall live also.' He rejoiced in the Lord's extraordinary supply of strength that enabled him to carry out a full slate of ministry responsibilities that day:

> God amazingly renewed and lengthened out my strength. I was so spent at noon that I could scarce walk, and all my joints trembled; so that I could not sit, nor so much as hold my hand still: And yet God strengthened me to preach with power in the afternoon; although I had given out word to my people that I did not expect to be able to do it. Spent some time afterwards in conversing, particularly with several persons about their spiritual state; and had some satisfaction concerning one or two. Prayed afterwards with a sick child, and gave a word of exhortation. Was assisted in all my work. Blessed be God! Returned home with more health than I went out with; although my linen was wringing wet upon me from a little after ten in the morning till past five in

the afternoon. My spirits were also considerably refreshed; and my soul rejoiced in hope that I had through grace done something for God.

After spending the following day 'under much weakness and disorder,' he again preached to his people on Tuesday afternoon, taking as his text Hebrews 9:27, 'And as it is appointed unto men once to die, but after this the judgment.' The occasion for such a solemn address, he reported matter-of-factly, was that 'some persons' in his congregation were 'lying at the point of death.' He provided no follow-up report in his diary about the outcome of that grave illness for those individuals.

The next day he went to Newark to attend a presbytery meeting, then spent the remainder of the week there and at Elizabethtown. On Sunday, July 6, he was still in Elizabethtown, to assist Jonathan Dickinson in a communion observance. His estimate of the conversation he had the following evening, presumably at Dickinson's home, is quite remarkable: 'In the evening, had the most agreeable conversation that ever I remember in all my life, upon God's being "all in all" (1 Cor. 15:28), and all enjoyments being just *that* to us which God makes them, and no more. 'Tis good to begin and end with God.'

Intending to administer the Lord's Supper to some of the Cranberry Indians on Sunday, he visited and spent time in serious conversation with them that Friday, July 11. The congregation devoted Saturday to fasting and prayer. He preached that morning and afternoon from Romans 4:25, 'Who was delivered for our offenses, and was raised again for our justification.' After the second sermon he led the native believers in 'fresh rededication of themselves to God' through a 'solemn renewal' of their Christian covenant.

Following the Sunday morning message, he administered the sacrament to thirty-one Indians. A number of other natives whom he considered qualified communicants were away from the settlement on that occasion. The communicants were deeply moved when it came time for the sharing of the elements: 'Oh, how they melted, even when the elements were first uncovered!

There was scarcely a dry eye amongst them when I took off the linen and showed them the symbols of Christ's "broken body" (1 Cor. 11:24).'

In concluding the solemnity the next morning he preached on Psalm 119:106, 'I have sworn, and I will perform it, that I will keep Thy righteous judgments.' He emphasized that all God's commandments are righteous and that His people, especially at the Lord's table, have pledged to keep them. As he had concluded the first communion observance with the Indians on April 28, so now he led them in renewing their earlier solemn covenant before God to watch over themselves and one another lest they should fall into sin and thus dishonor the name of Christ.

The rest of that week, starting the next morning, he traveled to Philadelphia and back. He did so even though he continued to be 'under a great degree of illness of body and dejection of mind.' Probably the purpose of the journey was to make arrangements for another itineration to the Susquehanna region.

On Monday morning, July 21, back in Cranberry, he discoursed primarily for the sake of 'some strangers' who had apparently just arrived at the settlement. After the message he shared with his congregation his intention to take another evangelistic journey to Susquehanna soon. He exhorted his people to pray that God would be with him in the journey, then chose various individuals to travel with him. Following the service he spent some time visiting with the newcomers and was 'somewhat encouraged with them.' By contrast, when he also cared for his people's secular business that same day he was 'not a little exercised with it.'

Two and a half weeks later, on Thursday, August 7, he rode to Crossweeksung to retrieve from his cottage there some unspecified items needed for the upcoming Susquehanna journey. He may have been surprised by the effect that being back at that location had on him: 'Was refreshed to see that place which God so marvelously visited with the showers of His grace. Oh, how amazingly did the "power of God" (Luke 9:43) often appear there!'

In Cranberry on Sunday he preached a pair of searching sermons from Acts 3:19, 'Repent ye therefore, and be converted, that your sins may be blotted out, when the times of refreshing shall come from the presence of the Lord.' Following the afternoon message he baptized three adults and three children. That evening he noted in his diary: 'I scarce ever in my life felt myself so full of tenderness, as this day.'

Considerable time was spent in prayer with the Indians on Monday for the purpose of seeking God's blessing on the impending itineration. After preaching and leading in prayer, his strength was so spent that he needed to leave the meeting to rest. The natives continued to pray and sing together at length. When he had recouped some energy, he returned, led in a benediction and dismissed the assembly.

Almost unbelievably in light of his limited physical strength, the very next day, August 12, he and the six Indians he had chosen to accompany him set out for the Susquehanna. This time, rather than retracing his usual route to the Forks of the Delaware and across the rugged mountain wilderness, he took a longer, southerly course through Philadelphia. From there they traveled west by northwest toward a lower point on the Susquehanna. He and his companions traveled just less than eighty miles in the first four days of the journey, arriving at Charlestown (now called Schuylkill on the river bearing the same name), about thirty miles west of Philadelphia, on Friday.

Richard Treat, who resided and pastored in Abington, a few miles north of Philadelphia, also ministered in Charlestown. Preparations were under way for a communion observance at the latter location that weekend, so Brainerd tarried in order to assist with that. Treat preached on Saturday morning, and Brainerd brought the afternoon message. Following the Sunday morning sermon by Treat, Brainerd and five of his native companions partook of the Lord's Supper. That afternoon he preached, as he had on at least two previous occasions, from Ezekiel 33:11.

He continued his westward trek, perhaps passing through Derry, now Hershey, and Paxton. After sleeping beside the Susquehanna on Tuesday night: 'Having lain in a cold sweat all night, I coughed much bloody matter this morning, and was under great disorder of body, and not a little melancholy; but what gave me some encouragement was, I had a secret hope that I might speedily get a dismission from earth and all its toils and sorrows.'

That day he rode to Chamber's Mills, a trading post on the Susquehanna, forty miles south of Shamokin. The company at his lodging place that night proved mixed: 'Was much afflicted in the evening with an ungodly crew, drinking, swearing, etc. Oh, what a hell it would be to be numbered with the ungodly! Enjoyed some agreeable conversation with a traveler, who seemed to have some relish of true religion.'

Thursday he ventured some fifteen miles further upriver, where he spent the night with a family 'that appeared quite destitute of God.' He tried to visit with the husband about spiritual matters but 'found him very artful in evading such conversation.'

His diary reveals that his native companions rejoined him as he continued his course upriver on Friday. Perhaps they had camped on the island of Juniata while he lodged at Chamber's Mills and with the white family on Wednesday and Thursday. There is no record that he stopped to minister at Juniata on this occasion. Having left behind the last English settlements, that evening they slept in the open woods. There with his Christian Indians he enjoyed 'more comfort than while among an ungodly company of white people.'

When he arrived at Shamokin the next day, August 23, he felt somewhat exercised but not as downcast as in recent days. On Sunday afternoon he visited with 'the king and others' who seemed disposed to consider his teaching. He sent out his native companions on Monday 'to talk with the Indians, and contract a friendship and familiarity with them, that I might have a better opportunity of treating with them about Christianity.' Those visits accomplished their intended purpose, with the result that the following day he addressed 'a considerable number of Indians.' His message seemed to make an impression on some who were very serious as he spoke. He also invited his Christian companions to share their testimony for God, which they did.

A thick smoke that nearly choked him filled the house where he slept that night. He awoke the next morning with distressing pains in his head and neck. A cold easterly storm was gathering, so he could not remain comfortably either inside the smoky dwelling or outside in the raw air. 'I was this day very vapory, and lived in great distress, and had not health enough to do anything to any purpose.'

On Thursday he was 'full of concern for the kingdom of Christ,' and for its expansion he prayed earnestly both privately and 'in my family.' (The latter phrase designates his Christian native companions and reveals the close, familial relationship he had with them.) He felt poorly and found few of the Delawares at their homes on Friday. The next morning he visited a trader who had come down the river sick and who 'appeared as ignorant as any Indian.' On Sunday he spent much time in secret duties, then met with his Christian natives (whom he again referred to affectionately as 'my dear family') for singing and prayer as well as reading and expounding of God's Word. He afterwards sought to speak the Word to some of the Susquehanna Indians, but only a few were present to listen.

In his previous Susquehanna itinerations, he had never ventured further west than Shamokin. On Monday, September 1, however, he and his companions set out for The Great Island, now Lock Haven, fifty miles up the west branch of the Susquehanna. He hoped to share the Christian message with the Shawanese Indians who resided there. Some of that tribe were considered dangerous, having sided with the French.

The second day and night of that leg of their journey proved especially difficult for him:

> Was very weak, on this as well as the preceding days: Was so feeble and faint that I feared it would kill me to lie out in the open air; and some of our company being parted from us, so that we had now no axe with us, I had no way but to climb into a young pine tree, and with my knife to lop the branches, and so made a shelter from the dew. But the evening being cloudy and very likely for rain, I was still under fears of being extremely exposed: Sweat much in the night, so that my linen was almost wringing wet all night. I scarce ever was more weak and weary than this evening, when I was able to sit up at all. ...

On Wednesday they arrived at 'the Delaware-town' where they found many people 'drinking and drunken.' They were able to visit with some of the natives there, and Brainerd noted that his interpreter was 'much engaged and assisted in his work.' A few individuals listened intently to what they had to share. That afternoon the evangelists paid a short visit to 'a small town of Shauwaunoes' about eight miles away, then returned to the Delaware town to spend the night.

The next morning he again spoke to the local Indians about Christianity, with his interpreter 'carrying on the discourse to a considerable length' even after he had finished. Then, realizing he lacked the strength to reach Great Island, he set out back toward Shamokin, with the Christian natives following behind on foot later that same day. At his campsite that night:

> Was in very uncomfortable circumstances in the evening, my people being belated and not coming to me till past ten at night; so that I had no fire to dress any victuals, or to keep me warm, or keep off wild beasts; and I was scarce ever more weak and worn out in all my life. However, I lay down and slept before my people came up, expecting nothing else but to spend the whole night alone and without fire.

He was so weak on Friday that he could scarcely ride: '. . . it seemed sometimes as if I must fall off from my horse and lie in the open woods.' But late in the afternoon he reached Shamokin, where: 'Felt something of a spirit of thankfulness that God had so far returned me: Was refreshed to see one of my Christians whom I left here in my late excursion.'

The following day he was again coughing and spitting blood and had very little appetite. He was able to carry out little ministry that day, but did manage to 'discourse a while of divine things' to his fellow Christians and to a few other Indians. He remained in much the same 'weak state of body and afflicted frame of mind' on Sunday. He again read and expounded a portion of Scripture and spent some time in prayer with 'my own dear family.' In addition, he discoursed briefly to some of the pagan Indians.

Leaving Shamokin on Monday afternoon, the missionary band made its way a few miles downriver. They traveled nearly thirty more miles on Tuesday, part of the way through a thunderstorm. That evening Brainerd had occasion to correct the misled notions of 'some poor ignorant souls' (presumably settlers and mere professing Christians) on what constituted convincing evidences of genuine spiritual life. The issue arose when the settlers were amazed to observe the Christian natives asking a blessing at dinner, and took that as 'a very high evidence' of God's saving grace at work in them. The settlers were further 'astonished' when he insisted that neither prayers at mealtime nor even secret prayers were 'any sure evidence of grace.'

Another twenty miles were traversed the following day. Somewhere, perhaps where he lodged that evening, he was 'much solicited to preach' but was 'utterly unable' to comply due to his weakness and illness: 'Was extremely overdone with the heat and showers this day, and coughed up considerable blood.' Again on Thursday as he traveled along: 'Had a very importunate invitation to preach at a meetinghouse I came by, the people being then gathering; but could not, by reason of weakness.'

The long journey was taking its toll on his fellow evangelists as well, and that weighed heavily on his mind: 'Was resigned and composed under my weakness; but was much exercised with concern for my companions in travel, whom I had left with much regret, some lame, and some sick.' Likely the Indians had encouraged him to continue on so he could receive help from his acquaintances to the east. Doubtless they also assured him they would follow along later after they had had opportunity to rest and recuperate.

Able to travel more quickly alone, he pressed to cover some fifty miles on Friday, and arrived at nightfall at 'a Christian friend's house, about 25 miles westward from Philadelphia.' The identity of the friend and the precise location of his home are not known. Brainerd was doubtless back in the vicinity of Charlestown and Norriton. The friend, who appears to be differentiated from Richard Treat, provided kind and refreshing hospitality for the exhausted, ailing itinerant.

He heard Treat preach on Saturday afternoon and that evening had a refreshing conversation with him. At the desire of Treat and his parishioners, the missionary spoke briefly both Sunday morning and afternoon. Monday was spent with Treat in seeking to help some members of that local congregation reconcile their differences. 'There seemed to be a blessing on our endeavors,' he was able to report. That evening he officiated over an infant baptism service, then conversed about spiritual matters till late at night.

But the following day he was too weak 'to perform any business' and could scarcely sit up. Though still coughing and spitting blood, he managed to ride to Philadelphia on Wednesday. Turning north, he rode to Treat's home in Abington on Thursday. The next day he proceeded northeast to the home of John Stockton in Princeton, New Jersey. Stockton served as judge in the Court of Common Pleas for Somerset County. His house later became the official residence of the Governor of New Jersey. Stockton's son, Richard, a signer of the Declaration of Independence, was sixteen years old at the time of Brainerd's overnight stay in their home.[1]

The missionary traversed the final eight miles to his home in Cranberry late on Saturday, September 20. He had been away thirty-nine days. When he arrived, the Indians were praying. Entering their meeting, he gave them a partial account of how God had helped him and his companions on the journey, then prayed with them. Both his report and prayer seemed to touch the natives, with several of them responding with tears.

Still being extremely weak, he soon had to leave the meeting to go to his lodgings. There he wrote: 'Thus God has carried me through the fatigues and perils of another journey to Susquehanna, and returned me again in safety, though under a great degree of bodily indisposition. ... Many hardships and distresses I endured in this journey: But the Lord supported me under them all.'

---

1. Pettit, *Life of David Brainerd*, p. 427.

27

FINAL MINISTRY AMONG THE INDIANS

From the time Brainerd returned to Cranberry in September of 1746, his diary entries became more periodic due to his sharply declining health and strength. Of his first Sunday back at Cranberry, September 21, he recorded that he was too weak to visit or preach to the Indians that morning. In the afternoon, however, he rode out to see them. Sitting on a chair rather than standing, he preached from Romans 14:7-8 on living and dying to the Lord. Afterwards: 'I returned to my lodgings extremely tired; but thankful that I had been enabled to speak a word to my poor people I had been so long absent from. Was able to sleep very little this night, through weariness and pain.'

Throughout the remainder of that week he was not only very weak but also suffered from a violent cough and a fever. He had no appetite, and frequently and quickly threw up what little he did eat. It was difficult for him to rest in bed because of pains in his chest and back. He did ride the two miles from the house where he boarded to the Indian settlement each day in order to 'take some care of' those who were then in the process of constructing a cottage for him there. Sometimes he was scarcely able to walk, and not one day that week was he able to sit up throughout the day. He had little strength to pray or meditate and none to read or write.

But despite his illness and accompanying thoughts about the possibility of death, his overall outlook remained positive and peaceful:

Was calm and composed and but little exercised with melancholy damps, as in former seasons of weakness: Whether

> I should ever recover, or no, seemed very doubtful; but this was many times a comfort to me, that life and death did not depend upon my choice. I was pleased to think that He who is infinitely wise had the determination of this matter ... But through divine goodness I could with great composure look death in the face, and frequently with sensible joy. Oh, how blessed it is to be habitually prepared for death! The Lord grant that I may be actually ready also.

The following Sunday, September 28, though still very weak, he attempted to preach to the Indians from 2 Corinthians 13:5, 'Examine yourselves, whether ye be in the faith.' After speaking for about half an hour, he was forced to desist, and for a time he felt faint. With great difficulty he rode back to his lodgings, where he lay in bed almost delirious with fever for several hours. Finally, near dawn the next morning, his fever broke. 'I have often been feverish and unable to rest quietly after preaching,' he divulged, 'but this was the most severe, distressing turn that ever preaching brought upon me. Yet I felt perfectly at rest in my own mind because I had made my utmost attempts to speak for God, and knew I could do no more.'

Some time before, he had given notice to the Indians, including those at the Forks of the Delaware, that he intended 'with leave of Providence' to observe communion at Cranberry the first Sunday in October. That Friday, October 3, he found himself feeling 'wonderfully revived and strengthened.' Perhaps taking that as an indication of the Lord's intent to prosper his plan, he preached a preparatory sermon that afternoon.

He felt 'surprisingly strengthened' while speaking, but immediately afterward had to return to bed. Fortunately, he did not need to ride back to his lodging that day, because at some undisclosed time during the week he had moved into his new cottage at the Indian settlement. That evening his soul was refreshed as he conversed with some of his people about spiritual matters while lying on his bed.

On Saturday he visited several of the intended communicants, then preached from Zechariah 12:10: 'And I will pour upon the house of David, and upon the inhabitants of Jerusalem, the spirit of grace and of supplications: and they shall look upon me whom they have pierced, and they shall mourn for him, as one mourneth for his only son ...' As a result, there was 'a tender melting and hearty mourning' on the part of a number of individuals over their own sin. Brainerd and most of the congregants were deeply touched by the humble, brokenhearted confession of a backslidden person who had come under heavy conviction the previous day. Again that evening, though extremely tired, he discoursed to his people about spiritual matters from his bed.

He was still very weak the next morning and 'considerably afraid' that he would not be able to carry out the work of the day. Before administering the sacrament, he expounded on John 1:29, 'Behold the Lamb of God, that taketh away the sin of the world.' Following the message he baptized two individuals. That brought the number of natives whom he baptized to its final total of eighty-five – they make up the total forty-three adults and forty-two children. After the baptisms he administered the Lord's Supper to nearly forty Indians as well as to 'divers dear Christians of the white people' who were present that day.

At the conclusion of the service he needed assistance to traverse the one hundred or so yards back to his dwelling: 'was supported and led by my friends, and laid on my bed.' Sometime that evening he was again able to visit with friends while sitting up in bed. 'Oh, how was this day spent in prayers and praises among my dear people!' he later exclaimed. 'One might hear them all the morning before public worship, and in the evening till near midnight, praying and singing praises to God in one or other of their houses.'

Early that same week he took two days to ride the thirty miles to Elizabethtown. His intention was to attend a synod meeting there, but he was disappointed to learn it had removed to New York. Because of his continuing precarious health, he remained in Elizabethtown throughout that week and the next. Late in the afternoon on Saturday, October 11, he was seized with chills, followed by 'a hard fever and considerable pain.'

He remained very weak and hardly able to do anything throughout the week that followed. On Thursday he 'rode out about four miles' on his horse but 'took cold' in the process. As the week wore on he was grieved to see the hours slip away while he was unable to do anything active in God's service. After attending public worship the following Sunday, October 19, he reflected: 'Was composed and comfortable, willing either to die or live; but found it hard to be reconciled to the thoughts of living useless. Oh, that I might never live to be a burden to God's creation; but that I might be allowed to repair home when my "sojourning" (1 Pet. 1:17) work is done!'

By riding a short distance each day, he was able to return to Cranberry in the first half of the next week. When he arrived home, thoroughly spent, on Thursday: 'Went to my own house and set things in order. Was very weak and somewhat melancholy: Labored to do something, but had no strength; and was forced to lie down on my bed, very solitary.'

On Friday he oversaw and directed the Indians in mending a fence to protect their wheat. Likely he was a bit disheartened when he related: 'Found that all their concerns of a secular nature depended upon me.' Still, the beneficial activity of the day was encouraging to him: 'Was somewhat refreshed in the evening, having been able to do something valuable in the daytime.'

Feeling 'much better in body than usual' the next day, he visited several of the natives and spent some time in writing. Late in the afternoon he felt so well that he started entertaining thoughts of preaching on the morrow. But such prospects vanished when his health took another sudden downturn and he spent the night coughing and spitting blood.

Throughout the following day – Sunday, October 26 – he was pained to see the members of his congregation wandering about 'as sheep not having a shepherd' (Mark 6:34), waiting and hoping that he would be able to preach to them. 'It could not but distress me to see 'em in this case, and to find myself unable to attempt anything for their spiritual benefit.' Feeling a little better late in the afternoon, he invited the Indians to his house, where he expounded on Matthew 5:1-16 while sitting down.

As he emphasized the final verse of that passage, a number of the congregants seemed concerned that their own lifestyle might be deficient to recommend the true religion of Christianity to others. One man in particular, who some time earlier had fallen back into drunkenness, 'was now deeply convinced of his sin and the great dishonor done to religion by his misconduct, and discovered [manifested] a great degree of grief and concern on that account.' Those responses were refreshing to the missionary: 'And though I had no strength to speak so much as I would have done, but was obliged to lie down on the bed: yet I rejoiced to see such an humble melting in the congregation; and that divine truths, though faintly delivered, were attended with so much efficacy upon the auditory.'

He was visited by two 'dear friends' on Monday afternoon and spent some time in conversation with them. Perhaps at the invitation of those unidentified friends, he rode the eight miles to Princeton the next day. Along the way, however, he was overtaken by 'such a violent fever' that he had to stop and lie down for a time at the home of another anonymous acquaintance. Apparently he was able to complete the journey to Princeton later that same day, and it appears he stayed there the remainder of the week.

Late that Tuesday afternoon four of his acquaintances from Pennsylvania arrived to visit him. Facilitating this visit likely was the primary reason for his having been invited to Princeton. His visitors included Richard Treat of Abington, Charles and Anne Beatty of Neshaminy (who had wed just four months earlier), and 'another friend' whose identity was not revealed. They were doubtless well aware of his precarious health. Their visit shows the esteem and concern that they had for him.

The next day he rode about ten miles with those friends before parting company with three of them. According to David, one of the friends, who again was not identified, 'stayed on purpose to keep me company and cheer my spirits.' After the exertions of the day, he was extremely weak and feverish that night.

He rode the three or four miles to Kingston on Thursday to visit Eleazer Wales. Despite continued weakness and fever, Friday was passed 'among friends in a comfortable frame of mind' back in Princeton. The following afternoon he bid farewell to his friends, then rode back to Cranberry.

That night he was oppressed with a cough, a fever and a sharp pain in his chest. Throughout the next day – November 2, 1746, his final Sunday in Cranberry – he was barely able to sit up. As on the previous Lord's Day, so now his greatest distress came from not being able to minister to the spiritual needs of his beloved congregation:

> Was grieved and almost sunk to see my poor people destitute of the means of grace; especially considering they could not read, and so were under great disadvantages for spending the Sabbath comfortably. Oh, methought, I could be contented to be sick if my poor flock had a faithful pastor to feed them with spiritual knowledge! A view of their want of this was more afflictive to me than all my bodily illness.

He took leave of his congregation the following day. Perhaps his friends had encouraged him in that direction during their visits of the previous week. Of the reasons for his decision as well as his immediate future plans he wrote: 'Being now in so weak and low a state that I was utterly incapable of performing my work, and having little hope of recovery, unless by much riding, I thought it my duty to take a lengthy journey into New England and to divert myself among my friends whom I had not now seen for a long time.'

Before leaving his people, he spent most of the day visiting them in their respective homes. Ever one to admonish the natives for their own spiritual welfare, he now sought to leave each one with a parting word that would be 'most proper and suitable' for their individual circumstances. He was grateful to experience great freedom and assistance in doing that. Tears were shed in many homes as the Indians considered his fervent farewell remarks and contemplated the imminent departure of their devoted pastor. Given his precarious health, doubtless some wondered if they would ever see him again.

After making a final visit and address to the children at the school, he rode, late in the afternoon, two miles to the house where he had previously lodged. As he spent the night there, he reflected: 'Was refreshed this evening, in that I had left my congregation so well disposed and affected, and that I had been so much assisted in making my farewell addresses to them.'

28

ILLNESS AT ELIZABETHTOWN

The next day, Tuesday, November 4, Brainerd rode twenty miles northeast to Woodbridge, where he lodged with John Pierson. A 1711 graduate of Yale, Pierson pastored at Woodbridge from 1717 until 1752. He had helped form the independent Synod of New York along with Jonathan Dickinson and Ebenezer Pemberton.[1]

Brainerd continued on to Dickinson's home in Elizabethtown on Wednesday. It was his intention to prosecute his journey into New England as soon as possible, but within an hour or two after arriving at Dickinson's he took a marked turn for the worse. For nearly a week he was confined to a bedroom and had to spend most of his time in bed. After that he was able to move about the house, but was still confined indoors.

As he continued to recover, he often (though not always) enjoyed periods of intense praise and petition:

After I had been in Elizabethtown about a fortnight, and had so far recovered that I was able to walk about the house, upon a day of thanksgiving kept in this place, I was enabled to recall and recount over the mercies of God in such a manner as greatly affected me and filled me (I think) with thankfulness and praise to God: Especially my soul praised Him for His work of grace among the Indians and the enlargement of His dear kingdom: My soul blessed God for what He is in Himself, and adored Him, that He ever would display Himself to creatures: ...

1. Pettit, *Life of David Brainerd*, p. 437.

> After this comfortable thanksgiving season, I frequently
> enjoyed freedom and enlargement and engagedness of soul
> in prayer, and was enabled to intercede with God for my
> dear congregation, very often for every family and every
> person in particular; and it was often a great comfort to me
> that I could pray heartily to God for those to whom I could
> not speak, and whom I was not allowed to see. But at other
> times my spirits were so flat and low, and my bodily vigor so
> much wasted, that I had scarce any affections at all.

In December he recovered far enough that he was able to go for walks out-of-doors and visit friends. Around Christmastime, however, he caught another cold. His health again began to decline, and continued to do so through the end of January, 1747. A violent cough, high fever, 'asthmatic disorder,' a complete loss of appetite and an inability to keep down the food he forced himself to eat reduced him to so low a state that his friends generally despaired of his life. For quite some time, some of his acquaintances scarcely thought he could live to the end of each new day.

On Sunday, February 1, he received special comfort and encouragement while contemplating Luke 11:13: 'If ye then, being evil, know how to give good gifts unto your children: how much more shall your heavenly Father give the Holy Spirit to them that ask Him?' He was enabled, 'with a childlike spirit,' to plead that passage in his own behalf, and was reminded that God in His faithfulness had dealt with him 'better than any earthly parent can do with his child.' That season of prayer and meditation so refreshed his soul that his body also seemed to benefit from it. From that time on he began gradually to recover.

After having been in Elizabethtown for nearly four months, on Tuesday, February 24, he was able to ride to Newark to visit Aaron Burr. Upon returning to Dickinson's home the next day, he wrote: 'My spirits were somewhat refreshed with the ride, though my body was weary.'

An Indian from his Cranberry congregation, perhaps Moses Tattamy, visited him on the Saturday of that same week. The native brought letters and a positive report of the 'sober and good behavior' of the Christian Indians in general. 'This refreshed my soul,' Brainerd commented. 'I could not but soon retire and bless God for His goodness; and found, I trust, a truly thankful frame of spirit, that God seemed to be building up that congregation for Himself.'

The following Wednesday, March 4, he received a rebuke from a friend concerning an undisclosed matter. Though thinking the reproof was not actually deserved, he nonetheless perceived that God used it for his spiritual good. But not surprisingly, the reproof led to further introspection and melancholy:

> I met with reproof from a friend, which although I thought I did not deserve it from him, yet was (I trust) blessed of God to make me more tenderly afraid of sin, more jealous over myself, and more concerned to keep both heart and life pure and unblameable: It likewise caused me to reflect on my past deadness and want of spirituality, and to abhor myself and look on myself [as] most unworthy. This frame of mind continued the next day; and for several days after, I grieved to think that in my necessary diversions I had not maintained more seriousness, solemnity, heavenly affection and conversation. And thus my spirits were often depressed and sunk; and yet, I trust, that reproof was made to be beneficial to me.

A day of corporate prayer and fasting was held in Elizabethtown one week later, March 11. For the first time since the previous December 21st he was able to attend public worship. For him it was an occasion of thankfulness to God for preserving his life as well as consecrating his life anew to God's glory.

He was again able to attend public worship service the following Lord's Day, March 15. Significantly, as he did: 'felt some earnest desires of being restored to the ministerial work: Felt, I think, some spirit and life to speak for God.' Consequently, on the Wednesday and Thursday of that week he rode to Cranberry to visit his native congregation. His physical and emotional condition was probably not strong enough for the twenty-six mile journey, for as he rode he found himself 'under great dejection.'

Still, he rose early on Friday morning and walked around visiting the Indians and inquiring about their 'state and concerns.'

Upon hearing 'some things disagreeable,' he was left with an even heavier burden on his spirits. Praying about his concerns failed to bring relief: 'I endeavored to go to God with my distresses, and made some kind of lamentable complaint; but notwithstanding, my mind continued very gloomy.'

Around ten o'clock that morning he gathered his congregation. After explaining a psalm and singing it with them, he led in a time of prayer. The natives were deeply stirred: 'There was a considerable deal of affection among them; I doubt not, in some instances, that which was more than merely natural.'

An hour later he left Cranberry for the final time. That Friday – March 20, 1747 – was the last occasion he ever saw his beloved native congregation in this life.

He made his way back to Elizabethtown that afternoon and the next day. There, his strength completely depleted, he 'continued for a considerable time under a great degree of dejection.'

'Violent griping pains' seized him the following Saturday, March 28. For several hours his distress was so extreme and constant that it seemed impossible for him to live another full day. Through God's blessing on an undisclosed treatment, his pain abated, though he was left excessively weak. His weakness lingered for several days as he continued to suffer from a fever, cough and night sweats.

Judging by the activities he was able to participate in beginning the second week of April, however, it seems clear that his health had improved somewhat by that point. On Tuesday, April 7, he rode to Newark in order to officiate at the wedding of Jonathan Dickinson and Mary Crane that evening. This was Dickinson's second marriage. Somewhat shocking to modern sensibilities is the fact that while Dickinson was fifty-nine years old at the time, his new bride was but twenty-seven.[2] The considerable age difference of the couple apparently was not at all unsettling to Brainerd. According to his diary, after performing the ceremony he returned to Elizabethtown 'in a pleasant frame, full of composure and sweetness.'

2. Wynbeek, *Beloved Yankee*, p. 237.

Two days later he was back in Newark for the ordination service of Nathaniel Tucker followed by the licensure examination of Caleb Smith. (As is still the case in some denominations today, ministers of that day were licensed for a time before receiving their permanent ordination.) Tucker was born in Milton, Massachusetts, in 1725 and graduated from Harvard in 1744. According to Jonathan Edwards, he was 'a worthy, pious young gentleman.' Sadly, just eight months after his ordination, he became ill on a journey and died in Stratfield, Connecticut.[3]

Smith, a 1743 graduate of Yale, was engaged to Dickinson's youngest daughter, Martha, at the time of his licensing. Following his licensure, he served for a year as the first tutor of the newly formed College of New Jersey. (The establishment of that institution will be considered later in this chapter.) He was then called to take Aaron Burr's place as pastor at Newark, after the latter assumed the presidency of the infant college.[4]

After spending Friday morning in other Presbyterial business, Brainerd rode back to Elizabethtown that afternoon. There he discovered that his brother John had arrived, and they spent some time in conversation. But following the exertions of the busy week, Brainerd's body was 'extreme weak and outdone,' his spirits 'considerably sunk' and his mind 'dejected.'

The following Monday, April 13, he assisted in the examination of John, who was being considered as his replacement to minister to the Indians at Cranberry. John had graduated from Yale the previous year and had subsequently been approached by the Scottish Society commissioners about assuming oversight of the native congregation during his brother's absence due to illness. Having been approved to take his brother's place, John left the next day for Cranberry.

David Brainerd had his twenty-ninth, and as it turned out final, birthday six days later, on Monday, April 20. He was still in a 'very disordered state' physically and spent much of the day in bed. Thankfully, however, he 'enjoyed a little more comfort' spiritually than he had for several days.

3.   Pettit, *Life of David Brainerd*, p. 441.
4.   Ibid., p. 442.

When he first left Cranberry early the previous November, he had intended to attempt to recover his health by riding back to New England to visit friends and relatives. Now, five and a half months later, he determined to prosecute that plan once again. Consequently, the following day he set out on the next leg of that journey by traveling to New York.

An historically significant development that had been taking shape the past six months, and of which Brainerd would have been fully aware, is well worth noting before continuing on with the narrative of his life. In recent years Jonathan Dickinson and some of his colleagues had become increasingly convinced that a new college was needed to train sound, progressive Evangelical ministers who could serve the rapidly growing number of congregations that held to New Side convictions. To that end the College of New Jersey (later to become Princeton College) was chartered in October of 1746, and Dickinson was chosen to be its first president.

It is generally agreed that Brainerd's expulsion from Yale almost certainly played a definite role in hastening the establishment of the College of New Jersey. In his 1857 work, *The Geneaology of the Brainerd Family in the United States*, David Dudley Field testified: 'I once heard the Hon. John Dickinson, son of the Rev. Mr Dickinson, of Norwalk, say that the establishment of Princeton College was owing to the sympathy felt for David Brainerd because the authorities of Yale College would not give him his degree, and that the plan of the college was drawn up in his father's house.' The John Dickinson here cited by Field was Chief Judge of the Middlesex County Court of Connecticut, and his father was Moses Dickinson, pastor of the church in Norwalk, Connecticut.

Archibald Alexander, in his 1851 volume, *Biographical Sketches of the Founder and Principal Alumni of the Log College*, similarly records:

> Messrs. Dickinson and Burr, the former pastor of the Presbyterian Church in Elizabethtown, and the latter in Newark, took the lead in this enterprise [the establishment of the College of New Jersey]. Both these distinguished divines were graduates of Yale College; but just at this time

their minds probably experienced some alienation from their alma mater on account of the harsh treatment which Mr David Brainerd had received from the officers of that college; for he had been expelled merely for a harsh word spoken in private company and overheard by a student who happened to be passing the door, who knew not to whom it referred.

The attachment of all the members of the New York Synod to Mr Brainerd was warm, and deservedly so. This affair, it is probable, quickened the zeal of these excellent men to get up a college of their own. Some years ago the writer [Archibald Alexander] heard the relict [widow] of the late Dr Scott, of New Brunswick, say that when she was a little girl she heard the Rev. Mr Burr declare in her father's house in Newark, 'if it had not been for the treatment Mr Brainerd received at Yale, New Jersey College would never have been erected.'

Thomas Brainerd, in his 1865 biography of David Brainerd's brother, John, concluded: 'This testimony of the Rev. Dr Alexander so corroborates the statements of the Rev. Dr Field, that we may regard the question as settled, that the expulsion of David Brainerd from Yale led to the founding of Princeton College.'

When the College of New Jersey first opened at the end of May, 1747, classes were held in Jonathan Dickinson's house. Some have considered Brainerd to be the first student enrolled in the college since he resided in Dickinson's home that year. Such, however, seems clearly not to have been the case since he left Elizabethtown the month before the college actually opened.[5]

As Jonathan Dickinson and his family bid farewell to the still relatively frail consumptive that April 21, they may very well have wondered if he would indeed recover or, instead, soon finish his

5. The above summary is compiled from: David Dudley Field, *The Geneaology of the Brainerd Family in the United States* (New York, John F. Trow, Printer, 1857), pp. 265-6; Archibald Alexander, *Biographical Sketches of the Founder and Principal Alumni of the Log College* (Philadelphia, Presbyterian Board of Publication, 1851), pp. 77-8; Thomas Brainerd, *The Life of John Brainerd* (Philadelphia, Presbyterian Publication Company, 1865), pp. 56-7; Pettit, *Life of David Brainerd*, pp. 55-6; Wynbeek, *Beloved Yankee*, p. 94.

earthly course. They would have had no way of knowing that just a few short months from then Dickinson himself would suddenly fall ill and precede Brainerd in death by two days.

29

NEAR DEATH AT BOSTON

After leaving New Jersey, Brainerd slowly made his way back to his home area of Haddam, Connecticut, arriving there around the beginning of May, 1747. On Sunday, May 10, he was 'much exercised' while at Hadlyme, about seven miles southeast of Haddam, on the Connecticut River. His perturbation may have come from some spiritual misgiving in his own soul or, perhaps more likely, from having encountered an erroneous teaching on that occasion. Whatever the cause, he was grateful for the Scripture's teaching that a holy life provides the regenerate believer with assurance of salvation and eternal life:

> I could not but feel some measure of gratitude to God at this time (wherein I was much exercised) that He had always disposed me, in my ministry, to insist on the great doctrines of 'regeneration,' 'the new creature,' 'faith in Christ,' 'progressive sanctification,' 'supreme love of God,' 'living entirely to the glory of God,' 'being not our own,' and the like: God has helped me to see, in the surest manner, from time to time, that these, and the like doctrines necessarily connected with them, are the only foundation of safety and salvation for perishing sinners; and that those divine dispositions, which are consonant hereto, are that 'holiness, without which no man shall see the Lord' (Heb. 12:14): The exercise of these Godlike tempers, wherein the soul acts in a kind of concert with God, and would be and do everything that is pleasing to God; this, I saw, would stand by the soul in a dying hour;

for God must, I think 'deny Himself' (2 Tim. 2:13) if He casts away 'His own image' (Gen. 1:27), even the soul that is one in desires with Himself.

He traveled up the Connecticut River valley and into Massachusetts two weeks later. Sunday, May 24, found him five miles north of Enfield, Connecticut, at Longmeadow, Massachusetts, near Springfield. On Thursday he rode the nearly twenty miles north from Longmeadow to Jonathan Edwards' home in Northampton.

Given Edwards' vibrant Evangelical spirit, his prominence and the warm support he had lent Brainerd in petitioning the Yale officials nearly four years earlier, it is not at all surprising that the ailing missionary desired to pay a visit to the Northampton divine. Edwards, for his part, had both heard reports and read Brainerd's Journal account of the dramatic spiritual awakening among the Indians.[1] He would have welcomed the opportunity to receive the missionary's first-hand account of those events.

Edwards gives no indication that he had been anticipating a visit from the missionary. Brainerd's visit was likely unannounced, and would not have been considered at all rude or abnormal. Christian leaders of that era were accustomed to opening their homes on short notice to traveling fellow believers. It seems clear from Brainerd's many travels that he had often been hosted in the homes of fellow Christians without prior arrangements having been made.

Probably he planned to spend a few days at Northampton, then to move on and visit elsewhere. The sudden collapse of his health was doubtless responsible for the change in those plans.

From Edwards' editorial comment concerning Brainerd's arrival at Northampton on May 28, it appears that while he had received considerable second-hand information about the missionary, this was only their second personal meeting:

I had had much opportunity, before this, of particular information concerning him, from many that were well acquainted with him; and had myself once an opportunity

1.   Murray, *Jonathan Edwards*, p. 303.

of considerable conversation and some acquaintance with him at New Haven, near four years before, in the time of the commencement when he offered that confession to the Rector of the college, ... I being one he was pleased then several times to consult on that affair.

In the days that followed Brainerd's arrival, Edwards observed of him: 'I found him remarkably sociable, pleasant, and entertaining in his conversation; yet solid, savory, spiritual, and very profitable; appearing meek, modest, and humble; far from any stiffness, moroseness, superstitious demureness, or affected singularity in speech or behavior, and seeming to nauseate [detest] all such things.'

During the first week of June, Brainerd consulted with Doctor Samuel Mather at Edwards' home about his illness. Mather, a 1726 Yale graduate, was Northampton's first regular physician. He practiced medicine there for forty-three years, from 1736 till his death at age seventy-three in April of 1779.[2] His prognosis for Brainerd was not at all optimistic. He plainly told the missionary he was in a confirmed state of consumption. The physician could give him no encouragement he would ever recover.

Edwards reported that Brainerd received the news with perfect calm: 'But it seemed not to occasion the least discomposure in him, nor to make any manner of alteration as to the cheerfulness and serenity of his mind, or the freedom or pleasantness of his conversation.'

Mather and other physicians concurred in advising him to continue his horseback riding as the activity that would tend, above any other means, to prolong his life. For a time he was at a loss 'which way to bend his course next,' but he finally decided to ride to Boston, some eighty miles to the east.

The Edwards' determined that their second oldest daughter, seventeen-year-old Jerusha, should accompany Brainerd on the journey, to assist him in his weakened condition. Edwards would later testify that 'she had manifested a heart uncommonly devoted to God, in the course of her life, many years before her death.' He also revealed that she was 'generally esteemed the flower of the

2. Pettit, *Life of David Brainerd*, p. 446.

family.'[3] The latter remark likely was a reference to her physical as well as spiritual beauty and the attractiveness of her personality.

Jonathan Edwards' eldest daughter, named Sarah after her mother, was nineteen at the time of Brainerd's visit. Mrs Edwards had given birth to her tenth child just a few weeks earlier and likely needed her oldest daughter's assistance in caring for the younger children. In addition, Eleazar Wheelock was also a visitor in the Edwards' home at that time and was in very poor health. So serious was Wheelock's condition that Jonathan Edwards wondered if he would ever preach again.[4] Daughter Sarah would have been needed to help nurse him.

As has already been seen, some have postulated, based on highly speculative suppositions, that Brainerd and Jerusha's relationship was a romantic one and that they were engaged to be married. It is undoubtedly true that a special bond developed between them as she helped to care for him during the closing months of his life. It is known that they came to have a deep, mutual admiration and affection for each other. They shared much in common spiritually.

But during those months, as throughout the preceding years, not a single statement made by Brainerd or Jonathan Edwards indicates that a romantic attachment or commitment existed between the missionary and Jerusha. Taking the available evidence at face value leads to the conclusion that theirs was a relationship of respected, cherished friends and spiritual family members, but did not include a romantic aspect.

One other significant consideration reinforces that conclusion. In the final months of his life, Brainerd maintained his earnest desire to go to be with the Lord as soon as his earthly usefulness to Christ had come to an end. It seems unlikely that such would have continued to be his outlook if he had been nurturing a romantic relationship with Jerusha.

The pair set out for Boston on Tuesday, June 9. They traveled slow-ly and stopped now and again so he could make the

3. Pettit, *Life of David Brainerd*, pp. 70, 475.
4. Murray, *Jonathan Edwards*, pp. 309-10.

acquaintance of several ministers along the way. By averaging twenty miles a day, they arrived in Boston on Friday.

They were hosted in the home of Edward Bromfield, an eminent Boston merchant and a member of the Old South Church. Brainerd spent the first half of the next week visiting various ministers of the town, who received him with great respect.

Then on Thursday, June 18, he suddenly fell extremely ill, even being 'brought to the gates of death.' He had a high fever, a violent cough and extreme pain in his head and chest. At times he became delirious. He remained in that condition till Saturday evening, when he seemed to be in the throes of death. His host family stayed up with him till one or two o'clock Sunday morning, expecting every hour would be his last.

His attending physician was Joseph Pynchon, whose fame as a doctor had spread from Boston to Salem. The physician was also a preacher, a justice of the peace, and an overseer of Harvard College, from which he had graduated in 1726.[5] Pynchon, whose medical opinions were held in highest esteem, diagnosed Brainerd's difficulties as being due to the eruption of pus-filled ulcers in his lungs.

He seemed only slightly better on Sunday. Though his headache was less severe, he still had sharp pain in his chest and great difficulty breathing. Monday his condition was generally improved. But after being able to sleep only a little that night, he was again much worse the next morning. Jerusha included the physician's indefinite prognosis in a letter home to her family that same Tuesday, June 23: 'Doctor Pynchon says he has no hopes of his life; nor does he think it likely he will ever come out of the chamber; though he says he may be able to come to Northampton.'

When she wrote her family again the following Monday, his condition was still very grave:

> Mr Brainerd has not so much pain nor fever, since I last wrote, as before: Yet he is extremely weak and low, and very faint, expecting every day will be his last. ... He has hardly vigor enough to draw his breath. I went this morning into town, and when I came home Mr Bromfield said he never

5. Pettit, *Life of David Brainerd*, p. 453.

> expected I should see him alive; for he lay two hours, as they thought, dying; one could scarcely tell whether he was alive or not; he was not able to speak for some time: But now [he] is much as he was before. The doctor thinks he will drop away in such a turn. ... Doctor Pynchon says he should not be surprised if he should so recover as to live half a year; nor would it surprise him if he should die in half a day. ...

During the first two days of this illness he had sometimes been delirious. Beginning the third day, however, and continuing for the next four or five weeks, he experienced constant and exceptional mental and spiritual clarity. As he lay near death, he contemplated at length his beliefs and the assurance they brought him even at the brink of eternity.

He remained in an extremely weak condition for a few weeks. Frequently he was reduced so low that he became completely speechless, not even being able to whisper a word. Even after he had recovered well enough to walk around the house and to step outdoors, he continued to suffer daily spells of faintness that usually lasted four or five hours. During those times he could not carry on a conversation or even speak a single sentence without pauses for breath.

At that time he composed a number of letters to friends and relatives. Edwards preserved three of those in his account of Brainerd's life.[6] They brim over with the fervent, affectionate perspectives of one who anticipates imminent entrance into eternity and separation from his cherished earthly acquaintances. To his brother Israel at Yale he wrote:

> Boston, June 30, 1747
>
> My dear Brother,
>
> It is from the sides of eternity I now address you. I am heartily sorry that I have so little strength to write what I long so much to communicate to you. But let me tell you, my brother, eternity is another thing than we ordinarily take it to be in a healthful state. Oh, how vast and boundless! Oh, how fixed and unalterable! Oh, of what infinite importance

---

6.   Pettit, *Life of David Brainerd*, pp. 493-9.

is it that we be prepared for eternity! I have been just a dying now for more than a week; and all around me have thought me so: But in this time I have had clear views of eternity; have seen the blessedness of the godly, in some measure; and have longed to share their happy state, as well as been comfortably satisfied that through grace I shall do so: But oh, what anguish is raised in my mind to think of an eternity for those who are Christless, for those who are mistaken and who bring their false hopes to the grave with them! The sight was so dreadful I could by no means bear it: My thoughts recoiled, and I said (but under a more affecting sense than ever before), 'who can dwell with everlasting burnings' (Isa. 33:14)? Oh, methought, that I could now see my friends, that I might warn them to see to it they lay their foundation for eternity sure.

And you, my dear brother, I have been particularly concerned for; and have wondered I so much neglected conversing with you about your spiritual state at our last meeting. Oh, my brother, let me then beseech you now to examine whether you are indeed a 'new creature' (2 Cor. 5:17)? Whether you have ever acted above self? Whether the glory of God has ever been the sweetest, highest concern with you? Whether you have ever been reconciled to all the perfections of God; in a word, whether God has been your 'portion' (Ps. 73:26), and a holy conformity to Him your chief delight? If you can't answer positively, consider seriously the frequent breathings of your soul: but don't, however, put yourself off with a slight answer. If you have reason to think you are graceless [not possessing saving grace], oh, give yourself and the throne of grace no rest till God arise and save! But if the case should be otherwise, bless God for His grace and press after holiness.

My soul longs that you should be fitted for, and in due time go into the work of, the ministry. I can't bear to think of your going into any other business in life. Don't be discouraged because you see your elder brothers in the ministry die early, one after another: I declare, now I am dying, I would not have spent my life otherwise for the whole world. But I must leave this with God.

If this line should come to your hands soon after the date, I should be almost desirous you should set out on a journey to me: It may be you may see me alive; which I should much rejoice in. But if you can't come, I must commit you to the grace of God, where you are. May He be your guide and counselor, your sanctifier and eternal portion.

Oh, my dear brother, flee fleshly lusts and the enchanting amusements, as well as corrupt doctrines, of the present day; and strive to live to God.

Take this as the last line from

> Your affectionate, dying brother,
> D. Brainerd.

To the above letter Edwards added an important editorial note: 'Mr Brainerd afterwards had greater satisfaction concerning the state of his brother's soul, by much opportunity of conversation with him before his death.'

Brainerd's two other surviving letters from that time were written to his brother John and to 'a young gentleman, a candidate for the work of the ministry, for whom he had a special friendship.' The latter was probably Nehemiah Greenman, whose college expense Brainerd had underwritten.

30

Temporary Recovery

During his ongoing confinement in Boston, Brainerd was asked to edit the diary of a deceased New England pastor, Thomas Shepard (1605–49). The diary, which had been left to Shepard's son, had just recently come to light and was being prepared for publication later that year as *Meditations and Spiritual Experiences of Mr Thomas Shepard*. A popular preacher and writer in his lifetime, Shepard's writings were greatly appreciated by Jonathan Edwards. The Northampton divine had quoted Shepard no fewer than seventy-five times in his *Treatise Concerning the Religious Affections*.[1] Brainerd carefully read through Shepard's papers and 'made some corrections where the sense was left dark for want of a word or two.'

As his condition began to improve somewhat, he received numerous visits from ministers from both the city and surrounding countryside. 'He was much visited, while in Boston,' reported Edwards, 'by many persons of considerable note and figure, and of the best character, and by some of the first rank: who showed him uncommon respect, and appeared highly pleased and entertained with his conversation.' Brainerd related:

> I had many visitants with whom, when I was able to speak, I always conversed of the things of religion; and was peculiarly disposed and assisted in distinguishing between the true and false religion of the times: There was scarce any subject that has been matter of debate in the late day,

1. Pettit, *Life of David Brainerd*, p. 451; Wynbeek, *Beloved Yankee*, p. 240.

but what I was at one time or other brought to a sort of necessity to discourse upon, and show my opinion in; and that frequently before numbers of people; ...

He also received a visit from a delegation of commissioners in Boston representing the Society in London for Propagating the Gospel in New England and Parts Adjacent. The commissioners had recently been entrusted with a legacy from Daniel Williams, a nonconformist English divine and benefactor who toward the end of his life gave active support to missionary societies in both London and Edinburgh. Williams' bequest was to support two missionaries to American natives, and the Boston commissioners came to seek Brainerd's advice about the possibility of establishing a mission to Indians of the Six Nations. They were highly impressed with his understanding of native ministry, so asked him to search out and recommend two individuals whom he perceived would be fit for that line of ministry.

Another group of 'pious and generously disposed gentlemen in Boston' paid him a visit, learned that Bibles were needed for the native school and promptly purchased three dozen for that purpose. They contributed an additional fourteen pounds toward other needs of the Indian ministry at that time and later made further donations to the Cranberry work.

Israel Brainerd, upon receiving his dying brother's correspondence at Yale, hastened to Boston, hoping to visit with him once more before he died, but little expecting he would have the opportunity. David Brainerd rejoiced greatly to see his brother and to converse with him about spiritual matters, including Israel's own spiritual standing. Their joyous meeting was tinged by sorrow, however, for Israel brought the news that their sister, Jerusha, had recently fallen suddenly ill and died at Haddam. According to Edwards, 'a peculiarly dear affection and much intimacy in spiritual matters' had long subsisted between David Brainerd and this sister. He was stunned by the news of her sudden passing, but also comforted by the expectation that he would soon be reunited with her in heaven.

To the astonishment of himself and all who had witnessed his recent grave illness, Brainerd's health continued to improve.

On his last Sunday in Boston, July 19, he was taken in a chaise to the Old South Church, where he heard Joseph Sewall preach. Sewall, known as 'the weeping prophet,' had opened his pulpit to George Whitefield in 1740 and generally retained a favorable opinion toward the Great Awakening. He pastored the Old South congregation for fifty-six years, from 1713 until his death at age eighty-one in 1769.

That afternoon Brainerd heard a sermon delivered by Thomas Prince, noted co-pastor of the same church. Prince had been Sewall's colleague since 1718 and was Boston's leading champion of Whitefield. One year older than Sewall, Prince died eleven years before him, in 1758.[2]

On Monday Brainerd had occasion to discuss and debate a troubling theological issue of the day with an individual who, according to Edwards, had 'very publicly and strenuously appeared to defend that tenet.' The dogma was referred to as 'the doctrine of *particular* faith' and was characterized by the statement of belief 'that Christ died for me in particular.' According to the proponents of this view (and contrary to common Puritan teaching), before salvation a person did not need to pass through a protracted, troubled period of preparation in which he sensed his separation from God due to his sinfulness and cried out to Him for saving mercy. Rather, he simply needed to believe that Christ had died for him in particular (not just for sinners in general), and he would immediately be saved.

Some who were of that persuasion interpreted the doctrine of justification by faith so strictly that they taught that repentance, contrition, humiliation or love to God were not needed to receive saving faith. They insisted that any such qualifications were conditions that were contrary to the pure doctrine of justification by faith alone.

Some in that camp also leaned toward antinomianism. They stated that because the Bible teaches justification through faith alone, a person did not need a life of good works following a profession of faith in Christ to prove he had been genuinely saved.

2. Pettit, *Life of David Brainerd*, pp. 455-6.

Such a perspective ran counter to the Puritan understanding that while Scripture teaches justification by faith, it also insists on a holy life following conversion as the positive proof of the genuineness of one's profession of faith.

While it is not known with certainty, the individual with whom Brainerd debated that Monday, July 20, may well have been Andrew Croswell, the leading proponent of such perspectives at the time. Croswell, a 1728 Harvard graduate, was a controversial New Light minister who first pastored in Groton, Connecticut, before settling in Boston in 1746. He had stirred up much controversy through his extensive ministry as an itinerant evangelist and through the numerous pamphlets he published. An extremist, he had broken with, then attacked, such highly respected moderate New Lights as Edwards and Jonathan Dickinson.[3]

Using many scriptural and rational arguments on that occasion, Brainerd spoke forcefully against the doctrine of particular faith and the antinomianism it tended to promote. The debate took place in the presence of 'a number of considerable persons' who had come to say farewell to Brainerd, as he was planning to leave Boston for Northampton that afternoon. Those individuals seemed highly approving of his discourse and the strong rationale he used to confirm his assertions. Several of them expressed their appreciation and affirmation to him after the meeting concluded.

After bidding an affectionate farewell to his friends, he set out late in the afternoon on the first leg of the journey back to Northampton. He was accompanied by his brother Israel, Jerusha Edwards and an unidentified 'honorable person' from Boston who rode with them for several miles before returning home. A number of other gentlemen desired to accompany him for a ways as a testimony of their esteem and respect for him. But his aversion to anything that suggested pomp and show prevented them from doing so.

3. For an excellent summary of Croswell's ministerial career and theological perspectives, see: Leigh Eric Schmidt, ' "A Second and Glorious Reformation": The New Light Extremism of Andrew Croswell,' *William and Mary Quarterly* 43 (1986): 214-44.

Because of that same aversion, he was actually relieved to be leaving Boston. He knew that funerals there were often attended by considerable display. Only with much difficulty had he been able to reconcile himself to the prospect of dying there, knowing that much to-do would likely be made of his funeral and that great public honor would be paid to him. He was pleased, therefore, when God granted his desire, which he had clearly expressed, of returning to Northampton. He knew that if, as he anticipated, he were to die there, his funeral and burial would be a quieter, less publicized affair.

By riding about sixteen miles per day the trio was able to reach its destination by Saturday, July 25. Israel left for New Haven the following Wednesday. David Brainerd did not expect to see him again this side of eternity.

The doctrinal matters he had publicly debated the day he left Boston continued to weigh heavily on his mind. He started to compose a letter to the individual with whom he had contended. He wished to express his concern about the dangerous tendency of some of the tenets his opponent had expressed both during their conversation and in his published writings. According to Edwards, however, he lacked the strength to finish the correspondence.

But he did capitalize on another writing opportunity presented to him at that time. The same individuals who had enlisted him in Boston to edit Thomas Shepard's diary now desired him to write a preface for the intended publication of that volume. In complying with that request, Brainerd penned some of his perspectives on genuine and counterfeit Christianity, a theme that had been much on his heart in recent weeks. He pointed out what he considered to be various inadequate bases that numerous people in the recent Awakening had had for thinking themselves Christians. He also expressed concerns about the type of unspiritual fruit that had been produced in the lives of individuals who had experienced such so-called conversions.[4]

---

4. Brainerd's remarks on these subjects as prepared for the preface to Thomas Shepard's diary are preserved in Pettit, *Life of David Brainerd*, pp. 513-15.

Another topic he talked much about in the final weeks of life was 'that future prosperity of Zion that is so often foretold and promised in the Scripture.' Edwards revealed that though Brainerd had no hope of living to see the flourishing of Christ's kingdom on earth, his desires and prayers for that to come about actually intensified the closer he drew to death.

Brainerd was greatly surprised and perplexed that Christian ministers and their congregations were not more disposed to pray for the widespread expansion of Christianity throughout the world. He wondered that such a small part of their prayers in their families, churches and elsewhere was generally devoted to that theme. On a number of occasions he expressed his amazement that there had not been a more ready willingness on the part of American church leaders to comply with a related proposal that in recent years had come out of Scotland.

Three years earlier, in October of 1744, a group of ministers in Scotland formed a prayer union to intercede for the worldwide extension and prosperity of the kingdom of Christ. They agreed that some part of every Saturday evening and Sunday morning as well as the whole or part of the first Tuesday of every quarter would be given to 'united extraordinary supplications' to that end. Some of the Scottish divines subsequently corresponded with Edwards, sending news of the prayer concert, which was international in its objective. He immediately began promoting it to his congregation.

In 1746 the 'Concert for United Prayer' was renewed in Scotland for another seven years. A short 'Memorial' concerning the prayer union's purpose was drafted by the Scottish ministers, and nearly 500 copies were sent to New England. The following year Edwards sought to further the prayer accord in America and abroad by writing a book that provided a solid biblical and theological basis for such an emphasis. The work bore a long, descriptive title common in that era: *An Humble Attempt to Promote Explicit Agreement and Visible Union of God's People in Extraordinary Prayer, for the Revival of Religion and the Advancement of Christ's Kingdom on Earth, pursuant to Scripture – Promises and Prophecies concerning the Last Time.*

Edwards sent the volume to the printer by September of 1747, though it was not actually published till the following January.[5] Very likely he was finishing the writing of the manuscript while Brainerd was a guest in his home. Doubtless the two men talked at length about the accord and its glorious aim.

Brainerd sent as part of his dying advice to his native congregation in Cranberry an injunction that they should cooperate fully with the practices recommended in the prayer union. When Edwards published his account of Brainerd's life he was able to report that the Cranberry congregation had followed the missionary's directive in that regard 'with great cheerfulness and unanimity,' sometimes even 'with uncommon engagedness and fervency of spirit.' Edwards further noted that the Presbyteries of New York and New Brunswick as well as some other Christians in those areas had by that time 'with one consent fallen in with the proposal.'

5. The history of the development of the prayer union is discussed at more length in Murray, *Jonathan Edwards*, pp. 293-6.

31

Finishing the Course

Brainerd was so rejuvenated through his worship at Edwards' church on Sunday, August 16, 1747, that to himself and others it seemed that both his spirits and bodily strength had been greatly restored. The restoration proved fleeting, for Edwards reported: 'But this was the last time that ever he attended public worship on the Sabbath.'

Two days later Brainerd prayed with Edwards' family while the divine was away on a journey. He did so with great difficulty due to the return of his physical weakness. Again Edwards related: 'And this was the last family prayer that ever he made.'

Since returning to Northampton from Boston three weeks earlier, he had regularly ridden five or six miles per day in an effort to rebuild his health and strength. But that Thursday, August 20, marked the last time he was able to do so.

Throughout the week that followed he was too disordered from illness to read or write. Up to that time he had been staying in one of the Edwards' upstairs bedrooms. But by Friday, August 28, he had become too weak to maneuver the stairs, so the family made up a room for him on the ground floor.

A public lecture was held at the Northampton church the following Wednesday. Rev. Timothy Woodbridge, a 1732 Yale graduate and the pastor at nearby Hatfield, Massachusetts, was the featured speaker. Brainerd seemed heartened by the sight of the neighboring ministers gathering for the lecture and expressed a great desire to join in the meeting. He managed to ride the short distance to the church. Edwards later commented: 'He signified that he supposed it to be the last time that ever he should attend the public worship; as it proved. And indeed it was the last time that ever he went out at our gate alive.'

That Saturday, September 5, he was greatly encouraged by an unexpected visit from his brother, John. Brainerd rejoiced not only to see this brother who was especially dear to him, but also to hear the encouraging report that was brought about his beloved congregation at Cranberry. Thirty new Indians, including ten adults, had come since John's arrival the middle of April, bringing to 160 the number of natives settled there. All the newcomers seemed 'rationally convinced of the truth of the Christian religion' and under some degree of concern about their spiritual need. Most of them, in fact, appeared to be very concerned, and their convictions seemed to be genuine and abiding.

The Indians had also become 'much more comfortable' in handling their 'secular affairs.' That summer they had raised forty acres of English grain and nearly as many acres of Indian corn.[1]

Brainerd was further delighted, even 'exceeding glad,' when he learned that John had brought from Cranberry some of his private writings, including the personal diary he had kept the past few years. He was heartened as he began to read back through them in the days that followed:

> Lord's Day, September 6. I began to read some of my private writings, which my brother brought me; and was considerably refreshed with what I met with in them.

> Monday, September 7. I proceeded further in reading my old private writings, and found they had the same effect upon me as before: I could not but rejoice and bless God for what passed long ago, which without writing had been entirely lost.

Edwards later revealed[2] that as Brainerd had lain near death in Boston he was 'fully resolved' to leave 'absolute orders for

---

1.   Thomas Brainerd, *Life of John Brainerd*, pp. 116-18. This report of conditions at Cranberry is actually based on a letter that John Brainerd had written to Ebenezer Pemberton on June 23, 1747. Doubtless the verbal report that John was able to share with his brother at Northampton two and a half months later would have been quite similar.

2.   Pettit, *Life of David Brainerd*, p. 540.

the entire suppressing of his private papers.' Only through the considerable importunity of his acquaintances there was he restrained from giving such a binding injunction. But now, as he reviewed his personal writings in Northampton, he apparently perceived that others might profit from reading them. After that he was willing to acquiesce to the desires of friends. He entrusted his papers to Edwards to use after his death, in whatever way he thought would be most for God's glory.

However, unknown even to Edwards until after Brainerd's death was the fact that the missionary had ordered the destruction of a portion of his diary from his student days at Yale. He can hardly be faulted for keeping from publication private perspectives from that imbalanced period of his life. Those perspectives, first of all, were out of step with his later mature and spiritual outlook, and, secondly, would not have been beneficial for others to consider. The majority of prudent, spiritual Christians would likely make the same choice if faced with Brainerd's decision.

His feet had become noticeably swollen by Sunday, September 13, and continued to swell throughout the remaining days of his life. 'A symptom of his dissolution coming on,' Edwards commented.

John reluctantly left his ailing brother that Tuesday to attend to 'some business of great importance and necessity' back in New Jersey. He intended to return as soon as possible, hoping to see him once more before his death.

Early that same week Brainerd wrote a letter to the commissioners in Boston who had asked him to recommend two candidates to go as missionaries to the Six Nations. He proposed two acquaintances of his, Elihu Spencer of East Haddam and Job Strong of Northampton. Spencer was a second cousin of David and John Brainerd, and had graduated from Yale with John the previous year. Strong was a 1747 Yale graduate. Upon receiving Brainerd's recommendations, the Boston commissioners unanimously approved them, and in due time Spencer and Strong were sent out.

Thursday, September 17, was the last day Brainerd was well enough even just to leave his bedroom. His brother Israel returned from New Haven that day and thereafter remained with him until his death. That evening Brainerd suffered from diarrhea, which he saw as another sign of his approaching death. Of that prospect he exclaimed: 'Oh, the glorious time is now coming! I have longed to serve God perfectly: Now God will gratify those desires!'

'And from time to time,' Edwards testified further, 'at the several steps and new symptoms of the sensible approach of his dissolution, he was so far from being sunk or damped that he seemed to be animated and made more cheerful; as being glad at the appearances of death's approach.' He often referred to the day of his death as 'that glorious day,' and the closer death came the more he seemed to desire it. He talked much about it, speaking with perfect calmness of the future state he anticipated.

Late in the afternoon on Saturday, September 19, while attempting to walk a little in the confinement of his bedroom, Brainerd began to think, 'How infinitely sweet it is to love God and be all for Him!'

Presently an accusing thought was suggested to his mind: 'You are not an angel, not lively and active.'

Immediately – and somewhat amazingly, given his tendency toward self-censure – his 'whole soul' replied, 'I as sincerely desire to love and glorify God, as any angel in heaven.'

'But you are filthy, not fit for heaven,' came another accusatory thought.

Instantly, however, he thought of 'the blessed robes of Christ's righteousness' with which he was clothed in God's sight and in which he 'could not but exult and triumph.' As he contemplated 'the infinite excellency of God,' his soul 'even broke with longings' that God would be glorified.

The idea of receiving dignity in heaven occurred to him, but promptly a thought he had had in recent days returned, 'I don't go to heaven to get honor, but to give all possible glory and praise.'

According to Edwards, the 'extraordinary frame' Brainerd was in that evening could not be concealed from those around him, as he could not help but speak out of the overflow of his heart. Apparently the entire Edwards family, joined by their servants and likely Israel too, gathered in Brainerd's room as he shared some of the thoughts just noted from his diary as well as 'very many other extraordinary expressions.' Edwards afterwards recorded a sampling of those:

My heaven is to please God, and glorify Him, and give all to Him, and to be wholly devoted to His glory; that is the heaven I long for; that is my religion, and that is my happiness, and always was ever since I suppose I had any true religion; and all those that are of that religion shall meet me in heaven. ...

I don't go to heaven to be advanced, but to give honor to God. 'Tis no matter where I shall be stationed in heaven, whether I have a high or a low seat there; but to love and please and glorify God is all: Had I a thousand souls, if they were worth anything, I would give 'em all to God; but I have nothing to give, when all is done. ...

'Tis a great comfort to me to think that I have done a little *for* God in the world; Oh, 'tis but a very small matter; yet I *have* done a little; and I lament it that I have not done more for Him. ...

My greatest joy and comfort has been to do something for promoting the interest of religion and the souls of particular persons: And now, in my illness, while I am full of pain and distress from day to day, all the comfort I have is in being able to do some little char [or small piece of work (Edwards' interpretive bracket)] for God; either by something that I say, or by writing, or some other way.

Brainerd intermingled with those and other similar statements many earnest words of spiritual counsel to the members of his small audience, especially to the Edwards children and servants. He reinforced his admonitions by reminding the children that his were the words of a dying man: 'I shall die here, and here I shall be buried, and here you will see my grave, and do you remember what I have said to you. I am going into eternity: And 'tis sweet to me to think of eternity; the endlessness of it makes it sweet: But oh, what shall I say to the eternity of the wicked! I can't mention it, nor think of it: The thought is too dreadful. When you see my grave, then remember what I said to you while I was alive: then think with yourself how that man that lies in that grave counseled and warned me to prepare for death.'

The thought of such solemn, even morbid, perspectives being shared with young children seems somewhat shocking to modern sensibilities, but would have been much more commonplace among Christians of that day. Edwards' record of Brainerd's fervent interaction with his children on that occasion certainly indicates appreciation rather than disapproval. The Northampton pastor further related:

> His body seemed to be marvelously strengthened through the inward vigor and refreshment of his mind; so that, although before he was so weak that he could hardly utter a sentence, yet now he continued his most affecting and profitable discourse to us for more than an hour, with scarce any intermission; and said of it, when he had done, it was the last sermon that ever he should preach.

In the days that followed Brainerd visited with Israel about the importance of the work of the ministry and of the need for pastors to have God's grace and assistance in their sacred endeavors: 'When ministers feel these special gracious influences on their hearts, it wonderfully assists them to come at the consciences of men, and as it were to handle them with hands; whereas, without them, whatever reason and oratory we make use of, we do but make use of stumps instead of hands.'

He spent the first half of the next week in various writing projects. He read and edited 'a little volume of my private writings,' probably a portion of his private journal. That Wednesday, September 23, he dictated a letter to Eliab Byram in Rockciticus, New Jersey. The correspondence, which he viewed as being 'of great importance,' concerned the qualifications of ministers and the examination and licensing of candidates for pastoral ministry. With the help of Israel, he also started composing an autobiographical account of his spiritual experiences as a child and of his conversion as a young man. That account served as the opening section of Edwards' work relating the missionary's life story.

Apparently even those exertions were too much for his tenuous health, for of that same Wednesday evening he recorded: 'This night I endured a dreadful turn, wherein my life was expected [to last] scarce an hour or minute together.' Thursday morning he had only enough strength to fold and address the letter he had dictated the previous day. About two o'clock that afternoon he was forced back to bed with a burning fever, but was unable to gain any proper rest. His condition continued to worsen:

> In the evening I got up, having lain down in some of my clothes; but was in the greatest distress that ever I endured, having an uncommon kind of hiccough; which either strangled me or threw me into a straining to vomit; and at the same time was distressed with griping pains. Oh, the distress of this evening! I had little expectation of my living the night through, nor indeed had any about me: and I longed for the finishing moment!

That Friday, though 'unspeakably weak' and barely able to speak, he did manage to do a little writing. In the last sentences that he himself ever penned in his diary, he reflected: 'Oh, it refreshed my soul to think of former things, of desires to glorify God, of the pleasures of living to Him! Oh, my dear God, I am speedily coming to Thee, I hope! Hasten the day, O Lord, if it be Thy blessed will: "Oh, come, Lord Jesus, come quickly! Amen" (Rev. 22:20).'

A few additional diary entries were made in the week to follow, dictated by Brainerd and recorded by Israel. On Sunday, September 27, he related: 'This was a very comfortable day to my soul; I think I awoke with God. I was enabled to "lift up my soul to God" (Ps. 25:1) early this morning; and while I had little bodily strength, I found freedom to lift up my heart to God for myself and others. Afterwards, was pleased with the thoughts of speedily entering into the unseen world.'

A member of the Edwards family entered his room a short while later that same morning. So spiritually uplifted was he that he stated, 'I have had more pleasure this morning than all the drunkards in the world enjoy, if it were all extracted!' Edwards commented further of that remark: 'So much did he esteem the "joy of faith" (Phil. 1:25) above the "pleasure of sin" (Heb. 11:25).'

He was unusually hungry that morning and, for some unknown reason, took that as 'a sign of the very near approach of death.' Of that prospect he commented:

> I was born on a Sabbath Day; and I have reason to think I was newborn on a Sabbath Day; and I hope I shall die on this Sabbath Day: I should look upon it as a favor, if it may be the will of God that it should be so: I long for the time. Oh, 'why is his chariot so long in coming? Why tarry the wheels of his chariots' (Judg. 5:28)? I am very willing to part with all: I am willing to part with my dear brother John, and never to see him again, to go to be forever with the Lord. Oh, when I go there, how will God's dear Church on earth be upon my mind!

Edwards explained in an editorial note that Brainerd had previously expressed a desire, if it were God's will, to live till his brother, John, returned from New Jersey. When John left Northampton nearly two weeks earlier, he had expressed his intention of returning within a fortnight. The next day would mark the completion of that period. However, Brainerd's desire to be with the Lord in heaven had by this time become so strong that he was willing to forego the opportunity to see his brother once again in this life.

The spiritual welfare of his congregation in Cranberry remained very much on his heart, and he often spoke of the Indians. 'And when he spake of them,' Edwards revealed, 'it was with peculiar tenderness; so that his speech would be presently interrupted and drowned with tears.'

Early in the afternoon on Monday, September 28, he was able to spend a couple of hours reading and making a few corrections in his private journal. He found himself 'sensibly declined in all respects' and unable to write as he had formerly done. Yet he was heartened that he was still able to do something that he considered to be for God.

That evening, however, his slight strength gave out. He and those with him again thought he was dying. He was nearly speechless, but his lips moved slightly, and one sitting very near him heard him whisper: 'Come, Lord Jesus, come quickly (Rev. 22:20). Oh, "why is his chariot so long in coming" (Judg. 5:28).'

But after a time he revived. He then blamed himself for having been overly eager to be gone. When asked whether or not he had heard the prayer that was offered for him when he had sunk so low, he answered: 'Yes, I heard every word, and had an uncommon sense of the things that were uttered in that prayer. Every word reached my heart.'

Two unidentified ministerial candidates were among those who visited with him the next evening. His mind was so full of 'sweet meditations concerning the prosperity of Zion' that he asked the little gathering to sing a psalm on the subject. The group obliged by singing part of Psalm 102, probably including the stanzas based on verses such as 13 and 16: 'Thou shalt arise, and have mercy upon Zion: for the time to favor her, yea, the set time, is come. ... When the Lord shall build up Zion, He shall appear in His glory.'

The singing of that song so revived him that, though before he had hardly been able to speak, he afterwards proceeded with some freedom of speech to give his dying counsels to the two young candidates for the ministry. He earnestly recommended that they frequently devote themselves to secret prayer and fasting. To reinforce his counsel he shared from his personal experience the great comfort and benefit he had gained from those spiritual exercises. Of his own private disciplines he added: 'I should not mention [them], were it not that I am a dying person.'

Brainerd lay in his bed throughout the visit that evening. Until that time he had been able to sit up part of each day in a chair. But from that Tuesday forward he never rose from his bed.

Two nights later, he became delirious for a short time. But before long he fell asleep, and when he awoke his thinking was lucid once again. Afterwards he had a related statement of praise recorded in his journal:

Oh, blessed be God for His great goodness to me, since I was so low at Mr Bromfield's, on Thursday, June 18, last past. He has, except those few minutes [earlier this evening], given me the clear exercise of my reason, and enabled me to labor much for Him, in things both of a public and private nature; and perhaps to do more good than I should have done if I had been well.

The final entry in his diary was made the following day:

Friday, October 2. My soul was this day, at turns, sweetly set on God: I longed to be 'with Him' that I might 'behold His glory' (John 17:24); I felt sweetly disposed to commit all to Him, even my dearest friends, my dearest flock, and my absent brother, and all my concerns for time and eternity. Oh, that His kingdom might come in the world; that they might all love and glorify Him for what He is in Himself; and that the blessed Redeemer might 'see of the travail of His soul, and be satisfied' (Isa. 53:11). Oh, 'come, Lord Jesus, come quickly! Amen' (Rev. 22:20).

When Jerusha Edwards entered Brainerd's room the following Sunday morning, he looked at her very pleasantly and said: 'Dear Jerusha, are you willing to part with me? I am quite willing to part with you: I am willing to part with all my friends: I am willing to part with my dear brother John; although I love him the best of any creature living: I have committed him and all my friends to God, and can leave them with God. Though, if I thought I should not see you and be happy with you in another world, I could not bear to part with you. But we shall spend an happy eternity together!'

That evening someone came into his room carrying a Bible. Spotting it, he exclaimed: 'Oh, that dear book! That lovely book! I shall soon see it opened! The mysteries that are in it, and the mysteries of God's Providence, will be all unfolded!'

The closing days of his life proved extremely difficult. Edwards provided a graphic description of the consumptive's ongoing physical deterioration:

His distemper now very apparently preyed on his vitals in an extraordinary manner: not by a sudden breaking of ulcers in his lungs, as at Boston, but by a constant discharge of purulent matter in great quantities: so that what he brought up by expectoration seemed to be as it were mouthfuls of almost clear pus; which was attended with very great inward pain and distress.

On Tuesday, October 6, he lay near death for a protracted period. During that time he was heard to utter in broken whispers: 'He will come, He will not tarry. I shall soon be in glory. I shall soon glorify God with the angels.' But after a considerable period of time he again rallied.

His brother John finally arrived that Wednesday, some nine days later than he had originally intended. He had been detained at Cranberry much longer than anticipated by a mortal sickness that was prevailing among the Christian natives. His return had also been delayed, Edwards related obliquely, by 'some other things in their circumstances that made his stay with them necessary.' David Brainerd was both 'affected and refreshed' to see his beloved brother again. He seemed in complete agreement that the interest of religion and the souls of his people had required John's delay.

On Thursday he suffered 'great distress and agonies of body' and throughout most of the day was disoriented. That evening his mind was again clear, but his bodily pain continued and increased. He divulged to Edwards that it was impossible for any to comprehend the distress he felt in his chest. His pain was so intense that he said the thought of enduring it one minute longer was almost insupportable. He expressed great concern lest he should dishonor God by manifesting impatience in his agony. He requested that others would be continually lifting up their hearts in prayer for him, asking God to support him and to give him patience. He indicated that he expected to die that night, but seemed to fear a longer delay in his passing.

Even in the midst of such bodily extremity, he continued to think and talk about the interest of Christ's kingdom in the world. That evening he visited at length with one of the neighboring ministers, Edward Billing, pastor at Cold Spring (now Belchertown, about twelve miles east of Northampton), concerning the great importance of the work of the ministry.[3] After that David and John Brainerd talked late into the night, discussing the native congregation in New Jersey and how further to promote the interest of religion among the Indians.

Still later that night his physical agony seemed to rise to a higher level than ever before. In his distress he stated to those attending him that it was another thing to die than people imagined and that people were not fully aware what bodily pain and anguish is undergone before death. Mercifully, his suffering did not last much longer.

Toward the dawning of the new day his eyes became fixed. He continued to lie unmoving till about six in the morning on Friday, October 9, 1747, when he died. Edwards fittingly described that as the moment: 'when his soul, as we may well conclude, was received by his dear Lord and Master, as an eminently faithful servant, into that state of perfection of holiness and fruition of God which he had so often and so ardently longed for; and was welcomed by the glorious assembly in the upper world, as one peculiarly fitted to join them in their blessed employments and enjoyments.'

3.   Pettit, *Life of David Brainerd*, p. 476.

32

ONGOING INFLUENCE

Brainerd's funeral took place the following Monday, October 12, 1747, at Edwards' church. The high esteem in which he was held is readily perceived through Edwards' report that the service was attended by 'a great concourse of people' including eight neighboring ministers and seventeen 'other gentlemen of liberal education.'

Edwards officiated the service, delivering a sermon based on 2 Corinthians 5:8 entitled 'True saints, when absent from the body, are present with the Lord.' After expounding the Scripture text at length, he commented extensively on Brainerd's exemplary faith and life in the concluding 'Application' portion of the discourse.[1]

Brainerd's body was buried in the Northampton churchyard. An old Scottish woodcut reveals that at some subsequent time a table-type monument was erected over his grave. The monument consisted of four marble pillars, each about two feet high, supporting a slab of marble that measured three by six feet. The slab bore this inscription:

Sacred to the
memory of the
Rev. David Brainerd,
a faithful and laborious

---

1. The entire funeral sermon is included in Sereno Dwight's *Memoirs of David Brainerd*, pp. 473-504. Pettit's *Life of David Brainerd*, pp. 543-54, includes only the 'Application' section of the sermon, in which Edwards spoke of Brainerd.

Missionary to the
Stockbridge, Delaware
and Susquehannah
Tribes of Indians
who died in this town
Oct. 10, 1747
AE. 32 [2]

Late that same year, Israel Brainerd became gravely ill with what Edwards termed 'a nervous fever.' After about a fortnight's illness he died in New Haven, Connecticut, on January 6, 1748. He was only twenty-two years old.

A similar sadness befell the Edwards family less than six weeks later. After a sudden, serious illness of but five days' length, Jerusha passed away on February 14, 1748. She was not quite eighteen years of age. Some have speculated she contracted tuberculosis from Brainerd while caring for him the previous summer and fall, but that is not at all known with certainty. Edwards gave no indication that she had any type of consumption.

He did include in his account of Brainerd's life both David's and his own perspectives on Jerusha's Christian spirit and service:

> She was a person of much the same spirit with Mr Brainerd.
> She had constantly taken care of, and tended him in his
> sickness, for nineteen weeks before his death; devoting
> herself to it with great delight, because she looked on him
> as an eminent servant of Jesus Christ. In this time he had
> much conversation with her on things of religion; and in
> his dying state, often expressed to us, her parents, his great
> satisfaction concerning her true piety, and his confidence
> that he would meet her in heaven; and his high opinion of

2. A reproduction of the woodcut of the monument, a copy of its inscription and further description of the grave site is included in *Flagellant on Horseback, The Life Story of David Brainerd*, Richard Ellsworth Day (Philadelphia: Judson, 1950), pp. 232, 242-3. The inscription, as preserved to this day in the Northampton cemetery, contains two errors: Brainerd died on October 9, 1747, at age twenty-nine, rather than on October 10, 1747, at thirty-two years of age. Pettit, *Life of David Brainerd*, pp. 72-3, includes photographs of the tombstones of both David Brainerd and Jerusha Edwards.

her, not only as a true Christian, but a very eminent saint; one whose soul was uncommonly fed and entertained with things that appertain to the most spiritual, experimental, and distinguishing parts of religion; and one who by the temper of her mind was fitted to deny herself for God, and to do good, beyond any young woman whatsoever that he knew of. She had manifested a heart uncommonly devoted to God, in the course of her life, many years before her death; and said on her deathbed that she had not seen one minute for several years wherein she desired to live one minute longer for the sake of any other good in life but doing good, living to God, and doing what might be for His glory.[3]

Jerusha's grave was placed immediately next to Brainerd's. The inscription on her tombstone, including a citation of Psalm 17:15, reads:

Jerusha
Daughter of
Jonathan and Sarah Edwards
Born April 26, 1730
Died February 14, 1748
'I shall be satisfied when
I awake in Thy Likeness'

For the first few years following David Brainerd's death, John Brainerd experienced definite ongoing success in his ministry at 'Bethel,' the new designation he gave the Cranberry Indian settlement shortly after his arrival there the spring of 1747.[4] Despite a mortal sickness that claimed the lives of fully one-third of the Christian natives there, new Indians kept arriving, with a number of them coming under saving conviction and going on to become committed Christians. The school continued to grow and thrive. Some of the boys began to learn a trade and several

3. Pettit, *Life of David Brainerd*, pp. 474-5.
4. The following summary of John Brainerd's ministry and the subsequent history of the New Jersey Indians is gleaned primarily from *Life of John Brainerd*, Thomas Brainerd.

spinning wheels were procured as a source of industry for the women and girls.

As early as 1749, however, a few prominent settlers, especially Robert Hunter Morris, Chief Justice of New Jersey, were claiming legal rights to the Indians' land at Cranberry. The avaricious chief justice brought suit not only against the Indians but also against a number of settlers who had established farms in the area, eventually forcing many of them to move. After five years of lawsuits and relentless pressure, John finally deeded the native land at Cranberry to a Peter Deremer in July of 1754.

John eventually moved with the Indians to Brunswick, about ten miles northeast of Cranberry. In 1758 a 3,000-acre tract of land was set aside by the government of New Jersey on which natives of the colony could settle without fear of further molestation or displacement. The reservation, the only one ever established in New Jersey, was located nearly forty miles southwest of Cranberry. The new native settlement there was named Brotherton (later Indian Mills). About half the 200 Indians who remained in New Jersey at the time settled there.

Throughout the remainder of his career, until his death in 1781 at age sixty-one, John Brainerd divided his ministry efforts between natives and settlers. He established several new churches among the settlers as well as two Indian schools, one at Brotherton and the other fifteen miles northwest of there at Bridgetown (now Mount Holly), where he moved in 1768.

In 1801 the Brotherton natives received permission from the government to sell their lands. The following year, seventy to eighty Indians from there loaded their belongings onto a dozen wagons and set out for the Oneida Indian settlement in central New York. The Oneidas had their settlement at New Stockbridge on Oneida Lake, northeast of Syracuse, New York. The two tribes remained there until 1824, when the encroachments of settlers led both of them, along with other members of the Six Nations, to venture some 800 miles west to the vicinity of Green Bay, Wisconsin.

Rev. Cutting Marsh was a missionary who ministered for many years to Oneida, Delaware and Muncey Indians after their settlement in Wisconsin. One of his converts was the grand-daughter of the first Indian to be brought to saving faith under David Brainerd's ministry at Crossweeksung. (Her conversion story was related in chapter 16.) This granddaughter gave Marsh the conch-shell that first David Brainerd, then John, had used to summon their native congregations for worship.

Some Delawares migrated 600 miles southwest of Green Bay, settling in Kansas. In 1834 the testimony of an anonymous missionary ministering to 100 or more Shawnee and Delaware Indians in Kansas was recorded in a publication called the *Missionary Herald*. He told of meeting two Indian sisters, Elizabeth and Catharine, whose parents and grandmother had been members of David and John Brainerd's congregation in New Jersey. Inquiring about David Brainerd, the missionary asked the sisters, 'What did your grandmother say about him?' They replied:

> He was a young man – he was a lovely man; he was a staff – he was a staff to walk with. He went about from house to house to talk about religion: that was his way. He slept on a deer-skin or a bear-skin. He ate bear-meat and samp: then we knew he was not proud. ...
>
> But some of the people did not like him, and said, 'What has this white man come here for? We don't want him here!' And they told him to go off. When the Indians assembled to dance and have a feast, he would go there also, and go away in the bushes and pray for them. And then some said, 'We do not want this white man here; let us make away with him.' But others said, 'No, we will not kill him.' After a while they found that he was an honest man, and then they would do any thing he said.

An account of the ongoing influence of David Brainerd's life and ministry, to be complete, certainly must include consideration of the impact of the publication of his diary and Journal. As has already been seen, what became commonly known as *Brainerd's Journal*, the account in his own words of God's mighty work among the Indians from June of 1745 till June of the following year, was originally published in two parts in 1746. Edwards published his edited version of *The Life of David Brainerd*, which did not include the material previously published in *Brainerd's Journal*, in 1749. It was the first full-length missionary biography ever written and was destined to become the most popular of all Edwards' works.

Subsequent editions often combined materials from *Brainerd's Journal* and Edwards' *Life of Brainerd*. Amazingly, those works have never gone out of print since they were first published over 250 years ago; they have always remained in print in one edition or another![5]

The reason for such ongoing interest in Brainerd's life is the tremendous spiritual inspiration and instruction to be derived from it. From his day till the modern era testimonies to that effect have abounded. The following examples are but a small sampling:[6]

John Wesley (1703–91), the founder of Methodism, published several editions of Brainerd's Life and instructed in the handbook of the Methodist ministry: 'Let every preacher read carefully over the Life of David Brainerd. Let us be followers of him, as he was of Christ, in absolute self-devotion, in total deadness to the world, and in fervent love to God and man.' In 1767 he wrote in his journal: 'Find preachers of David Brainerd's spirit, and nothing can stand before them, but without this what will gold or silver do?'

'The father of modern missions,' William Carey (1761–1834), claimed three heroes – the Apostle Paul, Massachusetts pastor and Indian missionary John Eliot, and David Brainerd. Whenever Carey found his heart growing cold he always succeeded in rekindling it by reading Brainerd's memoir. One of the rules of his mission group was for each member to read Brainerd's Life three times annually! 'Let us often look at Brainerd in the woods of America, pouring out his very soul before God,' he admonished.

---

5.   Pettit, *Life of Brainerd*, pp. 74-9, lists more than sixty editions of Brainerd's life and journal that have been published through the years.

6.   These and other testimonies are cited in Pettit, *Life of Brainerd*, pp. 3-4; *David Brainerd, Pioneer Missionary to the American Indians*, John Thornbury (Darlington, England: Evangelical, 1996), pp. 298-300; *David Brainerd*, Ranelda Hunsicker (Minneapolis: Bethany, 1999), pp. 138-40.

'Prayer, secret, fervent, expectant, lies at the root of all personal godliness.'

Henry Martyn (1781–1812) was a brilliant scholar at Cambridge who originally intended to pursue a career in law. But as he studied the life of Brainerd in his early twenties he was deeply stirred and decided to devote himself to missions instead. Of Brainerd he wrote, 'I long to be like him; let me forget the world and be swallowed up in a desire to glorify God.'

The renowned Scottish revival preacher Robert Murray McCheyne (1813–43) was deeply moved and influenced by the lives and teachings of both David Brainerd and Jonathan Edwards. Of the former he wrote in 1832: 'Life of David Brainerd. Most wonderful man! What conflicts, what depressions, dessertions, strength, advancement, victories within thy torn bosom! I cannot express what I think when I think of thee. Tonight, more set upon missionary enterprise than ever.'

Adoniram Judson Gordon (1836–95), pastor of Clarendon Street Baptist Church and founder of Gordon College in Boston, was also a strong missionary leader. After visiting Brainerd's grave, he wrote:

> What if the writer confesses that he has never received such spiritual impulse from any other human being as from him whose body has lain now for nearly a century and a half under that Northampton slab? For many years an old and worn volume of his life and journals has lain upon my study table, and no season has passed without a renewed pondering of its precious contents. ...
>
> When we shut the book we are not praising Brainerd, but condemning ourselves, and resolving that, by the grace of God, we will follow Christ more closely in the future.

Jim Elliot (1927–56), who, along with four missionary companions, was martyred while trying to reach the Waodani (Auca) Indians of Ecuador, was inspired and challenged by Brainerd's example. In his own journal he wrote on more than one occasion of that influence: 'Confession of pride – suggested by David Brainerd's Diary yesterday – must become an hourly thing to me'; 'Oh, that I might receive the apostle's passion, caught from vision of Thyself, Lord Jesus. David Brainerd's diary stirs me on to such in prayer.'

For a quarter of a millennium, unnumbered thousands of Christian missionaries, pastors and lay people have been inspired and challenged through Brainerd's example to seek the Lord and His holiness with greater earnestness and to serve Him with increased faithfulness and sacrifice. To the greater glory of God, such blessed spiritual results are sure to continue flowing to countless people through the consideration of his life in the years to come till Christ returns.

Appendix

Brainerd's Depression

One feature of David Brainerd's life that has perplexed some is the pronounced depression with which he regularly wrestled. He disclosed of his boyhood disposition, 'I was, I think, from my youth something sober, and inclined rather to melancholy than the contrary extreme.'[1] Regularly he recorded in his diary feelings of 'melancholy' and 'dejection,' or speaks of his spirits being 'damped,' all expressions for depression. Sometimes he remained dejected for days or even weeks at a time.

Doubtless a variety of factors contributed to his tendency toward despondency. At its root, the trait appears to have been an inherited, genetic one. Writing more than a hundred years after David Brainerd's death, a family descendant related: 'It must, however, be confessed that in the whole Brainerd family for two hundred years there has been a tendency to a morbid depression, akin to hypochondria.'[2] Brainerd's austere Puritan upbringing and the fact that he lost both his parents at a young age likely played a part in his melancholy. In his early twenties he began to show signs of the tuberculosis that led to his premature death just a few years later. Undoubtedly there was a strong link between his physical and emotional struggles. He suffered a traumatic disappointment in connection with his college training and career aspirations that probably deepened his struggle with dejection.

1. Pettit, *Life of David Brainerd*, p. 101.
2. Thomas Brainerd, *Life of John Brainerd*, p. 168. Thomas was a descendant of David and John Brainerd's uncle, James.

Contributing to that struggle, too, were several very difficult and discouraging circumstances that attended his ministry to the Indians: hard, primitive living conditions; the apathy and hostility of many he tried to reach; virtually no fruit from his first two years of missionary labor; worst of all, protracted periods of complete isolation from fellowship with other Christians accompanied by the resulting loneliness. Almost certainly another significant factor was the intense spiritual warfare he was involved in and the direct spiritual attacks to which that warfare surely subjected him. As he wrestled against the rulers of the darkness of this world and spiritual wickedness in high places, doubtless those spiritual forces of evil struck back at him by attempting to exploit and compound his despondency.

Brainerd's ongoing struggle with depression did not indicate a spiritual deficiency on his part. It needs to be remembered that through the centuries several eminent and deeply pious Christian leaders have wrestled with the same malady. Among them have been (to name but a few) Martin Luther, Charles Spurgeon, Samuel Logan Brengle, A.B. Simpson and J.B. Phillips. Brainerd, of course, had no recourse to modern medicines to lessen his low periods. He was forced to endure the full weight and darkness of them. His only means of getting through them were dependent prayer and sheer dogged determination.

Rather than indicating spiritual weakness, the fact that he prevailed despite regular periods of depression underscores Brainerd's spiritual strength. Many others would have been defeated and sidelined by it. He always persevered through it and to a large degree overcame it. What is truly noteworthy is not that he struggled with persistent melancholy, but that, by God's grace, he accomplished all that he did despite such a handicap.

For Further Reading

Brainerd, Thomas. *The Life of John Brainerd*. Philadelphia: Presbyterian Publication Company, 1865. While the primary focus of this book is on John's life and ministry, it also contains considerable material concerning David Brainerd.

Christie, Vance. *Into All the World: Four Stories of Pioneer Missionaries*. Uhrichsville, OH: Barbour, 2004. Introductory biographical sketches on David Brainerd, Adoniram Judson, Robert Moffat and John Paton.

Day, Richard Ellsworth. *Flagellant on Horseback – The Life Story of David Brainerd*. Philadelphia: Judson, 1950. An unreliable biography that includes much unfounded (and sometimes outlandish!) speculation.

Dwight, Sereno Edwards. *Memoirs of the Rev. David Brainerd*. New Haven: Converse, 1822. In addition to combining Jonathan Edwards' *Life of David Brainerd* and Brainerd's Journal, this volume includes the full text of the sermon Ebenezer Pemberton preached at Brainerd's ordination service and the message Edwards delivered at his funeral. It also presents the complete appendix to part two of Brainerd's Journal.

Edwards, Jonathan. *The Life and Diary of David Brainerd*. Grand Rapids: Baker, 1999. Originally published by Moody Bible Institute of Chicago in 1949, this volume includes a biographical sketch of the life and work of Jonathan Edwards by Philip E. Howard, Jr. This edition presents Edwards' *Life of David Brainerd* and Brainerd's Journal in a readable and accessible fashion.

Hunsicker, Ranelda. *David Brainerd*. Minneapolis: Bethany, 1999. A good, brief introductory biography.

Murray, Iain H. *Jonathan Edwards – A New Biography*. Edinburgh: Banner of Truth, 1996. This comprehensive biography of Edwards includes much information concerning the Great Awakening and about the interaction of Edwards and Brainerd.

Pettit, Norman. *The Life of David Brainerd*. New Haven and London: Yale University Press, 1985. This is the scholarly edition of Jonathan Edwards' original account of Brainerd's life. It also includes extensive citations from Brainerd's Journal that did not appear in Edwards' original work. In addition, it provides a lengthy historical introduction and extensive correspondence relating to Brainerd's life and ministry. The volume is marred by Pettit's hypercritical analysis of Brainerd that sometimes produces unfortunate misrepresentations of him.

Piper, John. *The Hidden Smile of God: The Fruit of Affliction in the Lives of John Bunyan, William Cowper, and David Brainerd*. Wheaton: Crossway, 2001. Provides a devotional summary of Brainerd's life.

Thornbury, John. *David Brainerd: Pioneer Missionary to the American Indians*. Darlington, England: Evangelical, 1996. A sound biography that includes helpful historical background material.

Tucker, Ruth A. *From Jerusalem to Irian Jaya: A Biographical History of Christian Missions*. Grand Rapids: Zondervan, 1983. Chapter 4, 'American Indian Missions: Seeking the "Noble Savage",' provides valuable historical information. Regrettably, Tucker's analysis of Brainerd is overly and unfairly critical.

Wynbeek, David. *David Brainerd, Beloved Yankee*. Grand Rapids: Eerdmans, 1961. An excellent, engaging biography.

John And Betty Stam

Missionary Martyrs

Vance Christie

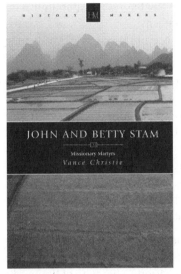

"*The fateful day began with deceptive normalcy at John and Betty Stam's missionary residence in Tsingteh, China. Both the wood-burning stoves had been lit and were starting to heat up nicely, helping to lessen the chill that gripped the large old house that cold, early December morning. The Stams, along with the six Chinese who lived with them in the house, had already eaten breakfast.*

"*John hoped to study and get some correspondence done that morning. Betty was preparing to give their three-month old baby, Helen Priscilla, a bath, with some assistance from the amah Mei Tsong-fuh. The cook, Li Ming-chin, busied himself in the kitchen. His wife, mother, and two children similarly had begun their various daily activities.*

"*John and Betty had been in Tsingteh for just two weeks. They had come there under the auspices of the China Inland Mission (CIM) to oversee the infant Christian work that had been established in the southern portion of Anhwei Province. There were very few Christians in the area, but the Stams were thrilled at the prospect of carrying out pioneer evangelistic work to help bring the Gospel to that needy part of China.*"

So begins this gripping story of missionary endeavour in China. The early church leader, Tertullian, said that 'the blood of the martyrs is the seed of the church'. This is just one story of the people who's witness is the cause of the spectacular growth of the church in China today.

ISBN 978-1-84550-376-5

Christian Focus Publications

publishes books for all ages
Our mission statement –

STAYING FAITHFUL
In dependence upon God we seek to impact the world through literature faithful to His infallible Word, the Bible. Our aim is to ensure that the LORD Jesus Christ is presented as the only hope to obtain forgiveness of sin, live a useful life and look forward to heaven with Him.

REACHING OUT
Christ's last command requires us to reach out to our world with His gospel. We seek to help fulfil that by publishing books that point people towards Jesus and help them develop a Christ-like maturity. We aim to equip all levels of readers for life, work, ministry and mission.

Books in our adult range are published in three imprints.

Christian Focus contains popular works including biographies, commentaries, basic doctrine and Christian living. Our children's books are also published in this imprint.

Mentor focuses on books written at a level suitable for Bible College and seminary students, pastors, and other serious readers. The imprint includes commentaries, doctrinal studies, examination of current issues and church history.

Christian Heritage contains classic writings from the past.

Christian Focus Publications Ltd
Geanies House, Fearn, Ross-shire,
IV20 1TW, Scotland, United Kingdom
info@christianfocus.com
www.christianfocus.com